READING RAYMOND CARVER

Reading
RAYMOND
CARVER

Randolph Paul Runyon

SYRACUSE UNIVERSITY PRESS

First Paperback Edition 1993
93 94 95 96 97 98 99   6 5 4 3 2 1

Frontispiece: photo by Tess Gallagher; courtesy of George Arents Room, Bird Library, Syracuse University.

The paper used in this publication meets the minimum requirements of American National Standard for Information Sciences—Permanence of Paper for Printed Library Materials, ANSI Z39.48-1984. ●™

Library of Congress Cataloging-in-Publication Data
Runyon, Randolph, 1947–
     Reading Raymond Carver / by Randolph Paul Runyon.
        p.   cm.
     Includes bibliographical references and index.
     ISBN 0-8156-2631-2 (pbk.)
     1. Carver, Raymond—Criticism and interpretation.   I. Title.
     PS3553.A7894Z86   1992   91-36790
     813'.54—dc20

Manufactured in the United States of America

For Elizabeth, Augusta, and Zeke

Contents

RANDOLPH PAUL RUNYON is Professor of French at Miami University in Ohio. He is the author of *Fowles/Irving/Barthes: Canonical Variations on an Apocryphal Theme,* *The Braided Dream: Robert Penn Warren's Late Poetry,* and *The Taciturn Text: The Fiction of Robert Penn Warren.*

Remembering Ray Carver

I first met Ray Carver in January 1978, at Goddard College, where we were both teaching in a two-week creative writing residency. He was just coming out of a bad time. Although he wasn't drinking, he was broke and feeling very fragile and uncertain about himself. He wanted to get away from his life out west and start a new one. He spent a lot of time in his room smoking and pacing around.

He wasn't equipped for the Vermont winter and wore a brown jacket that appeared to be made of vinyl and small shiny shoes that looked like a dancer's shoes, shoes oddly at variance with his great bearlike body. I remember him tiptoeing through the snow, setting his feet carefully in other people's tracks, and shaking his head as if the weather were just one more thing in an astonishing world.

He believed faithfully in catastrophe. Something awful would happen and all the stores would close. Consequently he was always leaving the dining hall with little packages of food wrapped in white napkins. Mostly they were sweet things because he had a terrible sweet tooth: packages of cookies, doughnuts, maybe a sandwich. One time someone took his package of brownies, replacing it with a package of stale bread. Ray carried it back to his room and eagerly opened it late at night. I would have been angry and hurt. He laughed, and for days he told everyone of the funny trick that had been played on him. And he was always forgetting these packages and leaving them around: in a classroom or after a reading. For years there were occasions when he would ride in my car and a week or so later I would discover a little white package of stale cookies under the seat.

At night at Goddard we would sit around and tell stories. His were always full of wonder: strange fish he had caught, narrow escapes he had had, outrageous behavior he had witnessed or participated in, dastardly deeds where one human being had let down or betrayed another. He had a story about how he had amused himself after he quit drinking by going to bingo games in California and how he had learned to cheat at these games and how the cheating was more interesting than the playing. He and his first wife would go up and down the coast seeking out bingo games while a posse of elderly women tried to catch them. And there was a story about how he and John Cheever, when they were both teaching at the University of Iowa, had walked a check at a fancy restaurant and got caught but never had to pay.

He would never tell a story to show himself off or brag. They would all deal with the strange predicaments we can find ourselves in. There wasn't much judgment. What Ray hated was cruelty and betrayal, but he had done those things too and sometimes a person couldn't help himself.

He read "Why Don't You Dance?" during the residency at Goddard. There were about a hundred of us in the audience. It was as if someone had slapped us. Most of us knew Ray's stories but this was something beyond *Will You Please Be Quiet, Please?*. What was wonderful about the story was how it dug its way inside your chest and squeezed your heart, also how it was about the impossibility of communication and how it communicated so perfectly. Ray loved stories that worked on as many of the reader's emotions as possible. He hated stories that were simply idea and surface.

When he left the residency at the end of two weeks, he borrowed a hundred bucks from one of his students and a hundred bucks from me and headed out to western Illinois. Somebody had given him the use of an empty house, and he thought he could hole up there and write. The house turned out to be fifteen miles from the nearest town. He bought an old Oldsmobile. I think it was a '63 or '64. He called it his Okie car. It was February and about fifteen below and after the first night the car wouldn't start. The house was a cheap little place furnished entirely with lawn furniture. He lasted about a week, then called me in Iowa City where I was teaching. The next night he was sleeping on my couch.

He stayed in Iowa City until the summer and we saw each other often. He got a room, then another, then his wife joined him, and they moved to a succession of rental cottages. Okie places he called them. He was writing a lot, both poems and stories, but he was beginning to feel trapped again. When he answered the phone it was always with a quick "Yes?" or "Lo?" as if he thought his creditors had finally found him.

He loved what he called swapping stories, a group of friends sitting around, each telling a story in turn. There were many evenings like that in Iowa City that spring. Ray would scratch his head and lean forward with his elbows on his knees and say, "You know, I remember a funny thing," then he would be off with some story about how a lawyer had sued him, trying to get his dog because Ray hadn't paid his bill, and how the judge had grown indignant, saying, "You actually want to take this man's dog away from him?" And there was another story about finding a corpse on the beach in California.

He was a great listener and when someone else was telling a story he would burst forth with oddly archaic interjections like "you don't say" and "think of that." Then he would shake his head and look around in amazement. And he had a great laugh. His whole body would collapse backwards as if he had been struck in the chest with something happy and his face would wrinkle and a high raspy noise would burst out again and again. There was nothing restrained about it. For a moment he was laughter's creature, then he would wipe his eyes and the story would resume or a new story would start.

He was also a tremendous enthusiast, and when I read a book I liked or a poem, or heard a piece of music or saw a movie that I liked, he was the person I thought to share it with, and we would have great talks about it. And he also always had a list of books or poems or stories that he would urge on people and they would be about how a person had lived, how he or she had survived and loved, how this person had dealt with being alive in a difficult time.

His writing was always original and critics loved to natter about his language, but the writing was the medium for something more important: the apprehension of human emotion—how does a person live, how does he connect with other human beings? This is what he loved about Chekhov and why he saw Chekhov as his main teacher. Emotion was the most important part of the story and he liked to quote that remark of Kafka's that literature should be an axe to smash the frozen sea of the heart. It is this emotion that makes many of his poems so wonderful. They are not a critic's poems. They are not decorative. They need no one to interpret them. They are reader's poems. They exist to define moments of emotion and wonder. Often the moments are very simple, like getting a haircut from his wife. Here is one called "Near Klamath."

> We stand around the burning oil drum
> and we warm ourselves, our hands
> and faces, in its pure lapping heat.
>
> We raise steaming cups of coffee
> to our lips and we drink it
> with both hands. But we are salmon
>
> fishermen. And now we stamp our feet
> on the snow and rocks and move upstream,
> slowly, full of love, toward the still pools.

I can think of no contemporary American poet who could locate this sort of small yet intensely emotional moment as well as Ray could. They are the moments we mostly don't have time for. Unfortunately, they are also the moments that give life its significance. Ray's work constantly tried to remind us of that. He was the celebrator of those small occasions of fragile contentment, of time lived instead of time passing. Without him, we return to the constant rush, the crowded streets and honking horns.

Now he has been dead for three years and his work is increasingly popular and the critical work accumulates. He would have been both amused and proud of the attention. A few weeks ago I gave a copy of Ray's last book of poems to a truck driver who is a recovered alcoholic and after reading and re-reading it he said, "I been there. That man lived my life!"

I can't remember Ray's reading much criticism. Although a passionate reader, he had no interest in the various Isms and all the theories. His language worked to establish a particular tone and that tone became the vehicle for the emotion. In any case, although he took care of his stories and made sure they got published, the story or poem he liked best was always the next one. He was constantly pushing away from the confines of the present and into the future. In a letter I received from him two weeks before he died of cancer, he wrote that in a week or ten days his new collection of poems would be done. "Then we'll take a holiday—a week's salmon fishing in Alaska." And he also wrote that he wanted to go to London and Amsterdam in August where selections of his stories were being published. "I've been feeling very house-bound," he added.

Writing itself was a form of exploration for him. I once asked him how he had happened to write the story "Put Yourself in My Shoes" and he said that the first sentence popped into his head and he had to follow it. The first sentence reads, "The telephone rang while he was running the vacuum cleaner." That's all. But Ray knew that something had to come after those words, so he set off looking, which meant opening his mind to possibility and discovery.

I was also struck by how many of the odd details of his stories came from stories he had heard or from his own experience. In the story just mentioned one of the characters tells about a son beaning his father with a can of tomato soup and sending him to the hospital. This was a story Ray used to tell long before he wrote "Put Yourself in My Shoes." He'd tell it and shake his head and say, "Think of that," in his hollow, breathy voice that sometimes reminded me of a great owl.

But strange things happened to him as well. That first January at Goddard he returned to the dorm one day and it looked as if some vicious aminal had attacked his head. His hair seemed half chewed off. He had gone for a haircut to the one barber in Plainfield. The old man was just recovering from a stroke and had been forced to learn how to cut hair with his left hand. And his left hand shook terribly. Ray was the barber's first customer since returning to his shop. Looking at the man's shaking hand, Ray had considered not getting a haircut after all, but he had been afraid of hurting the man's feelings.

Then in Iowa City Ray rented a room from a man whose first name was the same as his last name. The man had a fierce wife who slept in a king-sized bed and made her husband sleep nearby on the floor. The man spent long hours telling Ray his troubles, until Ray could stand it no more and fled.

One of the things that made Ray a wonderful writer was the honesty with which he approached the endeavor of writing. He would begin without knowing where he was going and he would turn away from nothing that might show up. The story was in charge and it didn't matter how odd something was or who it might offend or that *The New Yorker* might find it in bad taste. After those initial drafts, of course, he would revise sometimes for years, until he could think of nothing else, until he found himself putting back commas he had taken out earlier. For him starting a story was like getting into a fast car with a questionable driver. There was no telling where they would wind up. Yet he trusted it and gave himself over to it. Even though dangerous, the story required that he surrender himself to the mystery. The poet Rainer Maria Rilke once wrote in a letter, "Works of art are indeed always products of having-been-in-danger, or having-gone-to-the-very-end in an experience, to where one can go no further." [1] Ray always tried to do this in his writing. He was a brave man and the stories and poems we are still gladly reading are the results of that bravery, the results of his passionate investigation of the world.

In his last letter to me in July 1988, he described his mar-

---

1. Rilke, Rainer Maria, *Letters of Rainer Maria Rilke*, trans. Jane Bannard Greene & M. D. Herter Norton (New York: W. W. Norton, 1945), vol. 1, 285.

riage to Tess Gallagher in Reno about three weeks earlier. "[We] got hitched by the world's oiliest minister, a pomaded man who was wearing a string tie, cowboy boots and a $15.00 sport coat. But it was official, and then we walked a block into the heart of the gambling center, and played roulette (Tess won nearly $400.00; I lost). But we had a good time."

Had Ray lived, the world's oiliest minister would have turned up in a short story.

STEPHEN DOBYNS

Syracuse, New York
September 1991

Acknowledgments

I would like to express my appreciation to Miami University for the Assigned Research Leave that gave me the time to begin this book, and to Gary Knock, Dean of the Graduate School, and to Karl Mattox, Dean of the College of Arts and Science, for making funds available to cover the costs of securing permission to quote from Carver's works. Heartfelt thanks are due to Cynthia Maude-Gembler, Acquisitions Editor of Syracuse University Press, for suggesting and encouraging this book, and to Tess Gallagher for her hospitality and advice.

Permission to quote from materials listed below is gratefully acknowledged.

From A NEW PATH TO THE WATERFALL by Raymond Carver. Copyright © 1989 by the estate of Raymond Carver. Reprinted with permission of Atlantic Monthly Press.

From AMPLITUDE: NEW AND SELECTED POEMS by Tess Gallagher. Reprinted with the permission of Graywolf Press.

From WILL YOU PLEASE BE QUIET, PLEASE?; WHAT WE TALK ABOUT WHEN WE TALK ABOUT LOVE, CATHEDRAL, ULTRAMARINE, A NEW PATH TO THE WATERFALL by Raymond Carver. Reprinted for use in the United Kingdom and the British Commonwealth excluding Canada by permission of HarperCollins Publishers Limited.

From FIRES: ESSAYS, POEMS, STORIES; WILL YOU PLEASE BE QUIET, PLEASE?; and ULTRAMARINE by Raymond Carver. Reprinted by permission of International Creative Management, Inc.

READING RAYMOND CARVER

1

Introduction

A premature silence descended in August 1988 when Raymond Carver died, in the prime of his career. Yet something of that silence was always there in his taciturn stories, in a style that seemed to say so little but somehow suggest so much. As Susan Lohafer has described the experience of reading him, "While it might seem that we could be bored by Carver's lean style (as we surely are by imitations of Hemingway), we are in fact kept alert by having to look through the interstices for the meaning—and by being rewarded for doing so" (*Coming to Terms with the Short Story*, 65). Lohafer is speaking of the interstices within a story, the "holes" that a Faulkner or a James would have "stopped up with *more* language. . . . Carver teases us into collaboration by noting the salient points of a scene we must work to fill in, while Faulkner makes us work hard to take in all the points he's hidden in a field of more points." In Carver there is a prevailing absence, a silence, an empty space between the lines that his texts invite us to fill.

But the collaboration his stories ask of the reader extends —and this is the thesis of my book—to the interstices *between the stories* as well. The reader is invited to consider, for example, why it is that two of Carver's stories about neighbors are themselves neighbors. Or why the two stories in the numerical middle of a collection should each feature freshly delivered letters folded in half by the recipient (who in one case is not the

1

addressee).[1] When something like that happens it is reasonable
to wonder whether we ought not to extend the definition of
the text we are reading to include the sequence itself—the book
—and not just the story, and from there be led to wonder if
there might not be another story hidden in the text, one in
which the stories themselves become protagonists and behave
like the eavesdropping and apartment-invading protagonists
within them, somehow eavesdropping on each other, somehow
invading their neighboring stories' space. Or if the double instance of doubled envelopes (doubled, that is, by having been
"folded . . . in half," "folded . . . in two") shouldn't lead us to
the conclusion that each of the two contiguous stories in which
this happens is in some way the double, the other half, of the
other.

What I want to present here is, as readers familiar with the
minimalist controversy with which he has been associated may
have already guessed, a different Raymond Carver than the
one we thought we knew. *Minimalism* as a term applied to the
American short story renaissance that dates from the late 1970s
may have begun to take hold on the occasion of the special
number the *Mississippi Review* devoted to the phenomenon in
1985, but the editor of that issue made clear even then her
discomfort with the word. It "is not a good term. It is not a
useful term. We would like to get rid of it, to replace it with
something appropriately descriptive. . . . It has shown itself to
be, at best, misleading, and at worst devaluative. But it is, for
now, what we have" (Herzinger, 9). In "A Few Words About
Minimalism," which appeared in the *New York Times Book Re-*

---

1. The two halved envelopes are as prominently hidden as the one likewise halved in "The Purloined Letter"—"torn nearly in two, across the middle—as if a design, in the first instance, to tear it entirely up as worthless,
had been altered, or stayed, in the second." For Poe's clever thief placed it
likewise precisely *in the middle:* "just beneath the middle of the mantel-piece"
(695). It could only be spotted by someone who realized the importance of
"the hyperobtrusive situation of this document, full in the view of every
visiter, and thus . . . strongly corroborative of suspicion, in one who came
with the intention to suspect" (696).

view 28 December 1986, the avowed maximalist John Barth both praised and defined it thus:

> Minimalism (of one sort or another) is the principle (one of the principles, anyhow) underlying (what I and many another interested observer consider to be perhaps) the most impressive phenomenon in the current . . . literary scene. . . . I mean the new flowering of the (North) American short story (in particular the kind of terse, oblique, realistic or hyperrealistic, slightly plotted, extrospective, cool-surfaced fiction associated in the last 5 or 10 years with such excellent writers as Frederick Barthelme, Ann Beattie, Raymond Carver, Bobbie Ann Mason, James Robison, Mary Robison and Tobias Wolff, and both praised and damned under such labels as "K-Mart realism," "hick chic," "Diet Pepsi minimalism" and "post-Vietnam, post-literary, postmodernist blue-collar neo-early-Hemingwayism"). (1–2)

Considering that in "The Literature of Replenishment" Barth locates himself in the postmodernist camp, and that in "The American New Novel" he puts Carver and company in the category of "Post-Alcoholic Blue-Collar Minimalist Hyperrealism," which he describes as something quite "else" (256) from the postmodernism in which he sees himself engaged, surely the last term in his *New York Times Book Review* piece should be amended to read "*post*postmodernist blue-collar." In any case, Barth was no doubt asked to write the article because his expansive *(The Sot-Weed Factor, Giles Goat-Boy)* and metafictional *(Lost in the Funhouse, Chimera, Letters)* works are thought to be about as far from minimalist as one can conceivably get. If so, his response to the invitation was typically generous, though not unleavened by more than a hint of genuine reproach. There is room for both, "less is more" (or can be sometimes), and in fact the minimalists are performing a necessary function: "Beyond their individual and historically local impulses [they] are re-enacting a cyclical correction in the history . . . of literature. . . . Renaissances beget Reformations, which then beget Counter-Reformations." But as his historical examples proliferate, his *parti pris* becomes apparent: "the seven fat years are succeeded by seven lean, after which we, no less than the people of Genesis, may look forward to the recorrection." The lean years in Egypt were, of course, a time of starvation that could be endured only because Joseph took the precaution of storing up vast silos of grain. Barth is even more critical a few paragraphs earlier when he complains that rarely in minimalists' prose "will one find a sentence of any syntactical complexity. . . . Dick-and-Jane prose tends to be emotionally and intellectually poorer than Henry James prose." Though he does acknowledge that "among the great minimalist writers, this impoverishment is elected and strategic: simplification in the interest of strength or of some other value (25)."

I certainly have no intention of defending minimalism, if it exists, against such a critique, for I would personally tend to side with Barth anyway on the question of the relative value of the simple versus the complex. This is a book on Carver, not on the genre. And he in fact rejected the term's applicability to himself: "In a review of the last book, somebody called me a 'minimalist' writer. The reviewer meant it as a compliment. But I didn't like it. There's something about 'minimalist' that smacks of smallness of vision and execution that I don't like" (*Conversations,* 44). The problem here may be that Carver has been the most influential minimalist ("the most influential stylist since Donald Barthelme," according to David Bellamy [38]) while at the same time the least representative.

Carver is in fact a self-reflexive metafictional writer—not the practitioner of "extrospective" fiction Barth takes him to be but an extremely *intro*spective one. When Barth published his book of short stories—*Lost in the Funhouse* (1968)—he made explicit claims for the volume that Carver never made for his but that I would like to make for him. "This book," Barth wrote in the Author's Note, "differs in two ways from most volumes of short fiction. First, it's neither a collection nor a selection, but a series; though several of its items have appeared sepa-

rately in periodicals, the series will be seen to have been meant
to be received 'all at once' and as here arranged" (ix). In Barth's
Funhouse the bottle with a contentless message that floats up on
the Maryland shore in one story turns out to have been sent on
its voyage in ancient Greece in a later one. As Max Schulz
demonstrates in his recent and brilliant analysis of the volume,
each of several "self-reflexive fictive voices" (9) in the several
stories "will in turn recover the bottled water-message of the
unknown original tale-teller with its undesignated greeting, un-
signed conclusion, and blank lines between—and each will se-
riatim fill in the blanks with written words" (10). What gets
repeated from story to story, that is, often (like this water-
message) refers, self-reflexively, to the notion itself of text,
and in particular to the kind of text in which it appears. The
order in which Barth's stories appear is also, as he makes clear,
significant: "as here arranged." As Schulz points out, for
example, "Petition," wherein one Siamese twin lusts in vain
after the woman his brother possesses, immediately precedes
"Lost in the Funhouse," in which the protagonist lusts in
vain for his older brother's girlfriend (squinched up next
to him in the family car en route to Ocean City, Maryland,
and thus recalling the "so near yet so far" syndrome the less-
lucky Siamese twin suffered in the story before). "Petition"
is preceded by "Water-Message," which concerns the same
Maryland protagonist and his rivalry with his older sibling.
"Given its pivotal place between the two stories," Schulz
comments, "the rivalry of the 'Petition' brothers resonates
allegorically with the sibling tensions joining and separating the Mensch brothers" (2). One could also go as far as to
say that this sandwiching of the twin story between the two
Mensch ones itself resonates with the sandwiching in close
quarters the Siamese petitioner suffered when his twin made
love to Thalia.

The burden of my book will be to show that things like this
happen in Carver too—like the two doubled or halved envelopes in the two central stories of *Will You Please Be Quiet,
Please?*—though nowhere does Carver, like Barth, make a

point of telling us they do.[2] Perhaps the difference between a
postmodernist and whatever it is that Raymond Carver is
(which is not a minimalist) is the difference between a self-
reflexive metafictionist who says he is one and a self-reflexive
metafictionist who leaves that to the reader to decide. Frederick
Barthelme speaks of the minimalist's reticence in his (even
more cleverly titled) *New York Times Book Review* contribution to
the ongoing discussion ("Convicted Minimalist Spills Bean"). If
you are accused of being a minimalist, he concludes, "Tell them
that you prefer to think you're leaving room for the readers, at
least for the ones who *like* to use their imaginations; that you
hope those readers hear the whispers, catch the feints and
shadows, gather the traces" (27). Kim Herzinger's account of
the moment in literary history through which we are now passing, however, presents the best explanation of the difference—
and the continuity—between Carver and Barth:

> The Postmoderns . . . showed their public the tubes and
> wires of fiction; we could not taste the product without being
> fully aware of the methods of its manufacture. But . . . it be-
> came apparent that things could not be spoken of directly in
> any case. This Postmodern revelation, once declared, made
> everything possible, including a return to story, character,
> and the conventions of representation. . . . The effect . . . is
> to revitalize certain literary values once thought exhausted,
> and to defamiliarize what we thought was familiar. . . . And
> far from collapsing into a kind of journalistic representation
> of life in our time, [the minimalists] may well be creating
> literary constructs as formally rigorous and linguistically
> savvy as their Postmodern predecessors. (20)

2. Marc Chénétier is the only other critic I know of who has spoken of
the self-reflexivity of Carver's work. "The Lie" (an early story reprinted in
Fires), he points out, "demonstrates in a perfectly circular manner the emp-
tiness of a text which is 'about' nothing but its own structure. . . . 'I want the
truth,' the male protagonist says . . . and this is exactly what the overall structure of the text makes sure the reader cannot attain" (176). Carver will tell
another such tale in "Blackbird Pie," one of his last stories (to be discussed
later in these pages). Chénétier too (though he doesn't mention the folded
envelopes) says he "cannot but be struck by abundant occurrences of what I

Metafictional self-reflexivity is at least as old as part 2 of *Don Quixote* ("with *Don Quixote,* the novel may be said to *begin* in self-transcendent parody and has often returned to that mode for its refreshment" [Barth, "The Literature of Replenishment," 205]). There was plenty of it going on, as I have elsewhere shown ("The Oblique Gaze," "Montaigne's Larceny") in the *Essays* of Montaigne—and, as Barth himself reminds us, in *The 1001 Nights:* the plots of the first two stories, suspended in midsentence at the end of night number one, "have to do with innocent victims under imperious and imminent threat of death, the first of whom, like Scheherazade herself, is playing for time by telling his would-be executioner a story! We are reminded for the 1001st time that 'self-reflexivity' is as old as the narrative imagination" ("Don't Count on It," 265–66). The particular forms it takes in short story and poetry (and in Montaigne's case, essay) sequences have only recently begun to attract the attention they deserve. In fact, while considerable work has been done on the short story collection as a genre, I have not been able to find any study that focuses in quite the way I intend to here on the importance of the *order* in which stories appear—though Robert M. Luscher's essay in Lohafer's *Short Story Theory at a Crossroads* does come tantalizingly close. Alluding to Forest Ingram's pioneering 1971 study *Representative Short Story Cycles of the Twentieth Century: Studies in a Literary Genre,* Luscher writes:

> Ingram's term, *short story cycle,* which critics most commonly use, draws attention to the recurrence of theme, symbol, and character, but does so at the expense of deemphasizing the volume's successiveness. While Ingram's name evokes a distant kinship with epic cycles, the term *short story sequence* sug-

---

will call here 'halving' " (189). Carver's characters are so often "halfway between possibilities," like "the couple provisionally caught on the landing between two doors in 'Neighbors' " (184). Nor does he fail to notice that "subrevelatory moments will occur over a double gate" in "I Could See the Smallest Things." "Reversals, parallels, contradictions, and paradoxes" in the stories "perpetually suggest that surfaces tend to have two sides and that the one we see is not the one that matters" (185).

gests the form's kinship with the sonnet sequence and the modern poetic sequence, thus highlighting the close alliance between the short story and lyric poetry. Since the reader's dominant experience as he negotiates the text and tentatively assembles its patterns is sequential, the [latter] term is more accurately descriptive.

I say "tantalizingly close" because in his next sentence Luscher begins to go in a different direction, though of course a quite valid and useful one, from the one this book will take: "As in a musical sequence, the story sequence repeats and progressively develops themes and motifs over the course of the work; its unity derives from a perception of both the successive ordering and recurrent patterns, which together provide the continuity of the reading experience" (149). Progressive development, while no doubt characteristic of many short story sequences, is not as far as I can tell a feature of the ones we will be reading here. That refusal on Carver's part to continue the story within the story is perhaps part of the stubborn silence that pervades his work, even in the subtext that can be glimpsed in the interstices between his stories.

We will not, then, find a single buried narrative from beginning to end in the short story sequences considered here. But we will find other stories, metastories in which the stories themselves, together with their constituent motifs, images, and turns of phrase, are part of the plot.

What Luscher says is valuable not only because it asks us to focus our attention on the sequence in which stories appear but also for its insistence on the blurring of boundaries between fiction and poetry that takes place in such sequences. In fact, some work has already begun on the poetic side of the question. Neil Fraistat, in *The Poem and the Book: Interpreting Collections of Romantic Poetry* (1985) and in *Poems in Their Place: The Intertextuality and Order of Poetic Collections* (1986), has focused on what happens when we read poetic sequences with an eye to their sequential connections. In *The Braided Dream: Robert Penn Warren's Late Poetry* (1990), I read Warren's last sequences in just this way.

Carver was a poet of considerable gifts, and I will conclude with a glance at a few of the poems—and a bit of the sequential structure—of his strongest collection, *Ultramarine* (1986). Some of the recent poems of Tess Gallagher, Carver's companion for the last ten years of his life and his collaborator on the arrangement of the poems in *Ultramarine*, betray, perhaps not surprisingly, a similar interest in the possibilities of sequence.

It may be time to invent a new word. *Intratextuality* may be the proper coin to account for what can happen when the texts in a text (poems or stories in an intelligently assembled sequence) begin to refer to each other in ways that seem to refer to their doing so (for a quick example think of the two envelopes folded in half, referring both to themselves as doubles of each other and to the larger text of which they constitute the halving fold). It remains to be seen whether the kind of *intra*textual connections that characterize Carver's fiction can be discovered in short story sequences by other hands, though it will certainly be worth a try. The unity of such explicitly unified collections as Eudora Welty's *Golden Apples,* Sherwood Anderson's *Winesburg, Ohio,* Faulkner's *Go Down, Moses,* or E. L. Doctorow's *Lives of the Poets,* however, is of a different sort. In their stories, characters with the same names actually reappear from one story to another. Those collections approach the point of becoming novels; Carver's stories do not so clearly affirm their coherence. The intratextuality at work in Carver is less obvious, more subtle, goes against the grain of the reader's normal expectation. His stories keep their individuality, their sullen separate existence, yet despite this they find ways to communicate, with each other and with us, if we have ears to hear. Carver's text, to adapt what the protagonist of his penultimately published story ("Blackbird Pie") says of the disturbing text he is still trying to interpret (and in whose conflicting terms we can see the insistent struggle between saying nothing and saying something), is one suffused with *both* "silence and innuendo."

2

Will You Please Be Quiet, Please?

"Fat"

"That's a funny story, Rita says, but I can see she doesn't know what to make of it" (6). What are *we* to make of "Fat," the first story in Carver's collection *Will You Please Be Quiet, Please?*, for whom Rita is perhaps a less than ideal listener? Minimalist as Carver's stories are supposed to be (and bear in mind that Carver rejected that description of them), we are told that there is more than enough in this one for Rita to have figured it out: "But I won't go into it with her. I've already told her too much," the narrator tells us. Which means we have been told too much already too, but what exactly have we been told?

An extraordinarily fat man appears in the restaurant where the narrator is a waitress. "Everything about him is big. But it is the fingers I remember best. . . . They look three times the size of a normal person's fingers—long, thick, creamy fingers" (1). He speaks in the first person plural "I think we're ready to order now, he says. . . . Believe me, he says, we don't eat like this all the time. . . . You'll have to excuse us, he says" (1, 3). He consumes an enormous amount of food—lamb chops and baked potato, several servings of bread, two desserts. The fat man is the talk of the restaurant staff, including the narrator's husband, Rudy, who works in the kitchen. "Rudy says, Harriet says you got a fat man from the circus out there. That true? . . . Rudy, he is fat, I say, but that is not the whole story" (5).

11

The rest of the story may be what emerges in the following exchange between the narrator and her customer. "Believe it or not, he says, we have not always eaten like this. Me, I eat and I eat and I can't gain, I say. I'd like to gain, I say" (5). At this point, the listener, Rita, asks, "What else? . . . This story's getting interesting now." But, she is told, the story is over. "That's it. Nothing else. He eats his desserts, and then he leaves and then we go home, Rudy and me" (5). Actually, the story really isn't quite over yet, but as far as the narrator is concerned, what is essential in it has been recounted, apparently in that last bit of conversation with the fat customer. "That's it": the narrator's desire to gain weight. In fact, it is not just that she wishes to stop being skinny, but she positively wants to be fat. She wants to *become* the fat man. For later—and this is the rest of the story —when she and her husband are home in bed, and he begins selfishly to impose his lust upon her (for it was, she says, "against my will"), "When he gets on me, I suddenly feel I am fat. I feel I am terrifically fat, so fat that Rudy is a tiny thing and hardly there at all" (6). It is at this juncture that Rita says it's a funny story and the narrator tells us she can see that Rita doesn't know what to make of it, and furthermore that she feels "depressed," having "already told her too much" (6).

Rudy is a tiny thing and *has* a tiny thing. And that might prompt us to remember the part of the fat man the narrator said "I remember best," his fingers, "three times the size of a normal person's fingers—long, thick, creamy." Long and thick, to be blunt, like an ideal penis—and creamy, full of milk-white sperm. "God, Rita, but those were fingers" (2) (quite the opposite of the feminine digits of her listener, who at the end of the story "sits there waiting, her dainty fingers poking her hair" [6]). To be fat, then, is to be sexually powerful, even virile. For the waitress-narrator, to be as overwhelmingly large as the man in the restaurant is to be able to turn the tables on her usually dominant husband, who as a result has shrunk to practically nothing, "hardly there at all."

What else does it mean to be fat? Perhaps to be—or to have been—Raymond Carver, who in the poem "Harley's Swans" recalls, "Nobody, then, who could love me, / the fattest kid on the block, except my parents" (*Where Water Comes Together With Other Water*, 83). The waitress-narrator, already a figure for the author in her capacity as narrator, wants to acquire the fatness the author himself once had. Carver, that is, has written a story whose teller seems to want to become Raymond Carver. No wonder the fat man addresses himself as "we." He is multiple —not just a character, but narrator and author too.

He may even stand for the story itself, though one might at first be more inclined to take him for its antithesis—a maximalist out of place in a minimalist genre, if one thinks of the reputation Carver's stories have of being thin, even if Carver once was not. But we have the narrator's word for it here that there is more to what is recounted than meets the eye, that there is even "too much" already.

That Carver should place "Fat" first among the twenty-two stories of *Will You Please Be Quiet, Please?* may tell us something about how we might read the others. In these terse narratives perhaps there is something big, and aggressively potent, screaming to get out, if we could only hear it.

"Neighbors"

This woman's fantasy of becoming as fat as the man in the restaurant in order to assume sexual dominance and in the process change her sex finds a curious counterpart in the following story's account of a man who entered his neighbors' apartment and "rummaged through the top drawers until he found a pair of panties and a brassiere. He stepped into the panties and fastened the brassiere, then looked through the closet for an outfit. He put on a black and white checkered skirt and tried to zip it up. He put on a burgundy blouse that buttoned up the front. He considered her shoes, but understood they would not fit" (12). Bill Miller's visits to that apartment across the hall increase his sexual potency too. He comes home early from work and proposes to his wife that they go directly to bed before supper. Arlene Miller is willing to go along with this, for her own visits to the Stones' residence, fully authorized

by their having volunteered to feed the Stones' cat and water
their plants, have given her as much of an erotic thrill as they
have her husband.

Could it be just coincidence that these first two stories in
Carver's collection appear to echo each other so closely? Perhaps so, but consider one telling detail on the last page of "Fat,"
one that almost seems to announce the story to come—in fact
to link their titles, to show the essential equivalence of *fat* and
neighbor: Rudy recalls a "fat guy" he knew once. "We called him
Fat, the kid who lived next door to me. He was a neighbor" (6).

If, as I have suggested, "Fat" names itself as fat with an
excess of meaning that belies its supposedly minimalist genre,
so too does "Neighbors" name itself—given the way Bill Miller's
desire echoes the waitress's—as being significantly placed in the
immediate neighborhood of the story (and, as I hope to show,
the stories) next door.

The conclusion of "Neighbors" sounds, however, a caution-
ary note. The Millers become so fascinated with the apartment
across the hall that they forget the reason they were allowed
there in the first place, neglecting to feed the cat or to water
the plants. What is worse, they lock themselves out of their own
apartment, having forgotten to bring along the key. The kind
of reading I am proposing here may court a similar danger, if
one is so concerned with the way Carver's stories look at each
other from the outside in that one neglects to tend to what life
does dwell in each (let this serve as sufficient acknowledgment
of the warning). It is a risk, though, that evidently fascinated
Carver, who in "Locking Yourself Out, Then Trying to Get
Back In" found that "it was something to look in like that,
unseen, / from the deck. To be there, inside, and not be there"
(*Where Water Comes Together With Other Water*, 33).

The Millers' fascination with visiting the Stones' apartment
culminates, just before they realize they have lost their way
back, in their discovery of certain *pictures.* " 'I guess I should
tell you. I found some pictures.' He stopped in the middle of
the hall. 'What kind of pictures?' 'You can see for yourself,' she
said, and she watched him. 'No kidding.' He grinned. 'Where?'
"In a drawer,' she said. . . . And then she said, 'Maybe they

won't come back,' and was at once astonished at her words"
(13). It is astonishing that she should say that, but it is astonishing too that this penultimate moment in "Neighbors" should so
nearly echo what happens at about the same distance from the
end of "Fat": Rudy, remembering his childhood neighbor Fat,
and another equally obese kid named Wobbly, says "Wish I had
their *pictures*" (6). That desire to see a neighbor's picture is
strangely met in what Arlene Miller discovers in her neighbors'
drawer.

"The Idea"

The Millers' fascination with their neighbors is answered by
the fascination exerted on the couple in "The Idea" by *their*
neighbors, as well as by the fascination those neighbors themselves find for the very idea of voyeurism. Every three nights
or so, Vern and his wife can see the man next door "standing
and looking into his own bedroom window" (16)—pretending,
that is, to be a voyeur, playing an elaborate sex game with his
wife in which he imagines that he is peering into a stranger's
house, and that his wife is someone else.

> I could make out someone behind the curtain now. It
> must have been her undressing. But I couldn't see any detail.
> I strained my eyes. Vern was wearing his reading glasses, so
> he could see everything better than I could. Suddenly the
> curtain was drawn aside and the woman turned her back to
> the window.
> "What's she doing now?" I said, knowing full well. . . .
> "She's taking off her clothes," Vern said. "What do you
> think she's doing?"
> Then the bedroom light went out and the man started
> back along the side of his house. He opened the screen door
> and slipped inside, and a little later the rest of the lights went
> out. (16–17)

It is perhaps not without significance that this scene can be best
viewed through *reading* glasses (which in fact ought not to be

the case, since such lenses correct for near, not far, vision), for
what Vern is seeing is what the reader can see repeatedly inscribed in the very structure of Carver's text, the way his stories
catch illicit views of their neighbors. It is a reading scene, self-
referentially emblematic of the manner in which we—the readers—may glimpse the interplay transpiring in the short story
cycle of which "The Idea" is a part. We can read the book as
Vern reads his neighbors.

So as not to commit the Millers' sin of forgetting to take
care of what legitimately dwells in the apartment one is supposed to be tending (the cat, the plants), I should not neglect
to point out that within "The Idea" itself Vern's wife's figura-
tive denomination of the woman next door as "that trash" (17,
19) finds concrete realization in the garbage in her own kitchen
that, to her dismay, attracts a steady stream of ants. And of
course her frenzied defense against these invaders, as she
sprays insecticide everywhere, echoes her abhorrence of invading eyes: " 'Anybody comes looking in my window,' I said,
'they'll have the cops on them' " (18).

"They're Not Your Husband"

That repeated demonstrative pronoun—" 'Someday I'm
going to tell *that* trash what I think of her. . . . *That* trash,' I
said. 'The idea!' "—is repeated, in significantly different ways,
in the following story, where Earl Ober overhears one man say
to another, in the restaurant where his wife works as a waitress,
"Look at the ass on that" (20). And where Ober, pretending to
be a stranger to his wife, will later point her out to another man
and say "What do you think of that? . . . Don't you think that's
something special?' " (27) In both stories *that* is a woman, considered as a sexual object.

Between the first *that* and the second, several weeks pass,
during which Earl Ober puts his wife on a diet to make her lose
the fat that had attracted the derision of the man he overheard.
"The other man laughed, 'I've seen better,' he said. 'That's
what I mean,' the first man said. 'But some jokers like their

quim fat' " (20). If "Fat" gave us a fat customer who attracts the attention (and horror) of the waitresses, "They're Not Your Husband" presents a fat waitress who elicits a similar response from some customers. And while in one story a waitress dreams of being fat in order to triumph over her overbearing husband, in the other she is browbeaten by her overbearing husband into starving herself into thinness. " 'Just quit eating,' Earl said. 'For a few days, anyway' " (23).

Carver's fourth story symmetrically responds to his first. But it clearly echoes its immediate predecessor too, for just as Vern's neighbor would peer at his wife as if they were strangers to each other, so does Earl Ober come into the restaurant where his wife works and pretend he doesn't know her. This takes place after the weight-loss program had been in effect for a while:

> Another waitress came by with a coffeepot and filled Earl's cup.
> "Who's your friend?" he said and nodded at his wife.
> "Her name's Doreen," the waitress said.
> "She looks a lot different than the last time I was in here," he said.
> "I wouldn't know," the waitress said. (26)

Disappointed in his attempt to elicit some positive comment about his wife's appearance, he tries again.

> "What do you think of that?" Earl said to the man, nodding at Doreen as she moved down the counter. "Don't you think that's something special? . . . Look at the ass on her. Now you watch this now. Could I have a chocolate sundae?" Earl called to Doreen.
> She stopped in front of him and let out her breath. Then she turned and picked up a dish and the ice-cream dipper. . . . Earl looked at the man and winked as Doreen's skirt traveled up her thighs. (27)

By asking for ice cream he managed to get Doreen to turn her back to him and the man, which would place her in the same

position, as she bent over to dip it out, in which she had been
at the beginning of the story when the customer had made his
disparaging remark. Making her turn her back would place her
as well in the position the neighbor's wife had assumed when
she began her display for her husband: "Suddenly the curtain
was drawn aside and the woman turned her back to the window" (16).

"Are You a Doctor?"

When Earl Ober made his wife turn around to make a
chocolate sundae and winked at the stranger, the other waitress
asked Doreen, " 'Who is this character?' . . . 'Who?' Doreen
said. . . . 'Him,' the other waitress said and nodded at Earl.
'Who is this joker, anyway?' " (27–28). These questions at the
end of "They're Not Your Husband" anticipate the ones that
will be asked at the beginning of the next story, when Arnold
Breit receives a late-evening telephone call he assumes will be
from his wife. " 'Who is this?' a woman asked. 'Well, who is
this?' he said" (29; Carver's emphasis).

She is Carol Holt, and she claims to have gotten his phone
number from a call the baby sitter took when she was out. The
sitter obviously made a mistake in transcribing it, but Mrs. Holt
mysteriously persists in prolonging the conversation. She presumes a familiarity with Breit, calling him by his first name
and asking for a heart-to-heart talk, that is hardly justified. She
thus recalls the protagonist of the immediately preceding
story by virtue of doing precisely the opposite of what he did,
for we remember that Earl Ober pretended to be a stranger
to someone with whom he could hardly be more intimately
acquainted. At first annoyed but eventually intrigued, Breit
accepts her invitation, repeated in two subsequent calls, to
visit her apartment. She claims her daughter Cheryl is sick,
and when Arnold arrives she asks him, absurdly, "Are you a
doctor?"

The error the sitter must have made in understanding the
number is echoed by the conversational exchange Breit has

with the daughter before the mother returns from a trip to the drugstore for aspirin and cough syrup: " 'What is your name? Isn't your name Shirley?' 'Cheryl,' she said. 'C-h-e-r-y-l.' 'Yes, now I remember. Well, I was close, you must admit' " (34). Breit was about as close as the babysitter must have been when she mistakenly wrote down what turned out to be his unlisted number.

Carver's stories persist in giving us tantalizing clues to how we might read between their lines, for this business about misplaced letters and numbers strangely parallels the risks and opportunities of that very interlinear reading. Had the sitter not made the error Breit himself duplicates we would not have had a story. Breit would not have had the opportunity of risking an extramarital affair with Carol Holt (from which an awkward kiss, at least, results—more, perhaps, could eventually ensue). The parallel lies in the possibility that while we may think we see stories emerge in the space between Carver's stories (the story, for example, of how his stories behave like voyeuristic neighbors), as we pay attention to what gets repeated from one to the next, this may all be just a fiction, based on an error in perception. We may be seeing—reading—what isn't really there, or what is nothing more than chance and coincidence.

There is no way of knowing for sure. Yet there are at least two ways of reducing the element of doubt. One is to look at what revisions Carver may have made in his stories between their first publication and their appearance in book form. I will later show how some of these changes set up resonances with neighboring stories—so that the order in which they appear will turn out to be important, as was that of the letters of Cheryl's name. For it is possible to retrace the steps of Breit's mistake and to discover that he more or less had the right letters (or sounds) but had put the last two in the wrong order, getting "Shir*ley*" for "Cher*yl*."

The other aspect of Carver's text that provides some degree of reassurance that there may be indeed something to read between the lines, which is to say between the stories, is the way what is repeated is itself sometimes part of what appears to be a self-referential allusion to the fact of its repetition. That is, Carver's text seems to anticipate our discovery of contiguous repetitions, seems to be waiting to second our discovery with a resounding echo of its own. We have seen this for example in the neighborliness of "Neighbors" toward the stories on either side. We may see it as well in the babysitter's mistake that allowed the events of "Are You a Doctor?" to take place: " 'That's my *number*,' he said. 'How did you get it?' 'I don't know. It was written down on a *piece of paper* when I got in from work,' the woman said. 'Who wrote it down?' 'I don't know,' the woman said. 'The sitter, I guess. It must be her' " (29; emphasis added). For at the heart of the immediately preceding story lie numbers on a piece of paper too. They are an essential part of the weight-loss program Earl Ober forced on his wife so that he could return to the restaurant and point out her now svelte figure to the other customers: "Each morning he followed her into the bathroom and waited while she stepped onto the scale. He got down on his knees with a pencil and the *piece of paper*. The paper was covered with dates, days of the week, *numbers*. He read the *number* on the scale, consulted the *paper*, and either nodded his head or pursed his lips" (25; emphasis added). The parallel is rather striking: The numbers the babysitter wrote down on a piece of paper were close to the sequence she heard, though not quite close enough, with the result that the story "Are You a Doctor?" tells can take place. But that act of writing numbers down on a piece of paper is itself so close to what Earl Ober was doing that something seems to take place between the two stories that did not take place in either story considered separately. It is something like an event, like a piece of narrative outside the narrative—dwelling in the space between the stories, residing in the order of their appearance. That order is itself a text, the result of a choice.

But does this fragment of narrative really exist? It may indeed be an error to think it does, but the second of these two stories has already led us to ponder how narrative can arise from an error in transcription (which is to say an error in reading): Not close enough is precisely good enough for that. This kind of error, in other words, is already inscribed in the text of the sequence. We are invited, that is, by Carver's short story cycle to make precisely this very "error"—which strongly suggests that it is in fact no error at all.

"The Father"

When Arnold Breit returns home, his wife calls. Instead of answering with a "hello, dear" (29), as he had apparently been in the habit of doing before Carol Holt entered his life, since no one but Mrs. Breit knew the unlisted number, he replies, "Arnold. Arnold Breit speaking" (38). His wife perceives his change of tone immediately. "Arnold? My, aren't we formal tonight! . . . Are you there, Arnold? You don't sound like your self" (38). The very last words of this story—*like yourself*—announce the whole plot of the next, which in two pages recounts the conversation the father of a newborn baby overhears from the next room. It is a conversation that culminates in the question of who the self of that father is like:

> "Who does the baby look like?"
> "He doesn't look like anybody," Phyllis said. And they moved even closer.
> "*I* know! *I* know!" Carol said. "He looks like *Daddy!*" Then they looked closer at the baby.
> "But who does Daddy *look* like?" Phyllis asked.
> "Who does Daddy *look* like?" Alice repeated, and they all at once looked through to the kitchen where the father was sitting at the table with his back to them.
> "Why, nobody!" Phyllis said and began to cry a little. . . .
> "Daddy doesn't look like *anybody!*" Alice said.
> "But he has to look like *somebody*," Phyllis said, wiping her eyes with one of the ribbons. And all of them except the grandmother looked at the father, sitting at the table.
> He had turned around in his chair and his face was white and without expression. (39–40; Carver's emphasis)

Daddy in fact looks like the baby, who has a similarly expressionless face: "He did not smile or laugh" (39).

Both "The Father" and "Are You a Doctor?" are medita-
tions on identity, in particular on putting one's identity into
question—as even the title of the latter does. Carol Holt practically forces on Arnold Breit an identity he hadn't possessed,
behaving as if he were someone who would find it quite natural
to pay her a visit. While still in the first of their phone conversations, Arnold found it necessary to go look at his own reflection to figure out who he was to provoke such declarations
from this perfect stranger as "You sound like a nice man" (30)
and "You're kind to say that, Arnold" (31). " 'Will you hold the
phone a minute?' he said. 'I have to check on something.' He
went into the study for a cigar, took a minute lighting it up
with the desk lighter, then removed his glasses and looked at
himself in the mirror over the fireplace" (31). His identity in
fact becomes the subject of their telephone conversation: " 'I'm
an old man,' he said. 'Oh, you're not,' she said. 'Really, I'm old,'
he said" (31). At the end of his story, as a result of what was
apparently a troubling experience, Arnold doesn't sound like
himself any more, as his wife can realize all too well. No longer
who he was, it is not clear who he has become. Similarly, at the
end of the following story, the father's identity seems as blank
a slate as his face is "white and without expression."

"Nobody Said Anything"

In "The Father" the father overheard the conversation
about his son from the kitchen: "The father was *in the kitchen*
and *could hear them.*" (39; emphasis added). These words are
echoed in the very first line of "Nobody Said Anything,"
though the situation is now reversed. A son overhears his father in conversation *in* the kitchen: "I *could hear them* out *in the
kitchen*. I couldn't hear what they were saying, but they were
arguing" (41; emphasis added). The story begins and ends with
the parents locked in argument in that kitchen. Between these
early-morning and late-afternoon disputes the parents leave
for work and return, and the son, identified for us as "R" from

the signature on the note he writes his mother (45), plays hooky from school to go fishing.

R tells his mother he's too ill to go to school, of course; his "asshole" (41) brother George tries the same tactic but with no success. Our protagonist is extremely curious about sex, and his fishing expedition is continually interspersed with adolescent erotic dreams. Before he leaves the house he rummages through his parents' bedroom looking for rubbers and finds a jar of Vaseline in which he invests much mystery. "I knew it must have something to do with it, but I didn't know what" (44). On the way to Birch Creek a woman in a red car gives him a ride, and he fantasizes about the possibilities to which this gives rise. "You always see yourself getting picked up by this woman. You know you'll fall for each other and that she'll take you home with her and let you screw her all over the house. I began to get a boner thinking about it" (46). The first thing he does when he gets to the creek is to relieve his sexual tension. "I hurried down the embankment, unzipped, and shot off five feet over the creek. It must have been a record" (47).

He will catch two fish that day, the first extraordinary for its color, the second for its size. The degree to which sex and fishing are intertwined for the boy can be seen when the first of these fish makes its appearance on the scene. He has been daydreaming again about the woman in the car. "I followed her. I watched as she pulled down her pants and sat on the toilet. I had a big boner and she waved me over with her hand. Just as I was going to unzip, I heard a plop in the creek. I looked and saw the tip of my fly rod jiggling" (49). It was an easy catch, as the fish didn't put up much of a struggle. But it "looked strange . . . he was a trout. But he was green. I never saw one like him before. He had green sides . . . a greenish head, and like a green stomach . . . the color of moss, that color green" (49–50).

The boy had never seen a fish like this before, but we have seen something like it earlier in the story. Before he left home, he had allowed himself the pleasure of rereading, for "about the fifth time" (44), the chapter in Edgar Rice Burroughs's *The*

Princess of Mars "where Tars Tarkas falls for a green woman, only to see her get her head chopped off the next morning by this jealous brother-in-law" (43). Of the two fish he will catch that day, one will be green and the other will get its head chopped off because of a dispute with a jealous fellow angler who greatly resembles the protagonist's brother. The consequence is double: We can appreciate how well-constructed Carver's story is, since even what the boy reads that day is tied to what he will catch, and we can realize that not only is the fishing trip interlarded with erotic reverie, but the fish he will land are for him in some sense a woman.

It was the other boy, "a kid about George's size" (50), who saw it first, a fish "at least two feet long, queerly skinny, but bigger than anything I had ever caught" (55). Like George, R's rival for this monstrous catch was an "asshole idiot kid" (52)—an idiot because he did not follow R's instructions to the letter when they decided to work together to catch the fish. In the end R had to wrestle it to the ground himself. But the other boy claimed it was his since he saw it first. "Then I had an idea. 'We could half him,' I said. 'What do you mean?' . . . 'Half him. I got a knife. We cut him in two and each take half' " (56). They will have to halve him, that is, to have him. Though they disagree over who gets the better half, the other boy is finally content to take home the green fish and the tail half of the big one.

R is eager to take his half of the fish home to show his father and to bask in the pride of his accomplishment. But there a great disappointment awaits, for mother and father are arguing again in the kitchen and have no inclination to look at his fish. Besides, it's a disgusting sight. When he holds the creel out to his mother, she almost throws up, screaming for him to take it away. His father at first refuses to look; when he does his mouth falls open. "Take that goddamn thing out of here! What in the hell is the matter with you? Take it the hell out of the kitchen and throw it in the goddamn garbage!" (59) In the end R is left alone outside with his fish, or rather his half of it: "I lifted him out. I held him. I held that half of him" (59).

"The Kitchen," a poem in Carver's final collection, *A New Path to the Waterfall*, tells a hauntingly similar tale of a boy gone fishing, yet with some interesting—and revealing—differences. While in the short story the boy's masturbation was interrupted by—or perhaps even conjured into existence by—the fish that, like the woman in his favorite story, was green, in the poem it culminates in the sudden loss of his fishing pole (and we remember how phallic his fly rod had been in the story, how its tip began jiggling just as he was about to unzip). The way he tells it, it is as if his penis had fallen off, in divine retribution.

> I pushed a forked branch
> into the sandy bank, rested the pole in the fork,
> watched the bobber for a while, then beat off.
> Grew sleepy then and let my eyes close. . . . When
> suddenly, in my sleep, I heard a plop, and my eyes
> flew open. My pole was gone!
> I saw it tearing a furrow through
> the scummy water. . . .
> Began to run along the bank, swearing to God
> I would not touch myself again if He'd let me
> retrieve that pole, that fish. (37)

Like the short story, the poem concludes with a disgusting discovery in the kitchen, but it is the boy who experiences it now. "My dad was drunk / and in the kitchen with a woman not his wife, nor / my mother either" (38). She was sitting on his lap; they had been drinking. His father stared at him without recognition, then asked what was the matter. Like Noah's accursed son, Carver saw his father—figuratively—naked: "My dad waited . . . the bulge in his pants / subsiding." He could only respond—to the loss of his pole, to his father's infidelity, to the sight of that bulge—with "stuttered syllables . . . words made to cling / as anguish that poured from my raw young mouth" (38).

If the poem is autobiographical, as many of Carver's appear to be, then the short story that so strangely resembles it may be an earlier, disguised version of the event. But there is at least one specific detail in the story, not present in the poem, that points to another, still earlier version of these events. The detail

is the one to which the title alludes. As is almost always the case
with a Carver story, the title reappears somewhere in the text
of the narrative. If that title at first seems enigmatic, the place
where it reappears will make its meaning clearer. But sometimes, as here, the passage appears to have very little to do
with the rest of the story: "It was nice out. It was fall. But it
wasn't cold yet except at night. At night they would light the
smudgepots in the orchards and you would wake up in the
morning with a black ring of stuff in your nose. But *nobody said
anything*. They said the smudging kept the young pears from
freezing, so it was all right" (45; emphasis added).

What does this digression about the reluctance of citizens
to demand clean air have to do with fishing? The answer lies in
one of the oldest stories extant about a boy who goes fishing
and comes to terms with his sexuality. It even involves cutting
open the fish. Young Tobias, in the Old Testament book of
Tobit (sometimes relegated to the Apocrypha, sometimes—for
example in Catholic Bibles—not), goes on a journey to do an
errand for his father. At the Tigris River, he is frightened by a
leaping fish, but is told by his traveling companion (the angel
Raphael in human guise) to catch it with his hands, and then to
cut it open with a knife. Later in his journey he makes the
acquaintance of a girl with whom he falls in love, and whom he
rescues from a demon. Upon his return home, he heals his
father's blindness and makes the young woman his wife.

Not every moment in the story of Tobias finds a counterpart in that of young R, but enough do to make it appear that
this ancient tale is lurking somewhere in the background to
Carver's story. First, consider the way R caught the monstrous
fish. He did not use his fly rod for this one; neither did Tobias.
"I scooped him with my hands and arms, *up, up, raising him,
throwing him out of the water*" (54; emphasis added). Tobias
caught his in mid-air, as it leapt from the water. Second, there
is the cutting open R and Tobias did to the fish immediately
after they caught it. Third, we have abundantly seen, through
the analogy between green woman and green fish, and between
her decapitation and that of the larger fish, not to mention the
constant undercurrent of sex, that fishing and looking for girls

are intimately related in Carver's story. And so they are in the
Bible too, for Tobias, who is just as lacking as R in practical
experience with the opposite sex, finds a woman through his
fishing, winning her hand by making magic use of part of what
came out of the fish to free her from her demon.

Just how he frees her is the fourth and perhaps most remarkable parallel Carver's story has to offer. On the angel's
advice, he burned the heart and liver he had taken from the
fish and made so much smoke that the demon fled. The parallel
would not be so remarkable if the only smoke in "Nobody Said
Anything" were that which came from the smudge pots to keep
the pear trees from freezing. But the interesting thing is that
that is not the only smoke, for the final scene of the story is full
of it as well: "I heard their voices and looked through the
window. They were sitting at the table. Smoke was all over the
kitchen. I saw it was coming from a pan on the burner. But
neither of them paid any attention" (58). His mother, who that
morning had taken the precaution of telling her son "Don't
cook anything. You don't need to turn the burners on for a
thing" (43), had left the pan on the burner. In the heat of her
argument with his father, she had forgotten all about it. Now,
even without bringing Tobias into it, we can realize an important connection between the two smoky events in Carver's story
and find the explanation for its puzzling title. *Nobody said anything*, at least anything R was expecting and wanting to hear,
about his wondrous fish. The title, baffling when linked to the
smudge pots alone, assumes its fuller resonance in this smoke-
filled final scene.

If Carver's story is a latter-day version of the Biblical tale,[1]
it is one that has gone horribly wrong. The elements—the boy,
the journey, the fish, the knife, the sex, the smoke—are there,
but this time things have not quite worked out. The father,

1. Tobias's fish surfaces in other modern texts as well. In my *Fowles/
Irving/Barthes: Canonical Variations on an Apocryphal Theme* it can be found in
texts as diverse as *The World According to Garp* and Goethe's *Werther*. In *The
Taciturn Text: The Fiction of Robert Penn Warren* (143–45) I trace its reappearance in Warren's 1955 novel *Band of Angels*.

whose biblical predecessor had his blindness cured by his son
(Tobias made a paste for his father's eyes from the gall that
came from the fish), is perhaps most at fault. He is the one R
wanted to show his fish to. He is blind to its wondrousness: "He
said, 'I don't want to look' " (59).

"Sixty Acres"

"Sixty Acres" is the third story in a row in this collection to
feature fathers and sons. In "Nobody Said Anything" a son
returns home from an adventurous journey, only to meet a
disappointing response from his father to what he has accomplished. In "Sixty Acres" it is a father who must return home
to disappointment: his own—"he could not understand why he
felt something crucial had happened, a failure" (70)—and his
sons'. He had gone out to deal with two boys who were poaching on his land, shooting for ducks on his sixty acres—R and
the other boy had been trespassing too, R having "climbed
under a fence that had a KEEP OUT sign on the post" (48).
He knows his sons will be disappointed in the leniency he shows
toward the boys. They had seen him take his double-barreled
shotgun and asked him if he wasn't going to load it. "Ever since
the call they had been after him—had wanted to know if this
time he was going to shoot somebody. It bothered him, kids
talking like that, like they would enjoy it" (61). When he returns
home, having done nothing more than get the poachers to
promise they will not do it again, he seems to anticipate the
complaint his sons will likely make that he should have done
more, saying to his wife, "I should've given them more of a
scare, I guess. . . . I could've killed them" (72). Indeed, shooting bird poachers is a possibility "Nobody Said Anything" likewise raises, for R points out that "Sometimes when you go by
the orchards you see pheasants running down the rows, but
you can't hunt there because you might get shot by a Greek
named Matsos" (45). When R first presented his half of the fish
to his parents, he told us, "My legs shook. I could hardly stand"
(59). When Leé Waite confronted the poachers he seems al-

most to be in R's same shoes: "his knees unaccountably began to shake" (69); and again, when he returned home: "His legs began to tremble" (74).

One of the senses of the title of "Nobody Said Anything," we found, was R's disappointment that nobody said anything about what a wonderful fish he had caught. In "Sixty Acres" Waite's return from the encounter with the poachers is met with a stony silence from his septuagenarian mother, who "sometimes . . . went two days without saying something. . . . It made him shiver when she did that. . . . 'Why don't you say something?' he asked, shaking his head" (62)

His mother's silence may signal rage for her son's having betrayed his ancestors—the Waites are American Indians—to the extent of permitting poachers to escape with their lives from invading their land. Lee Waite thus feels even more guilty about what he is thinking of doing, leasing out his sixty acres for a thousand dollars to a duck club. " 'That wouldn't be selling it, would it?,' his wife asked. 'If you lease it to them, that means it's still your land?' " Waite's testy response shows how defensive he is about the project. " 'Yes, yes it's still my land! . . . Don't you know the difference, Nina? They can't *buy* land on the reservation.' . . . 'What will Mama say?' . . . They both looked over at the old woman. But her eyes were closed and she seemed to be sleeping. . . . 'It's just a lease,' he said" (73–74).

"What's in Alaska?"

The next story, "What's in Alaska?," likewise concerns a man willing to abandon to another his claim to some empty land—and not only land, in this instance, but his wife. That she is having an affair with his best friend becomes apparent when Carl and Mary go to Jack and Helen's house to try out their hosts' new hookah. When Mary and Jack go into the kitchen together, for example, Carl sees "Mary move against Jack from behind and put her arms around his waist" (84). At another moment, Mary addresses Jack as "honey," then tries to explain it away: "I'll have another one too, honey. What did I say? I mean *Jack*. Excuse me. I thought I was talking to Carl" (86).

Before they left to go to Jack and Helen's, Mary announced to her husband that she had a job interview that day and believes that " 'they're going to offer me a job—in *Fairbanks.*' 'Alaska?' Carl asked. 'I've always wanted to go to Alaska' " (76). But when they arrive at their friends' house, it becomes increasingly unlikely that it is Carl who is going to get to go with her there. Under the influence of whatever was in the hookah, Jack's tongue is loosened and he appears to let slip the truth of the situation. Carl had told his hosts they were contemplating moving to Alaska; meanwhile Jack and Helen's cat Cindy has brought in a dead mouse: " 'What the hell,' Jack said. 'Cindy's got to learn to hunt if we're going to Alaska.' 'Alaska?' Helen said. 'What's all this about Alaska?' 'Don't ask me,' Jack said. . . . 'Mary and Carl said they're going to Alaska. Cindy's got to learn to hunt' " (87). In his stupor, Jack has sought to cover up for having said that *we*—apparently he and Mary—were going to Alaska, but evidently forgot to explain why his *cat*—his own and Helen's cat—would be going.

The question the story's title poses is asked several times in the course of the evening and is given an interesting answer by Carl: " 'There's nothing in Alaska,' Carl said. 'He's on a bummer,' Mary said. 'What'll you guys *do* in Alaska?' Jack said. 'There's nothing to do in Alaska,' Carl said" (85), evidently depressed by the realization of what has really been going on between his friend and his wife. There is nothing in Alaska, as there was nothing in Lee Waite's "untenanted and irresistible sixty acres" (60). There is nothing there, that is, for Carl; though for Jack, who apparently finds Mary as irresistible as the poachers find Waite's untenanted acres, there will be plenty to do, and someone to do it to. Mary and Alaska are interchangeable in "What's in Alaska?" as are Alaska and Waite's sixty acres in the parallel structure these two stories display. Waite and Carl are both willing to abandon their rights to a more powerful claimant. Like Waite, Carl's "knees trembled" (90) as he realized the full force of his weakness. And like Waite, who "squinted in the late-afternoon winter half-light" as he told himself that "he wasn't afraid" (61) (and later, when he returned home, stared at a gill net wrapped around a fishing spear as if he did not recognize it and "squinted at it" [71]), Carl too "squinted" (83) as he leaned forward to peer at his wife embracing his best friend in the kitchen.

The hunting motif so important in "Sixty Acres" is reintroduced here too, in the figure of Cindy the huntress cat, who hasn't exactly been poaching but *is* guilty of invading someone else's private space. "The cat carried the mouse out of the hall and into the bathroom. . . . 'I don't think I want her eating a mouse in my bathroom,' Helen said" (86). Later, the cat brought it into the living room, dragging "the mouse under the coffee table. . . . She held the mouse in her paws and licked slowly, from head to tail" (87). This scene is reminiscent of the conclusion of "Nobody Said Anything," when R brought his disgusting catch into his parents' kitchen. "What's in Alaska?" could perhaps have followed R's fishing story, though the parallel conflicts of fathers and sons link it to "Sixty Acres" rather better, as the theme of giving up one's interest in a stretch of empty land ties the Alaska tale more appropriately to the story that it follows in Carver's actual sequence. But we have seen how parallels persist for more than two stories—paternity, for example, in "The Father" and in the two immediately after.

"Night School"

In "Night School" the unnamed protagonist-narrator is sitting in a bar when he is approached by two women who make what appears to be a mildly sexual proposal, certainly an invitation to continue the party in less public surroundings. " 'We're on the loose tonight,' the other woman said. 'But Edith's car is in the garage' " (95). They want him to drive them to the house of a certain Patterson, their night-school professor. Patterson likes to drink, they say, and so they'll take a six-pack along and surprise him. The protagonist is at loose ends too—his marriage has fallen apart, and his girl friend is out of

town. He agrees to take them there if he can borrow his parents' car. He walks with them to his parents' apartment, leaves
them outside while he goes in to ask his father for the car. His
father talks him out of it, and he simply abandons the women
on his doorstep, neglecting to go back out to tell them the car
is not available.

This is a puzzling story, with the slightest of plots. It doesn't
exactly go anywhere, but then neither does its protagonist. In
this regard it is certainly a convincing portrait of male inertia.
Considered, however, in the context of its immediate surroundings in *Will You Please Be Quiet, Please?*, it begins to show
a more lively resonance. For the protagonist is another version
of Carl in "What's in Alaska?" whose wife proposed to him that
they go someplace together too—Alaska—but who in the end
will not be going there. Mary is less interested in Carl than in
Jack, as the women in the bar are less interested in the protagonist than in their night-school teacher, despite the apparently
sexual context of their encounter, given the ambience of the
bar. Our hero is just a means to an end; so, by now it seems, is
Carl.

Near the end of "Night School," the narrator remembers
telling his wife about something he once read in a book.

> There's a man who has a nightmare and in the nightmare he
> dreams he's dreaming and wakes to see a man standing at his
> bedroom window. The dreamer is so terrified he can't move,
> can hardly breathe. The man at the window stares into the
> room and then begins to pry off the screen. The dreamer
> can't move. He'd like to scream, but he can't get his breath.
> But the moon appears from behind a cloud, and the dreamer
> in the nightmare recognizes the man outside. It is his best
> friend, the best friend of the dreamer but no one the man
> having the nightmare knows. (98)

In the earlier version of "Night School" that appeared in the
North American Review Carver named the book: William Styron's
Set This House On Fire (50). Now at the end of "What's in
Alaska?" something rather similar had taken place: "Just as he

started to turn off the lamp, he thought he saw something in the hall. He kept staring and thought he saw it again, a pair of small eyes. His heart turned. He blinked and kept staring" (91). This is a figment of Carl's imagination, surely, but he had most likely gotten the idea of the pair of small animal eyes from Jack's huntress cat.[2] Yet what the cat and the pair of small eyes really represent is Jack himself, who was preying on, poaching on Carl's wife (and Alaska prospects) as the cat had preyed on the mouse and had displayed the fruit of its crime on the living room floor as Jack had displayed, though unintentionally, his desire for his friend's wife. And it is perhaps not by accident that the counterpart in the dream to the pair of small eyes "is his best friend" too, "the best friend of the dreamer but no one the man having the nightmare knows." For this dream of a dream, and story in the story, is an allegory of the ghostly counterpart to this story—the preceding story—and that is the importance of its being not the dreamer's best friend, but the best friend of the dreamer in his dream. Because it is the best friend not of the protagonist of "Night School" but of the protagonist of "What's in Alaska?" who is threatening to enter his bedroom. It is almost as if the protagonist of "Night School" were dreaming, or reading about dreaming, about the story we had just read.

Indeed the way the protagonist-narrator of "Night School" retells the nightmare from *Set This House On Fire* misrepresents Styron's text in such a way as to make it more relevant to what is going on in these two stories of Carver's than it might otherwise be. For it was not in fact a dream of a dream. In the dream Peter Leverett, Styron's narrator, is trying to sleep, but he has not fallen asleep:

> During that time I had incessant dreams of treachery and betrayal—dreams that lingered all day long. One of them especially I remember. . . . I was in a house somewhere, trying to sleep; it was dead of night, wintry and storming.

2. As Boxer and Phillips remark, the " 'pair of small eyes' . . . reminds us of the neighbors' cat who so blissfully licked the mouse" (85).

> Suddenly I heard a noise at the window. . . . I looked outside
> and saw a shadow—the figure of someone who moved . . .
> toward me menacingly. Panicky, I reached for the telephone,
> to call the friend who lived nearby (my best, last, dearest
> friend; nightmares deal in superlatives and magnitudes). . . .
> But there was no answer to all my frantic ringing. Then,
> putting the phone down, I heard a *tap-tap-tap*ping at the win-
> dow and turned to see—bared with the malignity of a fiend
> behind the streaming glass—the baleful, murderous face of
> that selfsame friend. (9)

So that it is a misreading of Styron to say, as Carver has his
narrator say, that the best friend is "no one the man having the
nightmare knows." That man is not to be distinguished from
the dreamer, Peter Leverett. This is not to say that Carver
himself misread the passage, but it does suggest how important
it was to him to find a way of introducing the notion of a dream
of a dream at this point in his book, one that so intriguingly
parallels the way that characters in two neighboring stories in
that book can dream of each other unawares.

"Collectors"

Mr. Slater, unemployed but waiting to hear about a job "up
north," lies in wait for the mailman. When someone knocks on
his door, and he knows it's not the mailman, he does not at first
answer. "You can't be too careful if you're out of work and you
get notices in the mail or else pushed under your door. They
come around wanting to talk, too, especially if you don't have a
telephone" (100). "They" in this instance are, evidently, bill
collectors—one of a number of meanings the story's title will
disclose. A vacuum cleaner salesman is at the door, and he talks
his way in, claiming that Mrs. Slater's name was drawn for a
prize. Once inside, he explains that she has won a free vacuum-
ing and carpet shampoo and proceeds to demonstrate the wonders of his machine. Mr. Slater, despite his protests that Mrs.
Slater doesn't live there anymore and that he hasn't the slight-

est interest in buying a vacuum cleaner, is powerless to stop him. In the course of the demonstration, a letter falls through the mail slot in the front door. "Twice I started for the letter. But he seemed to anticipate me, cut me off, so to speak, with his hose and his pipes and his sweeping and his sweeping" (106). The salesman eventually gathers it up himself. "He read the name on the letter and looked closely at the return address. He folded the letter in half and put it in his hip pocket. I kept watching him. That's all I did. . . . It's for a Mr. Slater, he said. I'll see to it" (107). Slater, in his initial effort to keep the salesman from entering, had never actually admitted that he was Mr. Slater. Having boxed himself into a corner both figuratively and literally, since he had gone into the kitchen to make a cup of coffee and was thus prevented from approaching the letter-stealing salesman by the newly shampooed carpet that lay between them, all he can say in response is, "You're sure that's who the letter's for?" (107) Having collected Slater's letter—as Boxer and Phillips point out: "At the end, the salesman also pockets ('collects') a letter" (87)—the salesman departs.

The only appearance of the word of the title (and here changed from noun to verb) occurs in the salesman's spiel: "You'll be surprised to see what can collect in a mattress over the months, over the years. Every day, every night of our lives, we're leaving little bits of ourselves, flakes of this and that, behind. Where do they go . . . ?" (103) Mattresses and seat cushions are thus "collectors" too, as is the salesman himself, since he has apparently stolen Slater's identity. "Methodically ferreting through the house," as Arthur Saltzman also observes, he "tries to draw in as many of the fugitive 'bits and pieces' of his prospective customer as he can" (46). Still another "collector," of course, is the vacuum cleaner itself.

"Collectors" is clearly a story about the invasion of one's house, of one's privacy; Slater's house is invaded and his letter, even his identity, stolen. This story thus continues the theme that had been stated three times in the preceding "Night School"—in the protagonist's recollection of the story of the dream of the intruder at the bedroom window, in his successful repelling of the two women at his parents' door, and in the women's desire to impose themselves on Patterson. They wouldn't phone him, they said, because "he could make an excuse. We just show up on his porch, he'll have to let us in." In fact, they appear to have some unspecified hold on their night-school teacher that would compel him to let them in, even if he didn't want to: "Wouldn't be much he could do, anyway. We have something on him. On Patterson" (95). Like the protagonist of "Night School," who "could hear [the women's] *footsteps* on the sidewalk over my *window*" (98; emphasis added) (and could even "hear them shaking the outside door"), Slater in "Collectors" looks "through the curtain" of his window for the mailman, when the salesman comes to the door "knew it wasn't the mailman . . . knew his *steps,*" and saw that "there was no chance of slipping into the other room and looking out that *window*" (100; emphasis added). Like Patterson, he is powerless to prevent the entry of this intruder. And like Patterson, of whom the women in the bar said, "We just show up on his *porch*" (95; emphasis added), he has a porch: "I heard someone walk onto the *porch,* wait, and then knock" (100; emphasis added) (later, when the mailman does arrive, "I heard steps on the *porch,* the mail slot opened and clinked shut" [105; emphasis added]).

Like the young man in "Night School" who "couldn't find a job" (92) and was separated from his wife, Slater "was out of work" (100) and no longer lives with Mrs. Slater. This is, of course, a fairly normal state of affairs in a Raymond Carver story. But it is something less than normal for the protagonists of two sequential stories to be asked if they have a car. We have seen the women ask it in "Night School"—" 'So do you have a car?' the second woman said to me" (92)—and are aware that the question is essential to the plot of the story: They want him to drive them someplace. But the funny thing is that the vacuum cleaner salesman asks Slater the very same question (because the vacuum could do an equally effective job on the car's interior): "Do you have a car? he asked. No car, I said. I don't have a car. If I had a car I would drive you someplace" (103). The question is not essential to the plot of "Collectors." But it is essential to the echoing effect by which "Collectors" collects "little bits"—to adopt the story's own turn of phrase—of the immediately preceding story and rearranges them into a fresh, yet hauntingly reminiscent narrative.

"What Do You Do in San Francisco?"

A remarkably congruent counterpart to "Collectors," "What Do You Do in San Francisco?" is likewise the story of a young man waiting for the mail to arrive, this time told from the postman's perspective. "This story has nothing to do with me," Henry Robinson tells us from the very first sentence. It has to do with Lee Marston and his wife, "beatnik" painters who move into a house on Robinson's route in Arcata, California. They came from San Francisco with no visible means of support. After several weeks, the wife runs off with another man and Marston is left alone. "Beginning the next day he was out there at the box every day waiting for me to hand over the mail" (117). As Saltzman observes, "As in 'Collectors,' here is someone waiting for a letter that will bring him out of his inertia" (47). Like Slater, who would "look *through the curtain* for the mailman" (100; emphasis added), Marston, the mailman tells us, would be "looking out at me *through the curtain*" (118; emphasis added). While Slater never acknowledged that his name was in fact Slater and thus forfeited the letter the salesman collected, Robinson repeatedly tries to get Marston to affirm his identity by painting over the previous occupant's name on the mailbox and writing his own. "You might want to change the name on the box" (112). "On Thursday I . . . reminded him about changing the name on the box" (113). " 'I'll have to change the name on that box one of these days [Marston said]. I'll get myself a can of paint and just paint over that other name.' . . . But he never did change the name on the box" (113–14).

Return addresses are closely scanned in both stories. Slater watched the salesman as he picked up the letter meant for him, read the name, and "looked closely at the return address"

(107); observing Marston, the mailman would "see him start scanning the return addresses even before I could get it handed over" (117). It is, however, in another gesture shared by the salesman and Marston that the most remarkable parallel emerges between these two stories: The former *"folded* the letter *in half* and put it in his hip pocket" (107; emphasis added), while the latter *"folded* it *in two* and went back to the house" (117; emphasis added). As we examine more closely these pieces of mail, we move beyond similarity into complementarity as a precisely balanced opposition takes shape—the complementarity, that is, of two pieces that together form a complete entity, as a sixty-degree angle completes a thirty-degree one to make a right angle (though two forty-five-degree angles might be an apter analogy in this instance). For what the salesman folded in half was a letter specifically addressed to Slater to which Slater felt compelled to renounce his claim because he preferred to dwell in anonymity, while what Marston folded in two was an anonymous circular addressed "Occupant" (117). "I'd dropped off at least seventy-five that morning" just like it, Robinson tells us (117). Within the context of Marston's story its meaning is practically nil, but in the light of that scene in Slater's its significance as evidence of how Carver's stories beg to be read together just about jumps out at the reader. Like either letter or circular, this short story cycle itself might be folded in half at any point between two stories in order that the two might be read one on top of—congruent with—the other. All the more so here, as it happens, for we are at the very midpoint of the book, "Collectors" and "What Do You Do in San Francisco?" being the eleventh and twelfth of its twenty-two stories, the point where the book itself could be folded into two equal parts. Halved, like R's fish.

Henry Robinson is prompted to tell the story of Marston and his wife because of a picture he saw in the newspaper. "I got to thinking about them again when I picked up last Sunday's newspaper and found a picture of a young man who'd been arrested down in San Francisco for killing his wife and her boyfriend with a baseball bat. It wasn't the same man, of course, though there was a likeness because of the beard. But

the situation was close enough to get me thinking" (109). Indeed, this mention of being "close enough" to take someone
for someone else may set us thinking as well—thinking that is
of Arnold Breit in "Are You a Doctor?," who "was close, you
must admit" when he misremembered Cheryl's name as Shirley. We found then that this closeness was itself close to the
misheard phone number that led to Breit's being in the Holts'
apartment in the first place, and furthermore that that transcription of a number onto a piece of paper was close enough
to Earl Ober's writing down numbers on a piece of paper in
the story before that to get us thinking. And furthermore that
such "closeness" seemed to allegorize the resemblances between
the two stories, and in particular to constitute some encourage-
ment to seek them out by providing some assurance that even
though the resemblances would never be exact they were in
fact there, and that their discovery can produce meaning, perhaps even narrative. The closeness between the number Carla
Holt's babysitter was told and the one she wrote down did indeed produce the story "Are You a Doctor?" tells. Precisely the
same thing happens here, when Henry Robinson tells us that
the closeness of the resemblance between the bearded man in
the paper and the bearded Marston made him remember the
story he is about to tell us. It actually does more than that, for
the force of the word *thinking* in "close enough to get me thinking" goes beyond mere recollection. The resemblance between
the man Robinson knew and the murderer in the news makes
Marston more interesting, sufficiently interesting now to tell a
story about.

     In fact in at least one small way Robinson—and in another,
Carver—tells the story in such a way as to make Marston resemble even more closely the San Francisco murderer. From what
information is given, we can probably identify the wife's lover
as a certain "Jerry" who sends them (her?) a letter with postage
due. The postman gives it to the wife and waits for his five
cents. " 'Let me see. Who's it from? Why it's from Jer! That
kook. Sending us a letter without a stamp. Lee!' she called out.
'Here's a letter from Jerry.' Marston came in, but he didn't look
too happy" (116). Now after Mrs. Marston subsequently aban-

dons her family (including three children, whom her husband
then took to his mother's house in another town) for another
man, Marston eventually receives "a plain white envelope addressed in a woman's curlicue handwriting" with "a Portland
postmark, and the return address showed the initials JD and a
Portland street address" (118). J, apparently, as in Jerry. Now
Arcata, where the story takes place, is in northern California
and Portland, Oregon, is to the north. Why then does Robinson
make a point of saying that the last time he saw Marston the
bereft young man was staring *south?* "The last time I saw him
he was standing at the window and looked calm and rested. . . .
I figured at the time he was getting his things together to leave.
But I could tell by the look on his face he wasn't watching for
me this time. He was staring past me, over me, you might say,
over the rooftops and the trees, south. He just kept staring
even after I'd come even with the house and moved on down
the sidewalk" (119). One would think he would be gazing in the
direction his wife had gone. "The feeling was so strong, I had
to turn around and look for myself in the same direction he
was. But, as you might guess, I didn't see anything except the
same old timber, mountains, sky. The next day he was gone"
(119).

What do we see if we, like Robinson, look in the same direction? San Francisco ("fourteen hours" [111] south of there, as
Marston's wife described their long drive in the U-Haul when
they first arrived), where an estranged husband was arrested
for killing his wife and her boyfriend. Robinson, in other
words, returns near the end of his story to his initial suspicion
that the bearded Marston may have really been the bearded
murderer in the newspaper. In the final lines he tells us he
does not in fact know where Marston went when he left Arcata,
for "he didn't leave any forwarding" (119).

It is at this juncture that we can finally savor the real enigma
of the title Carver gave this story. What indeed do you do in
San Francisco—murder your wife? It is otherwise a title of the
most tangential significance. When it appears in the body of
the text, it is, of all things, a question Marston's wife asks Henry
Robinson. " 'My, my,' I said and shook my head. 'San Fran-

cisco? I was just down in San Francisco, let me see, last April or March.' 'You were, were you?' she said. 'What did you do in San Francisco?'" (111) The story merits its title not, surely, because of what the *mailman* may have done there.

"The Student's Wife"

At this point we might expect to find another bearded man. After all, Arnold Breit's talk of close resemblances turned out to be part of a double echo between his mistake and the baby-sitter's, between her numbers on a piece of paper and Earl Ober's in the immediately preceding story. And indeed we do, as if Henry Robinson's talk of two bearded men being close should itself call into being, should magically evoke, a "close" likeness between his story and the one so "close" (in that other sense, which is evidently evoked here too by the word's reappearance), "The Student's Wife," right next to it in Carver's sequence. We get several bearded men, in fact. And their ultimate source is another young husband, the student of the title. He is reading aloud from Rilke to his wife, and his "confident sonorous voice" gets her to thinking: "It was a rich voice that spilled her into a dream of caravans just setting out from walled cities and bearded men in robes" (120). Marston's beard has considerable prominence in "What Do You Do in San Francisco?" Not only is it the basis for the visual resemblance the mailman noted with the picture of the man accused of murder, but Robinson also tells us that, in Arcata, "people here aren't used to seeing men wear beards" (111), and "people might stare at his beard if they met him pushing the grocery cart" (116). So prominent is it that the student could have been reading *that* story to his wife instead of Rilke, for it too could have provoked a dream about men in beards. In fact, we have seen in "Night School" how Carver can use an intertextual allusion (Styron, in that instance) to bridge the connection between two sequential stories, and the connection between text and dream (it was a passage about a dream, and it echoed the waking dream Carl experienced in the immediately preceding story).

The student's wife, who looked to her husband "like a hospital patient in her *white* nightgown" (121; emphasis added), is costumed to resemble Marston's wife in the story before, who wore "*white* jeans and a man's *white* undershirt" (110; emphasis added). Yet, like the two stories before "The Student's Wife," these stories complement each other too. Both are about unhappy marriages. Though in neither story is the husband or the wife the narrator, one focuses on the effect of a wife's unlovingness on her husband, and the other on that of a husband's unlovingness on his wife. The student's wife has our sympathy in the second story, the painter's husband in the first. Robinson found Marston's wife inattentive and negligent: "put me down for saying she wasn't a good wife and mother. She was a painter" (110). When the Welcome Wagon lady came to visit, "One minute the woman would be sitting and listening to Sallie run on—all ears, it seemed—and the next she'd get up while Sallie was still talking and start to work on her painting as if Sallie wasn't there" (114).

Nan, the student's wife, likewise has trouble getting her husband to listen to her. Mike, it seems, is quite willing to read poetry aloud but has no patience for listening to his wife. He is more interested in Rilke, and in listening to his own voice, than in her. He's drowsy; she can't sleep and wants to talk—about a dream of being cramped in a boat, about a camping trip they took together, about likes and dislikes. She wants him to talk to her in return, but he keeps falling asleep, or pretending to. Eventually, she cries silently against the sheet, gets up alone, and wanders the house, awaiting the dawn. "Not in pictures she had seen nor in any book she had read had she learned a sunrise was so terrible as this" (129).

Robinson had given some friendly advice to the abandoned husband in the preceding story: "Why don't you forget her? Why don't you go to work and forget her? What have you got against work? It was work, day and night, work that gave me oblivion when I was in your shoes and there was a war on where I was. . . ." (118; Carver's ellipsis). It seems to be a course of action that Nan's husband, the student, has followed all too well, so caught up in his studies, in his love for poetry (he had read from Elizabeth Browning and the *Rubáiyát* on their camping trip, she recalls), that he has effectively forgotten his wife.

Robinson, ever the careful observer, says, "Twice I saw a
little white sports car in front, a car that hadn't come from
around here" (115). This is immediately before he tells of the
arrival of the letter from Jerry, who is most likely the lover and
whose car it very probably is. The color of that car is surely no
accident. That little white vehicle outside the door eventually
becomes that wife's escape from the husband she no longer
loved, while the whiteness that the student's wife sees outside
her window after a sleepless night embodies her despair and
entrapment: "When it began to be light outside she got up. She
walked to the window. The cloudless sky over the hills was
beginning to turn white. . . . The sky grew whiter, the light expanding rapidly up from behind the hills." Never had she
known a sunrise as "terrible as this" (128–29). Its terror, as
Carver describes it here, is its whiteness.

And when she turns to look at her unloving husband asleep
on the bed, the dread whiteness confronts her once more, symbolizing the blankness of her life: "The room grew very light
and the pale sheets whitened grossly before her eyes. She . . .
got down on her knees. . . . 'God,' she said. 'God, will you help
us, God?' she said" (129).

"Put Yourself in My Shoes"

The longest story in the collection save for the title story,
"Put Yourself in My Shoes" is an almost incredibly complex
narrative, for not only is it a tangled skein of several stories that
seem to have strange connections to each other beyond the
ostensible purposes of their telling but one of these embedded
stories—in fact the most important—is told in such a way as to
make no sense.

Like the immediately preceding "Student's Wife," "Put
Yourself in My Shoes" is about a young married couple in
which the husband is caught up in literature. The husband in
this instance is not, however, a student of literature but a prac

titioner, a writer, and unlike Nan and Mike's marriage, the Myerses' is a happy one. As the story begins, he is unhappy, not with his wife but with his inability to come up with enough material to write about; "Put Yourself in My Shoes" is the story of how he found it.

As the story begins, Myers's wife calls him from work to invite him to the office Christmas party. Myers used to work there too but left to write a novel. She also relates the news of the suicide of Larry Gudinas, who used to work there but got "canned" (131). Myers declines the invitation but agrees to meet her at a bar later. There, she proposes that they drop in on the Morgans, whom they have never met but for whom they house-sat when the Morgans went to Germany. The Myerses had been less than ideal tenants, and that this had engendered some resentment is evident from the "insulting letter they sent telling us they heard we were keeping a cat in the house," as Myers points out to his wife. But she counters that they must have forgotten by now, and besides they sent them a Christmas card inviting them to stop by during the holidays.

Things go wrong from the start, as the Morgans' dog Buzzy knocks Myers down on the icy sidewalk before he can get to the front door. Their welcome seems friendly enough, though it "seemed odd to Myers" (135) that Edgar Morgan should remark that he was looking out the window when the dog attacked (and did not intervene in time to prevent it). Once inside, Myers noticed "Morgan staring at him again, not smiling now" (136) and later "heard a muffled word that sounded like a curse" when Morgan was in the kitchen fixing drinks. Having been told that Myers was a writer, Morgan decides to tell him a story that he might find of interest. A former academic colleague, "about my age or so" had an affair with one of his students and told his wife he wanted a divorce. Enraged, she ordered him out of the house. "But just as the fellow was leaving, his son threw a can of tomato soup at him and hit him in the forehead. It caused a concussion that sent the man to the hospital. His condition is quite serious" (139). The title of Carver's story puts in its appearance during their subsequent discussion of this anecdote. Edgar Morgan invites Myers to write the story from the professor's perspective, Hilda Morgan says it should be told from the wife's, Paula Myers from the son's, and then Edgar says, "But here's something I don't think any of you has thought about. . . . Put yourself in the shoes of that eighteen-year-old coed who fell in love with a married man. Think about *her* for a moment, and then you see the possibilities for your story" (139). This only echo of the title appears at first to be about as puzzlingly tangential as the question Mrs. Marston put to Henry Robinson in "What Do You Do in San Francisco?"

Yet it does serve to draw our attention to what will turn out to be the central motif of Carver's story. When they house-sat for the Morgans, the Myerses may well have gone too far in the direction of making themselves at home in someone else's shoes, for they were not supposed to use, as Morgan will later angrily point out, the Morgans' "kitchen utensils marked 'Don't Open,' " their dishes (which they broke), their "blankets and sheets" and "*bathroom* things" (148; Carver's emphasis). Bill and Arlene Miller, in "Neighbors," abused their license too in a parallel situation, Bill going so far as to put on his neighbors' clothes, refraining from putting himself in Mrs. Stone's shoes in a quite literal sense only because he "understood they would not fit" (12).

The motif the title expresses emerges as well in three other aspects of Carver's story: (1) the way characters in the stories that are told within the story change places, putting themselves in each other's shoes or least following in their footsteps; (2) the way the last and most important story the Morgans tell the Myerses is meant to put their listeners in the shoes of its protagonists (as Hamlet tried to shame his uncle by presenting a play that reenacted his crime); and (3) the way Edgar Morgan stumbles in his telling of that ultimate story in such a manner as to reveal a hidden desire to be in the shoes of one of his listeners.

You may have already guessed how the stories of the suicide of Larry Gudinas and the adulterous professor are connected by Carver's outlandish pun: both, after a fashion, got "canned." And there's even a little more to their resemblance than that. Both were former work colleagues—recall that Mor-

gan said "he was a colleague for a couple of years" (138) where
Morgan taught, and that Myers used to work in the same office
with Gudinas ("You remember Larry Gudinas. He was still here
when you came to work. He helped out on science books for a
while, and then they put him in the field, and then they canned
him?" [130–31]). And their canning was in both cases part of
their leaving: for Gudinas getting "canned" meant that he was
forced to leave, and it was "just as the fellow was leaving" that
his son hit the professor in the head with the can. If the professor were to die, and he might for "his condition is quite serious," then the resemblance would become even closer.

The second story the Morgans tell is likewise about someone who dies in the act of leaving. It is related by Hilda, who
returned home from a museum to discover she had left her
purse in the restroom. It contained $120 in cash and her hus-
band's monthly check. Just as Edgar was about to telephone
the museum a well-dressed woman emerged from a taxi outside their door, carrying two purses. She told Hilda that "she
too had visited the museum that afternoon and while in the
ladies' room had noticed a purse in the trash can. She of course
had opened the purse in an effort to trace the owner" (145).
The woman said she found Morgan's check but not the $120.
Hilda regretted the loss, but she was grateful for the return of
the purse and the check, and asked the woman to stay for tea.
"Suddenly, after we had had a very pleasant conversation for
an hour . . . she stood up to go. As she started to pass me her
cup, her mouth flew open, the cup dropped, and she fell across
our couch and died" (146). When the Morgans opened her
purse to find out the woman's address, they were astonished to
find that the missing $120 had been there all the time. The
attentive reader may have noticed that this story is closely related to the two that precede it not only because, as I have
already noted, it too discloses an intimate relation between leaving and dying (receiving a serious, and possibly fatal, injury in
the act of leaving in one instance, dying because one cannot
bear the fact or the manner of one's departure in the other)
but because yet another *can* is involved, right in the middle of
Hilda's story, the trash can that the mysterious woman might

have been better advised to leave alone. Or, what is more likely, the trash can that was in fact only a figment of her lying imagination, since she probably never found the purse there in the first place but only invented it—a necessary intermediary that would allow her to pretend to have discovered the purse in order to gaze upon the victim of her crime.

And therein lies another resemblance, this time to the frame story embracing all these. For the Myerses are returning to the victims of their crime too (as well as to its scene), as it becomes increasingly clear that the Morgans are of the opinion that it was indeed a crime, and a hideous one, for the Myerses to have gone beyond the terms of their lease and to have used the Morgans' personal crockery, linen, and bathroom items, to have brought a cat into the house, and even, according to Edgar Morgan's ultimate, and perhaps unjustified, accusation, to have made off with his two-volume record set of "Jazz at the Philharmonic" (149). That last complaint, making Myers into a thief, strengthens his resemblance to the stricken purse snatcher.

It is a resemblance that the Morgans do not apparently consciously intend. But Edgar does mean for the Myerses to see a resemblance between themselves and the next story he tells, which I must beg the reader's indulgence to quote in full, for the precise way he tells it, or tries to, is of the greatest significance:

"Consider *this* for a possibility, Mr. Myers!" Morgan screamed. *Consider!* A friend—let's call him Mr. X—is friends with . . . with Mr. and Mrs. Y, *as well as* Mr. and Mrs. Z. Mr. and Mrs. Y and Mr. and Mrs. Z do not know each other, unfortunately. I say *unfortunately* because if they *had* known each other this story would not exist because it would never have taken place. Now, Mr. X learns that Mr. and Mrs. Y are going to Germany for a year and need someone to occupy their house during the time they are gone. Mr. and Mrs. Z are looking for suitable accommodations, and Mr. X tells them he knows of just the place. But before Mr. X can put Mr. and Mrs. Z in touch with Mr. and Mrs. Y, the Ys have to leave sooner than expected. Mr. X, being a friend, is left to

rent the house at his discretion to anyone, including Mr. and
Mrs. Y—I mean Z. Now, Mr. and Mrs. . . . Z move into the
house and bring a cat with them that Mr. and Mrs. Y hear
about later in a letter from Mr. X. Mr. and Mrs. Z bring a cat
into the house *even though* the terms of the lease have ex-
pressly forbidden cats or other animals in the house because
of Mrs. Y's asthma. The *real* story, Mr. Myers, lies in the
situation I've just described. Mr. and Mrs. Z—I mean Mr.
and Mrs. *Y*'s moving into the Zs' house, *invading* the Zs'
house, if the truth is to be told. Sleeping in the Zs' bed is one
thing, but unlocking the Zs' private closet and using their
linen, vandalizing the things found there, that was against
the spirit and letter of the lease. And this *same* couple, the *Zs,*
opened boxes of kitchen utensils marked 'Don't Open.' And
broke dishes when it was spelled out, *spelled out* in that same
lease, that they were not to use the owners', the Zs' *personal,* I
emphasize *personal,* possessions." (147–48; Carver's emphases and ellipses)

It is no misprint, for the same slippage in Morgan's discourse
occurs on page 51 of the 1972 version of this story in the *Iowa
Review,* as well as on page 111 of its subsequent appearance in
the collection *Where I'm Calling From.* He really does get his Ys
and Zs confused. At first, as we see, he catches himself: "including Mr. and Mrs. Y—I mean Z." But, to compound the error,
when he begins to say Y for Z, it actually appears in the form
of a correction: "Mr. and Mrs. Z—I mean Mr. and Mrs. *Y*'s
moving into the Z's house." He gets back on the right track
again when he says "And this *same* couple, the *Zs,* opened
boxes" but then immediately gets it wrong once more: "were
not to use the owners', the Zs'. . . . " "Edgar Morgan was in his
forties" (135) and thus not old enough, surely, to be suffering
from senility. It is much more probable that his errors constitute a genuine Freudian slip, that there is a hidden desire behind his mistaking Y for Z—Morgan for Myers.[3] We can

3. Freud cites many cases of saying—and thereby unconsciously meaning
—exactly the opposite of what one consciously meant to say. In *A General
Introduction to Psychoanalysis* he writes: "In almost all cases of slips of the

practically see this unconscious wish struggling, with increasing success, to be expressed.[4] And what else could that desire be but the wish to change places with Myers, to enact the switch of identity his slip of the tongue allows him to pronounce?

He has already made some progress in this direction, having recently (that is, since their return from Germany) acquired a dog, despite the opposition of his wife, who suffers from asthma. "It's Edgar's dog. I can't have an animal in the house myself, but Edgar bought this dog and promised to keep him outside" (135). Myers, we remember, has a cat, and his having brought the cat to live with them in the Morgans' house figured prominently in the indictment against him. It is not clear that Edgar is living up to his promise to keep the dog out, since at one point the dog "began to whine and scratch at the door" and Edgar somewhat defensively remarked "I don't know what's gotten into that dog" (140–41). The force of his comment is that the dog is behaving strangely, which runs counter to his earlier confession, when the atmosphere had been a little more freer, that "He begs to come in the house, but we can't

---

tongue where the opposite of what is meant is said the interfering tendency expresses the opposite meaning to that of the intention interfered with, and the slip is the expression of the conflict between two incompatible impulses. 'I declare the meeting open but would prefer to have closed it' is the meaning" (65) of the slip the President of Parliament made when he said in his opening speech: " 'Gentlemen, I declare a quorum present and herewith declare the session *closed*' " (38).

4. It is so successful in fact that Mrs. Morgan becomes caught up in it as well. " 'And the bathroom things . . .' Mrs. Morgan said. 'It's bad enough using the Zs' blankets and sheets' " (148). In the *Iowa Review* version she had said "the Xs' blankets"—with the result that this earlier version pointed toward her having simply forgotten which letters stood for whom, while as the story appears in the book her slip seems, like her husband's, to be motivated by a desire to change places with the Myerses. She, like her husband, likes to tell stories; she likes to so much in fact that she revels in subsidiary detail too much for her husband's taste ("Come to the point dear," Edgar prompts, when she goes on at too great a length about the purse snatcher's life story) and likes to go in for the grand dramatic statement—the line "Fate sent her to die on the couch in our living room in Germany" (146) that causes Myers such mirth.

allow it, you know" (135). The later remark is a guilt-laden attempt to cover up the dog's having indeed been allowed into the house, for if it never had been inside it would not have whined and scratched at the door. It is not, by the way, a short-haired but a "bushy" dog (134), which would have made it a poor choice, given the state of Hilda's lungs.

Myers has already been presented to the reader, from the first page of the story, as a man subject to another's envious desire to be in his shoes. "Myers used to work for Carl. Carl always talked of going to Paris to write a novel, and when Myers had quit to write a novel, Carl had said he would watch for Myers's name on the best-seller list" (130). If Morgan did wish he were Myers, it would not be the first time a university professor longed for the freedom and the glory of a writer's life.

As Carver pointed out in an interview in 1986, "Put Yourself in My Shoes" is "the only story about a writer I've ever written" (*Conversations,* 162). Two facts from Carver's biography suggest that the story is even closer to his life than that. One is that the job Carver held as a science textbook editor at Science Research Associates in Palo Alto, California, from 1967 to 1970 sounds very much like the job Myers held before he left to pursue his writing full-time. Recall that Myers's former colleague Larry Gudinas "helped out on science books." Like Myers, Carver was able to devote all his energies to writing when he left SRA because, to use the story's term, he was "canned" and was thus entitled to unemployment benefits and severance pay. He didn't have to look for another job for a while. According to William Stull, "for the first time in his life he could write full-time. Over the next nine months, he produced more than half the stories that went into *Will You Please Be Quiet, Please?*" (*DLB Yearbook 1988,* 207), including, apparently, the one we are reading.

The other relevant biographical fact is that Carver once did to the novelist John Gardner what Myers did to Edgar Morgan. Carver was a student of Gardner's in a writing class at Chico State College in 1958. As he recalls in "John Gardner: The Writer As Teacher," his mentor was

already surrounded by a bit of mystery and romance. . . . For
it was said that Gardner was a real, that is to say a practicing,
writer. . . . I'd never laid eyes on a writer before, and I was in
awe. But where were these novels and short stories, I wanted
to know. Well, nothing had been published yet. It was said
that he couldn't get his work published and that he carried it
around with him in boxes. (After I became his student, I was
to see those boxes of manuscript. Gardner had become aware
of my difficulty in finding a place to work. . . . He offered me
the key to his office. . . . I spent part of every Saturday and
Sunday in his office, which is where he kept the boxes of
manuscript. . . . *Nickel Mountain*, grease-pencilled on one of
the boxes, is the only title I recall. But it was in his office,
within sight of his unpublished books, that I undertook my
first serious attempts at writing.) (*Fires*, 41)

But this is not the whole story. In a 1977 interview with Cassandra Phillips, Carver confessed that " 'in his office on the weekends I used to go through his manuscripts and steal titles from
his stories . . . I mean take his titles, which struck me as awfully
good, as I recall, and rephrase them, and put them in my own
stories.' When Gardner caught on to what his young protegé
was up to, Carver got a scolding, and was informed that the
invasion of another writer's privacy and the pilfering of his
words were basic improprieties" (Boxer and Phillips, 75; cf.
Conversations, 4). It is interesting that in the 1983 essay on Gardner he should speak of the *titles* of Gardner's manuscripts and
say that he could remember only one of them. In light of the
confession he had made six years before, this reads like an
attempt to repress a troubling memory (that only succeeds in
dredging it up).

"This incident curiously resembles one of Carver's own best
stories, 'Neighbors,' " Boxer and Phillips comment, and indeed
it does, as the "unglamorous Millers . . . wistfully envy the
'fuller and brighter life' of the peripatetic Stones" (75). But it
even more curiously resembles "Put Yourself in My Shoes," for
while the Stones did not complain about the pilfering, the Morgans, and Gardner, did. The scolding Myers gets, it now seems,

is the fictional projection of the scolding Carver himself received from John Gardner. Gardner is hidden yet displayed in the person of Edgar Morgan (as the -*gar* of his first name in fact suggests)[5] by a remarkable switch of opposites: Morgan envies Myers for being a writer, but at a deeper level this is the story of how Carver-Myers, the aspiring writer who has just left his job with the scientific textbook company to write full-time, wishes he were Gardner-Morgan, whose personal belongings he has pilfered. Or perhaps deepest of all, Carver wishes Gardner had reason to envy him, as Morgan does Myers!

The real extent and nature of the desire Morgan feels toward Myers may stand revealed when we pay Carver's choice of a title and his choice of a place to insert it in his story the careful consideration they deserve. It was puzzling, we recall, that the only place the title appears should be at a moment when something quite inessential was being said: " 'But here's something I don't think any of you has thought about. . . . Put yourself in the shoes of that eighteen-year-old coed who fell in love with a married man. Think about *her* for a moment, and then you see the possibilities for your story.' Morgan nodded and leaned back in the chair with a satisfied expression" (139). Why does Edgar say this? Why should he want to say that it is even more important to get inside *her* shoes than (as had been his earlier, but now corrected, suggestion) into the head of the man who had had an affair with her (she wasn't even there when it happened, by the way)? And why should saying it leave him with such a "satisfied expression" on his face?

The answer can be found by realizing first of all that Morgan probably wishes he were the professor having the affair (which does not preclude his wishing he were Myers—but that is another story, as we have seen). They have, after all, a lot in common. "This fellow was about my age or so. He was a colleague for a couple of years. We knew each other a little, and we had good friends in common" (138). If there is anything

---

5. All the letters of *Edgar* in fact appear in *Gardner*, while Myers's name suggests what is *mine*—Carver's—in this story about the abuse of others' personal property.

more likely than an academic wishing he had a writer's freedom and gift for creation, it is a professor wishing he could have an affair with one of students, fantasy not entailing such costs as what this tomato-canned man had to pay. Secondly, and more significantly, Morgan wants Myers to put himself in the shoes of the student because, despite—indeed perhaps on account of —the hatred he directs toward his former tenant, the young writer is in fact the object of his homosexual desire.[6]

The rich interplay among the several stories within this story, the persistent "canning" and linking of death and departure, embodies on a smaller scale the echoing phenomenon that has come to our attention on the level of the collection itself. "Put Yourself in My Shoes" takes part in that interplay as well in several ways, echoing "The Student's Wife," as already noted, through the parallel between the literary husbands. Secondly, both husbands are forced to listen to someone else (the wife in the first story, the Morgans in the second) bore them with stories. Nan's husband Mike, keeps trying to go to sleep; Myers keeps getting up to leave. Now these echoes together lead to a third that will, as it happens, strengthen the suspicion that Morgan's wish that Myers put himself in the shoes of the student means more than it may seem: for the husband in "The Student's Wife" is a *student,* and thus Myers is already placed in the position of resembling a student before Edgar Morgan even gets to express his disguised, and repressed, wish.

Let us not forget that Carver was Gardner's *student,* and that that professor-student relationship evidently lies behind a great deal of what happens in "Put Yourself in My Shoes." At this juncture the supreme significance of Carver's choice and use of titles becomes once more apparent. For why is it, we might especially now want to ask, that it was *titles* that he stole from Gardner to "rephrase them, and put them in my own stories"? To insert Gardner's title somewhere *in* his own story,

6. This is at least what Carver seems to suggest by the importance he gives Morgan's remark about putting Myers in her shoes, the honor that is of being the vessel of the title in the text. Yet even if he doesn't want to screw him, he at least wants to screw him over.

and thereby to surreptitiously incorporate part of the adored
(and beloved, if what I have suggested about Morgan's lust for
Myers holds true here too) in one's body, may have become a
mystic ritual for Carver, one reenacted in his practice of bury-
ing his own titles in his stories in places where one might sometimes least expect to find them.

The visit to the Morgans gives Myers the raw material he
needs to write the story he couldn't get started before. The last
lines of Carver's story show that he has found it. " 'Those people are crazy,' Paula said. Myers patted her hand. 'They were
scary,' she said. He did not answer. Her voice seemed to come
to him from a great distance. . . . He was silent and watched the
road. He was at the very end of a story" (150). At this moment
this husband comes close once more to finding himself in the
shoes of the other husband who tuned out his wife's words, this
He did not answer echoing (answering) such moments from "The
Student's Wife" as these:

> "Well, don't go to sleep before me," she said. "I don't want to
> be awake by myself." *He didn't answer.* (124; emphasis added)

> "Mike? Are you asleep?" She shook his shoulder gently, but
> *there was no response.* (126; emphasis added)

> "Mike," she whispered. *There was no answer.* (127; emphasis
> added)

At this moment he comes close as well (and again), as Boxer
and Phillips point out, to becoming Raymond Carver: "The
final line of the story . . . signifies much: 'He was at the very
end of a story.' At the end, Carver and Myers merge" (83).

"Jerry and Molly and Sam"

In the next story in the cycle the protagonist accomplishes
in two separate acts what the Myerses did in one, in their visit
to the Morgans, when he returns to the house where he and

his wife once lived and then returns there once again to what will by then have become the scene of his crime. And the Morgans' troublesome dog Buzzy, who had attacked Myers as he came up the sidewalk, returns as the equally troublesome (and similarly named, all but the initials) dog Suzy. "The moment the back door was left open and everyone gone, she'd pry open the screen, come through to the living room, and urinate on the carpet" (154). She chewed the dirty clothes, the antenna wires, Al's Florsheim shoes.

Al plotted her disappearance. He would lure her into the car and dump her somewhere—but where? He wanted her to find a good home. "Then he thought of the place. The neighborhood where they used to live, swarming with kids and just across the line in Yolo County"—so she wouldn't turn up at the local dog pound—"that would be just the right place" (157). As he drove along, with the dog in the car, "when he came to his old house he slowed down almost to a stop and stared at the front door, the porch, *the lighted windows.* . . . He had lived there—how long? A year, sixteen months?" (158; emphasis added). Myers likewise, in the immediately preceding story, had stared at the house (the Morgans') where he too had once briefly lived: "Something took him when he saw *the lighted windows,* saw snow on the roof, saw the station wagon in the driveway. The curtains were open and Christmas-tree lights blinked at them from the window" (134).

I had earlier said that there are some places where Carver changed his stories between their original magazine publication and their appearance in his books in such a way as to appear to heighten their sequential echoes. We have just arrived at such a place: "He thought of . . . autumns when he'd hunt pheasants behind Sam, *the setter's flashing red coat a beacon* through cornfields and alfalfa meadows" (158; emphasis added). The italicized passage does not appear in the original version of the story, published in *Perspective* in 1972: "He thought fleetingly of . . . fall when he'd hunt pheasants behind Sam, sending him into the cornfields and alfalfa meadows" (38). Now this passage appears in the same paragraph as the one quoted just before where Al is staring at the house where he used to live. It is the continuation of his thought, as thoughts of this house remind him of houses he had lived in before that, back to the one where he lived as a boy and to the dog he used to take hunting. It is therefore all the more significant that the flashing light, the beacon, of the dog's red coat should echo, as it can now that the passage has been added to the story, the blinking lights on the Christmas tree that Myers sees through the window of the house where *he* used to live, in a passage that has already been echoed once before on this same page of "Jerry and Molly and Sam" (and will be echoed once more, as we will see). In doing so, it sets up yet another echo, between these passages and one in "The Student's Wife," the story that immediately precedes "Put Yourself in My Shoes." The student's wife is staring out the window at the whitening dawn. "By stages things were becoming very visible. She let her eyes see everything until they fastened on the red winking light atop the radio tower atop the opposite hill" (129). I had not mentioned this winking light before, because though it is echoed by the blinking lights Myers sees, the true constellation of these intermittent lights, like the red winking one Nan saw, becomes entirely apparent only "by stages" and is "becoming very visible" only now—now that the third one has appeared. For the third one, the flashing red beacon of the dog's coat, confirms the echoing effect in a way the blinking Christmas-tree lights could not, for it, like the first, winking one, is also red.

What is the meaning of these winking, blinking, flashing lights? In their individual contexts, they seem to offer the viewer access to a deeper reality. Nan "fastened" her eyes on the radio tower's light as if she had found a beacon of hope in a world otherwise inescapably white. When Myers saw the lighted windows of the Morgan's house, with its blinking Christmas-tree lights, "something took him," exactly what is not clear. Perhaps it was a fuller recognition that this house, where someone lived who could write him an "insulting letter" (133) and which he had not wanted to visit (it was Paula who insisted they go), was nevertheless the place he had once called home. Home is certainly what the red beacon of his setter's coat means for Al, for thoughts of Sam lead him to thoughts of the house where he grew up. "He wished he could keep driving and driving tonight until he was driving onto the old bricked main street of Toppenish . . . stopping when he came to where his mother lived, and never, never, for any reason ever, ever leave again" (158).

In their collective context, these lights, as I have suggested, emerge "by stages" as we stare at the stories in the same way the student's wife stared at the gradually lightening dawn. There is, that is, an almost uncanny coincidence between her experience and ours, through which Carver's text tells us how it might be read. For we could do worse than to imitate her. "She let her eyes see everything until they fastened on the red winking light." We can, as attentive and careful readers, try to see everything we can in Carver's stories, and that includes seeing everything we can *between* the stories, until our eyes fasten on something that persists through the whirl of transitory detail: these repetitively intermittent lights. We can imitate Myers too, who "tried to see everything, save it for later. He was between stories" (132). For we too are between stories, in a different sense of course, but in one that can also, like Myer's, lead to the production of meaning.

The page from "Jerry and Molly and Sam" where Al gazes on the house he once lived in echoes the page from "Put Yourself in My Shoes" where Myers did the same in yet a third way, and it has to do with the objectionable dog. When Myers and his wife approached the Morgans' house Morgan's dog Buzzy came tearing down the sidewalk, heading straight for Myers, who slipped and fell on the ice. "Paula picked up a *handful* of snow and *threw* it at the dog" (134; emphasis added). Now when Al stopped his car on the street where he had once lived, having finally found the place where he could comfortably dump the dog, "without thinking any longer about what he was doing [he] scooped a *handful* of dog food up . . . *threw* the stuff out, and said, 'Go on, Suzy' " (158, emphasis added). Once again Carver has revised the story with the result that it more closely echoes the parallel scene in the story that immediately precedes it in the cycle, for the passage had originally read "without thinking any longer about what he was doing, *took the bread* from the glove compartment . . . threw the bread down and said" (39; emphasis added).

When Al got home, "it was all tears, confusion." His daughter "ran out to the car, crying, before he could get parked. 'Suzy's gone,' she sobbed. 'Suzy's gone. She's never coming back, Daddy, I know it. She's gone!' *My God,* heart lurching. *What have I done?*" (162). "He knew he must somehow retrieve the dog, as the night before he had known he must lose it" (165). He sped back to the field at the end of the street where he had once lived, back to the scene of his crime. Eventually he found the dog, in fact "understood he had been looking at it for a time" (167). Suzy looked at him, then turned away. Besides, a boy there had adopted her. Al sat down to think and realized that "he didn't feel so bad, all things considered. The world was full of dogs. There were dogs and there were dogs" (167).

"Why, Honey?"

And there are cats. Consider the beloved Trudy of "Why, Honey?" Like Suzy, she is inexplicably missing: "Our cat Trudy disappeared and was gone all night and the next day" (168). And as in Suzy's case, the perpetrator of the crime turns out to be a member of the family, "the man of the house" (169) as Al was of his: the miscreant son of the distressed mother who narrates this story in the form of a letter to someone who, now that her son has left home and become a famous politician, has discovered her identity. She had changed her name and moved away in the hope that her son would never find her. The cat had become the victim of a boyhood prank, firecrackers having been exploded "in Trudy's ears and in her you know what" (168).

The son is an accomplished liar, telling his mother that he earns eighty dollars from a parttime job when he really only brings in twenty-eight, that he went to the show when he went to the dance, and that he went on a field trip when he played hooky from school. The first two of these seem not to have merited the effort of a lie, as his mother well knows. "I would think what difference could it make, why doesn't he just be truthful, there is no reason to lie to his mother" (169). Al in "Jerry and Molly and Sam" was an inveterate liar too: "His life had become a maze, one lie overlaid upon another until he was not sure he could untangle them if he had to" (154). Al, by this point in his life, had to lie—he couldn't very well tell his wife that he was having an affair, or that he was going to get rid of the family pet. The son's mendacity seems to be more innate, though all we know about him is what his mother tells us. But even if we could hear his side of the story, how could we fail to be shocked by his apparent wickedness in the climactic scene in which he seems about to threaten her with violence?

> I want the truth, honey, that's all I've ever asked from you, the truth. Suppose you had a child who when you asked him something . . . never once told you the truth? . . . Why should he lie, you ask yourself, what does he gain I don't under-stand. I keep asking myself why but I don't have the answer. Why, honey?
> He didn't say anything, he kept staring, then he moved over alongside me and said I'll show you. Kneel is what I say, kneel down is what I say, he said, that's the first reason why.
> I ran to my room and locked the door. He left that night.
> (172–73)

This is one of the most chilling moments in all of Carver's work. What is the boy going to do, assault his mother? Ask her to join him in prayer? Or is he so fed up with her domination that he has decided to take up for real the mantle of "the man of the house" that she had foisted upon him, and to assert the domi-nance owed a husband—not to strike her, but simply to tower above her in order to announce that henceforth *he* is the master of the house?

An eerie silence surrounds this gesture, as we look in vain for what Carver may have carved away from this scene that might have explained what he had in mind. The ambiguity of that *he* is intentional, for in their common silence Carver and the son come remarkably, and scandalously, close. In Carver's poetry, which is more openly autobiographical than his stories, the mother is in fact presented as a meddling, tiresome woman who torments her son. In "What I Can Do," in *Ultramarine,* she keeps calling him on the phone. "My mother wants / to talk to me too. Wants to remind me again how it was / back then. All the milk I drank, cradled in her arms. / That ought to be worth something now. She needs / me to pay for this new move of hers" (63). In "Where the Groceries Went," which immediately precedes "What I Can Do" in *Ultramarine,* the mother, again on the phone, pleads to her son, "Honey, I'm afraid. / I'm afraid of everything. Help me, please. / Then you can go back to whatever it was / you were doing. Whatever / it was that was so important / I had to take the trouble / to bring you in this world" (62). Notice that she calls him *Honey.* With such a mother as that in the background, we should not find it un- thinkable that the narrator's sympathies in "Why, Honey?" might lie with the son.

"Whatever it was that was so important," as she puts it, is clearly, in the context of the poem, his writing. And we must not lose sight of the fact that the son in the story, like the author, is a writer, and that his mother chooses the very mo- ment he invites her to become his reader to lose her patience and confront him with her long-meditated indictment for lying. "I want to show you something, he said, and he showed me this essay he was writing for his civics class. I believe it was on relations between the congress and the supreme court. (It was the paper that won a prize for him at graduation!) I tried to read it and then I decided, this was the time. Honey, I'd like to have a talk with you" (172). Here begins the scene in which she asks him why he always lies to her, and he responds with his bizarre command.

Is there any other way to read this story? Can we put our- selves in his shoes? Is Carver asking us to try?

There is no father in this home, and the mother has had to raise her only child alone. Our sympathy goes out to her, as it would in any event because all we hear is *her* side of the story, but we also know that such a family situation can lead to some strained behavior on both sides. Husbandless, such a mother would naturally tend to cling to her son in a perhaps obsessive way, seeing him, as she says she does, as "the man of the house" (169). As she herself confesses, without perhaps realizing it was a confession, "I built up all these fears" (173) about her son's lack of truthfulness and about his perceived potential for violence. Perhaps she built them up on an inadequate foundation. If we come away from this story as afraid of her son as she, have we become the victims of an elaborate deception on the part of the author?

What exactly has he done? He may have been one of the two boys who abused the cat, though the story is told in such a way as to leave plenty of room for doubt. After all, the only witness to the event only *"thought* it was your son" (168; emphasis added), evidently not getting a good enough look to know for sure. And the reason Mr. Cooper thought it was her son may simply have been that he saw that "one of them ran this way" (168), that is, in the direction of her house. When the mother told her son about Trudy "he acted surprised and shocked" (169), offered to post a reward, and later tried to comfort her: "Don't take it too hard, mom, she was old, in cat years she was 65 or 70, she lived a long time" (169). In this already frightening narrative made all the more frightening for its ambiguity, it is not easy to tell how this should be interpreted. Was this a veiled threat against his mother, who had perhaps also lived a long time? Or was it genuinely an effort to reconcile her to the fact of Trudy's death? If he were innocent, how else could we expect him to act than in the way he did?

If he lied to her needlessly about where he spent his evenings or how much money he made, we can on the other hand see how he could have interpreted her behavior toward him as a persistent invasion of privacy. In fact his lie about being at the show when he really "went to the school dance or spent the evening riding around with somebody in a car" (169) is far from unnecessary, if we realize the extent to which he may have resented her wanting to know where he was at all times. He might quite justifiably think she had no right to know every detail of his social life and therefore intentionally mislead her

about exactly which of several innocent pastimes he was pur-
suing on a given night.

Besides, this mother is a bit of a snoop. She found out about
the salary discrepancy when she found the check stub in his
pocket in the dirty clothes. That discovery may have been innocent enough, but her tiptoeing into his bedroom when he
was asleep to filch his car keys was somewhat less so. She wanted
to peek into the trunk of his car, where her diligence was rewarded by finding a bloody shirt with his shotgun and hunting
knife. He said it had been a nosebleed, and it may well have
been—or something else equally innocuous he didn't want to
bother her about, perhaps the blood of an animal he had killed.
Perhaps we are, at least at first reading, supposed to think him
capable of murder, but if we sufficiently reflect on just how
unreliable a narrator we may have on our hands we may well
be entitled to second thoughts.

Perhaps her most egregious invasion of his privacy occurred on the evening that provoked the rupture between
them. He had come in late, and his mother, worried as usual,
had knocked on his bedroom door and then pushed it open
without waiting for a response, saying, "Would you like a hot
cup of tea, honey, I can't sleep" (172). She could evidently lie
as well as he, since obviously the desire to get him a hot cup of
tea is not the reason she barged in uninvited. "He was bent
over by the dresser and slammed a drawer and turned on me,
get out he screamed, get out of here, I'm sick of you spying he
screamed" (172). Horrible words, yet a cry from the heart that
many a teenager pestered by an interfering parent could
readily understand.

"I went to my room and cried myself to sleep. He broke my
heart that night." We can surely sympathize with both. The
mother, in her blindness, cannot see how her meddling looks
to her son, who surely has problems of his own he does not feel
obliged to share. The son, for his part, is evidently sorry for his
outburst, for when his mother came in the next evening "he
had supper ready. How are you? he said, he took my coat. How
was your day?" She told him she hadn't been able to sleep the
night before because of what he had said. "I'm not trying to

make you feel guilty but I'm not used to being talked to like that by my son." He does not, perhaps cannot bring himself to apologize, but he does respond in a way: "I want to show you something, he said, and he showed me this essay he was writing for his civics class. I believe it was on relations between the congress and the supreme court" (172). Nothing of course could be farther removed from the immediate demands of the present situation, in the mother's eyes, than such a topic as this. Yet from our perspective, a real parallel does emerge between the legislative-judical power struggle and the one going on between mother and son—one of which the son may even be aware, so that his offering her this essay to read in lieu of explaining his actions or apologizing for his behavior would in fact be a genuine attempt to communicate. Unfortunately, she is a poor reader, lacking the patience necessary to understand what he is trying to say. The parallel is based on the absence of the father, to which the mother alludes at this very moment: "It's especially hard for us having no father in the house, no man to turn to when we need him" (172). There should be, as in the American constitutional system, three parts to this family and its disputes. In the son's essay one of these parts, the executive, is missing. Were this branch missing as well in actual political life "relations between the congress and the supreme court" would be impossible to resolve. As it is, each of the three operates a check on the other: congress passes laws, the supreme court can rule them unconstitutional, and the justices are chosen by the president, as a husband chooses a wife, or a wife a husband. Once the choice is made, the president, and in this case the husband, may have to live with the consequence, but each has as well a certain intangible additional power that derives from the prestige of his office with which he can at least set the agenda and sometimes browbeat the other into submission. It is not by chance that the son eventually became a member of that missing executive branch, supplying what had been missing in his family by becoming the governor of a state.

Though the ambiguities of "Why, Honey?" may be beyond resolution, its place in the sequential structure of the book is clear. One of the most important things about the son and the

protagonist of the immediately preceding story is that they are
liars, as Saltzman also noted: "Al's attempts to resist victimiza-
tion strangle him in a web of deceit. But the alternative to being
a poor liar is not necessarily being honest, but being a proficient
liar. 'Why, Honey?' introduces a character who thrives on it;
having mastered the talent for lying as a child, he matures into
a social, if not moral, success" (58).

So important is Al's lying to that story, and to that story's
appearance in the book just before "Why, Honey?" that a desire
to emphasize this aspect of the narrative still more may explain
Carver's decision to change its title from "A Dog Story" (as it
appeared in *Perspective* in 1972) to "Jerry and Molly and Sam."
Molly is a woman Al tries unsuccessfully to pick up in a bar
after he let Suzy out of the car, and Jerry is the bartender who,
it turns out, is a good friend of Molly's (which may have ren-
dered the seduction impossible, since Al couldn't very well pick
her up from under the eyes of the guy who may be her boyfriend). Sam, of course, was his boyhood dog. It is, once more,
a real puzzle of a title. No one named in the story, surely, could
be less important to it than Jerry and Molly (though Sam has a
great deal of relevance, all the more so now that his flashing
red beacon of a coat comes to echo the winking and blinking
lights of the two preceding stories). Two more passages added
to the story since its original appearance shed some light on the
problem: "Sandy! Betty and Alex and Mary! Jill! And Suzy the
goddamn dog! That was Al" (153). And "he dressed and he
thought of Jill. He thought of Betty and Alex and Mary and
Sandy and Suzy. He felt drugged" (155). (Sandy is his wife's
sister and the one who gave them the dog, Betty is Al's wife,
Alex and Mary his children, and Jill his mistress.) These litanies
of names linked by "and," which appear early in the story before Al makes Jerry and Molly's acquaintance, are the closest
the title comes to reappearing in the text. The first of these
passages asserts that the list of names itself "was Al," that it
summed him up; the second makes it appear that he feels
drugged from having to think about them all (in the first version, the drugged feeling had a different cause: "He felt
drugged, like he'd had too much sleep" [36]). Al's life, as a

passage occurring on the page between these two passages tells us, "had become a maze, one lie overlaid upon another until he was not sure he could untangle them if he had to" (154). "He could never get used to the lying. Besides, he hated to use what little reserve he might have left with Betty by telling her a lie for something different from what she suspected. A wasted lie, so to speak. But he could not tell her the truth, could not say he was *not* going drinking, was *not* going calling on somebody, was instead going to do away with the goddamn dog and thus take the first step toward setting his house in order" (153–54). The three things Al has just said he could not tell her the truth about correspond with precision, even in their order, to the three names in the title: drinking with the bartender Jerry, calling on somebody with Molly (whom he would like to be able to call on as he does Jill), and the goddamn dog with Sam (the beloved dog that Suzy can never be).

Al and the mother's son, in addition to being extraordinary liars, are also both capable of doing away with their family pet. Though Al didn't actually kill the dog it wasn't for lack of desire: "The mere thought of all the twenty-five- or fifty-buck checks" that his sister-in-law Sandy kept touching him for "made him want to *kill* the goddamn dog" (153; Carver's emphasis). In fact, this murderous thought was added to the text for the story's appearance in the book, where it would come just before the story of the son who may have murdered the family cat. The passage had originally read: "The mere thought . . . caused his stomach to knot, and he opened and closed his hands convulsively in his pockets" (34). No mention of killing the dog here.

At the same time the son's walking out of his mother's house at an early age (even before he graduated from high school) and his never looking back ("I found out his address and wrote to him . . . there never was an answer" [173]) form a stark contrast to Al's nostalgic wish to drive his car to his old home town, "stopping when he came to where his mother lived, and never, never, for any reason ever, ever leave again" (158).

"The Ducks"

The way the wife in "The Ducks" makes love with her husband is strangely maternal: "Slowly she inched up in the bed,
gently moving his head down to her breast. He took the nipple
and began working it in his mouth" (181). So was Jill's calming
approach to Al in "Jerry and Molly and Sam": "She stroked his
hair with one hand and leaned over him, gazing into his eyes.
'Poor baby' " (161). "Why, Honey?," sandwiched between these
two stories, is the story of a perverted maternity in which a son
becomes his mother's "man of the house" and of the ambiguities and confused affections that result. Does this mother really
love her son, or is she only paranoid? And does he really hate
his mother, or is he just incapable of expressing affection? At
the very moment the husband in "The Ducks" makes that
childlike gesture, he raises the same question: "He tried to
think how much he loved her or if he loved her" (181). And he
uses, elsewhere in the story, the same term of endearment:
"Hon, why don't you go ahead and take your bath" (179).
"Hon, wake up" (182)

Both stories begin with a bang, as the firecrackers that did
in Trudy are echoed in the first sentence of "The Ducks": "A
wind came up that afternoon, bringing gusts of rain and sending the ducks up off the lake in black explosions looking for
the quiet potholes out in the timber" (175). These explosions
are not death-dealing, just the flapping of duck wings. But they
announce the husband's intention of going duck hunting the
next day, when explosions will in fact be as fatal to the ducks as
the other explosions had been to the cat. For a brief moment
we might have shared the mother's possible paranoia and
thought that her son's conceivably innocent remark about the
cat's already being old enough to die was a hint of the fate he
had prepared for her; likewise the ducks could be taken to
represent such a married couple as the husband and wife were,
for they flew in "groups of half a dozen, but mostly *doubles*"
(175; emphasis added). This initial paragraph of "The Ducks"
concludes with yet another set of explosions with an innocent
cause yet an undertone of mortality: "On his wife's clothesline,

strung up between the two sugar pines, sheets and blankets popped shotlike in the wind" (175).

Death is certainly stalking the neighborhood, for the husband returns prematurely from his night-shift job to report that the mill boss had dropped dead of a heart attack right in front of everyone, and that the shift was canceled. Before he had left for work she had asked him if we was going hunting again in the morning, and he had replied that he was. "She went back into the kitchen and shut the door and looked at him through the window. 'I just hate to have you gone all the time. It seems like you're gone all the time,' she said to the window" (176). So that when he comes back before the end of his shift, she finds that her wish has come true, but at a terrible cost: "That Granger man, that's a shame. It's nice to have you home, but I hate for something like that to happen" (177–78). This does not prevent her from seeking to make what profit she can from the situation. "She moved her fingers through his hair and dropped her hand and smoothed his neck. 'Maybe we'll have a little tonight. We never hardly get a chance to have a little.' She touched her other hand to his thigh, leaned over and kissed him. 'What do you think about that?' " (179) In the end, it does not really come to pass as she had wished, for even though she later takes the initiative of moving his head down to her breast, nothing happens. He even, at that point, as we have seen, begins to doubt his love for her. "He tried to think how much he loved her or if he loved her. He could hear her breathing but he could also hear the rain. They lay like this. She said, 'If you don't want to, it's all right.' 'It's not that,' he said, not knowing what he meant" (181). He is evidently haunted by thoughts of death, for after she falls asleep "he tried to think of Reno," where they planned to go in a few days, but when he tried to hear the sound of the roulette wheel and "tried to concentrate on the wheel" what he saw and heard were "the saws and the machinery slowing down, coming to a stop" (181), as they had when Granger dropped dead on the factory floor.

This may help us to understand a little better what may have happened in the immediately preceding story. For the mother in "Why, Honey?" may have been doing what the wife has done here—may have brought something into existence by her desire, through a kind of self-fulfilling prophecy. The way it comes about is different, and so is the final result, but there is yet something fundamentally the same. The mother so desired her son that she watched his comings and goings with a lover's jealous eye, with the result that he lied all the more in self-defense. Her suspicions were continually confirmed, as if these confirmations satisfied the desire that these suspicions be correct, the desire that her son in fact turn out to be the liar that his father may have been (we are not told whether he died or left her; if the latter, we may think we now know why). In "My Father's Life," Carver tells the story of his mother's putting his sleeping father's hand in a pan of warm water. "This would make him talk in his sleep, she told me. There were things she needed to know, things she was sure he was keeping from her" (*Fires*, 16).

Perhaps this is why when the wife makes that maternal gesture in "The Ducks" her husband should be wondering if he loved her at all. For she is in fact being more than maternal here: "She opened her mouth and kissed him, pulling his head *down* with her other hand. Slowly she inched up in the bed, gently moving his head *down* to her breast. He took the nipple" (181; emphasis added). She is assuming a position of dominance, reenacting a significant aspect of the terrifying scene in the immediately preceding story in which the son tried to turn the tables on his mother: "Kneel is what I say, kneel *down* is what I say" (173). That scene in "Why, Honey?," so troubling and so difficult to interpret, finds its counterpart, and perhaps its explanation, in this one in "The Ducks." The reading I had suggested for that scene—that it is not in fact as terrifying as it first appears, that the son was not about to strike his mother but merely choosing a dramatic manner to assert his dominance—now appears, in the light of what happens here, to have been correct. For the wife's gesture in "The Ducks" reminds us that a mother must place herself *above* her child's head if she is to give it milk, moving it down gently if she can, pulling it down forcefully if she must. When mothers give their milk in Carver they are not unaware of the power this gives them over their child, as we saw in "What I Can Do": "My mother wants / . . . to remind me again how it was / back then. All the milk I drank, cradled in her arms. / That ought to be worth something now."

"How About This?"

The husband in "The Ducks" is not entirely happy with his family's situation where they are, apparently a small mill town in northern California. "*I just want to leave.* We been here a long time. I'd like to go back home and see my folks. Or maybe go on up to Oregon. That's good country" (181; emphasis added). His wife is quite willing to do what he wants. " 'If that's what you want,' she said." Harry, the young husband in "How About This?," has the same idea, expressed in fact in the same words: "At first he wasn't too clear about where he wanted to go; he *just* knew he *wanted to leave* the city to try to start over again" (185; emphasis added). What he had in mind was "a simpler life . . . a more honest life somewhere in the country." His wife, Emily, as cooperative in this regard as the wife was in "The Ducks," is willing to pull up stakes and go with him. She suggests, "jokingly at first, her father's deserted place in the north-western part of Washington" (185). Thus their destination becomes, like the one the husband in the story before contemplated, a country place in the Pacific Northwest, "back home" in Emily's case (as close, that is, as she could come to doing that, as her parents are evidently deceased).

What happens in this story is that Harry soon loses his fervor for the outdoor life when he discovers how dilapidated the deserted house is, lacking plumbing, electricity, or even a fireplace. Emily, who neither pushed him toward moving there nor tried to dissuade him, is lovingly supportive. "You decide, Harry, if you haven't already. It's your decision. I'd just as soon go back if that makes it any easier for you" (190). "Harry, we have to love each other. We'll just have to love each other" (192).

Trying to decide what to do, Harry studied some old license plates nailed to the door of the barn. "Green, yellow, white plates from the state of Washington, rusted now, 1922–23–24–25–26–27–28–29–34–36–37–40–41–1949." In a sentence that did not appear in the original version of the story (in *The Western Humanities Review* in 1970), "he studied the dates as if he thought their sequence might disclose a code" (188). This story's protagonist, in other words, finds himself doing precisely what Carver's stories invite his readers to do—an invitation that is reiterated by this very act of wondering about the possibility of a code concealed in the sequence, for it happens only in the version of the story that appears *in sequence*, in the short story cycle that *Will You Please Be Quiet, Please?* forms.

Three more changes in the text of "How About This?" contribute to the feeling that the sequence of stories in which it now appears might disclose a code, a hidden language that would enable us to read between the lines. The first is the title itself, which was originally "Cartwheels," referring to those Emily turns as she waits for Harry to decide what to do. The new title comes from the same scene: "She turned two more cartwheels while he watched, and then she called, 'How about *this!*' [shortened from the earlier version's 'How about *this* now?' (382)]. She dropped lightly onto her hands and, getting her balance, began a shaky hesitant movement in his direction. Face flushed, blouse hanging over her chin, legs waving insanely, she advanced on him" (191-92). There are no cartwheels or walking on hands in "The Ducks," but the wife's question that the new title repeats is anticipated by two questions the wife of the earlier story asked *her* husband. "What do you think about that?" (179) she asks after having just made him the following proposition: "Maybe we'll have a little tonight. We never hardly get a chance to have a little" (178–79). A little later that evening, she steps naked from her bath, "smiled and draped the towel over her shoulder and made a little step in the tub and posed. 'How does it look?'" (179–80). Here she comes even closer to anticipating the scene in "How About This?" when Emily asks for Harry's reaction to her cartwheels and handstands (their visit to her parents' old place had reawakened her childhood dream of becoming a circus star) because she too is calling her husband's attention to her body and to what it can do.

The wife's two questions in "The Ducks" were clearly sexual advances, the first inviting her husband to respond to the suggestion they make love that night and the second asking him to comment on her unclothed figure. That "How about *this?*" is likewise a sexually loaded question is made apparent by yet another change Carver made as he revised this story for its appearance in this collection. In the earlier version, after walking on her hands she "let herself fall onto her shoulder and rolled onto her back, covering her eyes from the sun with an arm. Her breasts rose and fell with her deep breathing. After a minute, still resting, she said, 'Harry' " (382). This deep breathing was not particularly sexual, just the natural consequence of the cartwheels and handstands she had just performed. In the later version this evidence of exertion is gone, replaced by the sexual allure the narrator now sees in what she does with her breasts: "She let herself fall against her shoulder and rolled onto her back, covering her eyes from the sun with an arm as if to uncover her breasts. She said, 'Harry' " (192). This change in the text gives a different slant to the question announced in the title, for though Emily's "How about this?" is still sandwiched between cartwheels and handstands, these feats of physical prowess now eventuate in a come-hither pose. As such, it now bears a closer resemblance to the "What do you think about that?" and "How does it look?" the other wife asked of her husband.

Carver's characters at times like these show evidence of performing gestures that mean more than they realize, that seem to be part of another story than merely the one in which they appear, part of that fragment of extramural narrative that gradually emerges as we read these stories in the same way Harry read the license plates, itself an example of just such a gesture. Sometimes these gestures, repeated in sequentially appearing stories, appear to allude to their own existence and to that of this other, hidden agenda that seems to govern them. It

even happens, in these two stories, that the characters performing these echoing gestures express their ignorance of why they
do what they do and thereby suggest, without of course realizing it, that there is something here beyond their control. For
when Harry in "How About This?" says " 'We've got to decide,'
. . . *not really knowing what he meant*" (190; emphasis added), his
confession that he doesn't know the meaning of his words
strangely echoes the confession the husband makes (again,
through the narrator's telling us what he was really thinking) in
the immediately preceding story: "She said, 'If you don't want
to, it's all right,' " alluding to her husband's apparent lack of
sexual desire. " 'It's not that,' he said, *not knowing what he meant*"
(181; emphasis added). Clearly one of the things he didn't
know he meant was that this expression of ignorance should so
clearly anticipate his counterpart's in the neighboring story.

   We are in a position to know more than either husband,
since we can read both stories. But we are in a position to know
more even than that, for if we were to read both versions of the
second of these stories we would discover that Carver added
the echoing phrase "not really knowing what he meant" at the
time of the story's appearance in the book (originally, the line
had read, " 'We've got to decide,' he said vaguely [380]),
thereby reiterating his invitation to read the stories here as
Harry tried to read the numbers on the plates: "as if . . . their
sequence might disclose a code."

"Bicycles, Muscles, Cigarets"

   Gestures are again repeated, this time in more widely divergent circumstances, in "How About This?" and "Bicycles, Muscles, Cigarets." After turning cartwheels and walking upside
down on her hands, we recall, Emily had "let herself *fall* against
her shoulder and *rolled onto her back*" (192; emphasis added).
Two men engaged in a fight in the following story "*fell* heavily
onto the lawn. They *rolled* on the lawn, Hamilton wrestling
Berman *onto his back*" (201; emphasis added). It was not so
strange that Harry should, like the husband in the story before

his, find himself "not knowing what he meant," nor that Emily should seem to display her breasts for her husband as the wife in the story before had drawn her husband's head down to her breasts. After all, these echoing gestures were performed by characters who already bore some resemblance to each other— husband to husband, wife to wife. But that Emily's falling on the ground and rolling onto her back should now be reassigned to these wrestling men is a great deal more puzzling.

It would probably be a mistake in this case to try to interpret this echo by seeking some hidden analogy between the persons who perform these gestures. It would be better to acknowledge that the gestures outlive the characters who perform them, are perhaps in some sense more important than the characters, and in the final analysis may be something like characters them- selves. I mean to say that the characters who act in the fragmen- tary narrative sometimes glimpsed in the spaces between Carver's stories may be not people but gestures, words, and images.

"Rolling" in any case suddenly becomes, if only for a mo- ment, the most important act, or character, at this point in Carver's book. For the rolling in which Emily was first engaged (she is the first person to do any rolling in *Will You Please Be Quiet, Please?*) is not only echoed, as we have just seen, by the two fighting fathers (Hamilton and Berman) of "Bicycles, Mus- cles, Cigarets" and by Hamilton's young son, who "*rolled* onto his side and watched his father walk to the door" (205; empha- sis added) on the way out of the son's bedroom, but "rolling" itself comes to occupy center stage in this story. It becomes so important that the word now demands redefinition: " 'Kip and Roger used Gilbert's bike to help Kip deliver his papers, and then the two of them, and Gary too, they say, took turns rolling it.' 'What do you mean "rolling it"?' Hamilton said. 'Rolling it,' the woman said. 'Sending it down the street with a push and letting it fall over' " (196–97). Not only, by the way, does this rolling repeat once more the verb first applied to Emily, but the movement of the bicycle wheels recalls the spiraling turns of cartwheels she had so expertly performed.

Indeed, Emily's surprising athletic prowess is paralleled by

Evan Hamilton's, who quickly overpowered his opponent in a fight. Both had been summoned to appear by Gilbert's mother, for the bicycle was not only damaged but by this point missing. Mrs. Miller was trying to bring all the participants and their fathers together to sort out what had happened. Hamilton's son Roger admitted "rolling" the bike with Kip and with Gary Berman but denied stealing it. Gary and his father leave the room to have a secret conference, which strikes Hamilton as irregular. "He had the feeling he should stop them, this secrecy" (199). When they return, Gary says " 'It was Roger's idea to roll it.' 'It was yours!' Roger said. . . . 'You wanted to! Then you wanted to take it to the orchard and strip it!' 'You shut up!' Berman said to Roger. 'You can speak when spoken to, young man, not before' " (199–200). With this remark Gary's father has clearly stepped out of line, as he does again when his son complains of Roger, "He called me a jerk, Dad," and Berman responds, "He did, did he? Well, he's the jerk. He looks like a jerk" (200). Hamilton tells Berman to get control of himself. Berman brushes up against Hamilton on his way out the door, knocking him into the bushes. Hamilton "couldn't believe it was happening. He moved out of the bushes and lunged at the man where he stood on the porch. They fell heavily onto the lawn. They rolled on the lawn, Hamilton wrestling Berman on his back" (201) and begins to pound his head against the ground. The struggle ends when Mrs. Miller screams for someone to call the police.

On their way home, Hamilton, who probably realizes that the edginess he was already feeling for having just quit smoking may have led him to resort to physical violence when he shouldn't have, tells his son he's sorry he had to see something like that. He doubtless regrets, as well, that the lesson he wanted his son to learn about not damaging someone else's property has been obscured by the fight.

Later, as he meditates alone Hamilton thinks back to a fight his father once had. "It was a bad one, and both men had been hurt. . . . Hamilton had loved his father and could recall many things about him. But now he recalled his father's one fistfight as if it were all there was to the man" (203). Emily in the preceding story recalled an incident in her father's life too, one so important that it likewise seemed to sum up the kind of man he was. Like the paternal recollection that comes to Hamilton, this one involved a confrontation, under uneasy circumstances, with another man; it had, however, a much happier resolution. "Once Dad shot a deer out of season. I was about—I don't know—eight or nine, around in there." The game warden showed up and followed Emily into the barn, where her father had hung the deer in the loft. " 'The deer was hanging there, but the game warden didn't say anything. He offered Dad a chew of tobacco, but Dad refused—he never had liked it and wouldn't take any even then. Then the game warden pulled my ear and left. . . . I haven't thought about things like that in years. I don't want to make comparisons,' she said" (189). What comparisons she doesn't want to make are not entirely clear—a comparison between her father's taciturn and rough-hewn strength and her urban and artist husband's indecision and inability to cope with the rigors of country life?

Perhaps so, for Hamilton's son asks him about his father, wondering what comparisons could be made. "Dad, was Grandfather strong like you? When he was your age, I mean, you know, and you—" "And I was nine years old? Is that what you mean? Yes, I guess he was" (204). Emily was the same age —"I was about . . . eight or nine"—when her father had the confrontation with the game warden that had made such an impression on her. Hamilton's fear that his scuffle with Berman will be, as the fistfight his father had been for him, what his son will remember after his death "as if it were all there was to the man" finds some justification when we consider that both incidents occurred when the child—Emily, Roger—was at the evidently impressionable age of "eight or nine, around in there."

"What Is It?"

Leo is a bankrupt and ashamed of it. Unfortunately his father did not appear to share his sense of moral values. Leo "recalls when he was a kid his dad pointing at a fine house. . . .

'That's Finch,' his dad said admiringly. 'He's been in bankruptcy at least twice. Look at that house' " (209–10). Evan
Hamilton in the story just before is ashamed of what he's done,
of the fight he had in front of his son with another boy's father.[7] And he's afraid that all his son will remember of him is
what looms so large in his memory of his father, the fight that
he had with another man. Emily in the story before that has a
vivid recollection of an event that, when we read that story,
seemed to show her father in a positive light; especially by
comparison (a "comparison" she said she didn't want to make
but thereby makes inevitable) with her husband, who could not
have done any of what her father had done. But now in retrospect, in light of the subsequent reminiscences of a father in
the two stories since then, it may be important to note another
important detail about her recollection. Emily's father had been
guilty of breaking the law (he shot the deer out of season), as
Evan Hamilton's had of getting into a fight and Leo's of admir-
ing the fruits of bankruptcy. All three stories thus feature a
recollection of the wrong the father did (or could countenance
doing, in Leo's father's case).

Because of his impending bankruptcy, Leo's wife must sell
their convertible. She's an experienced salesperson—she used
to sell children's encyclopedias door to door. As the story pro-
gresses, it becomes apparent that she is experienced in other
ways as well (unless we consider it part of the ins and outs of
selling). For she doesn't return home until early the next morning, having evidently slept with the used-car salesman in order
to guarantee a good price.

The title of the story appears in the question the salesman
asks Leo, when it appears that Leo is about to pick a fight with
the man who has just slept with his wife. The salesman had
driven the convertible into their driveway to return the makeup
pouch she had left behind. " 'Look,' the man says, 'I have to go.

---

7. As they meditate on the wrong they've done both men sweat it out:
"The sweat had dried on [Hamilton's] forehead. He felt clammy under his
clothes" (202). Leo's "undershirt is wet; he can feel the sweat rolling from his
underarms" (210).

No offense. I buy and sell cars, right? The lady left her makeup. She's a fine lady, very refined. What is it?' " (215) But the real fight Leo gets into is with his wife. And when this happens, they together repeat the lunging and rolling that had figured so prominently in the fight in the immediately preceding story, between Evan Hamilton and Gary Berman's father. Then, Hamilton had "moved out of the bushes and *lunged* at the man. . . . They *rolled* on the lawn" (201). Now, Leo's wife "makes a noise and *lunges,* catches his shirt, tears it down the front. 'Bankrupt!' she screams . . . 'You son of a bitch,' she says, clawing. . . . He waits awhile, then splashes water on his face and goes to the bedroom. . . . He turns back the covers and *rolls* her in, naked" (215). The rolling that had once been a wife's in "How About This?", that became a man's in "Bicycles, Muscles and Cigarets," is now once more a wife's. But by a kind of thesis, antithesis, and synthesis, it combines the attributes of both its predecessors: it's a woman's body that rolls (as in the first of these three stories), but it's a man's violent hands that makes her do it (as it had been Evan who violently set Berman to rolling in the second).

"Signals"

The salesman's declaration that Leo's wife is a real lady— "She's a fine lady, very refined"—is echoed at the beginning of the next story, "Signals," in what the restaurant owner says to Wayne about *his* wife: "Aldo personally conducted them to a table, seated Caroline, and then turned to Wayne and said, 'A lovely lady,' before moving off—a dark, small, impeccable man with a soft accent" (216). He says it again at the end of the story, as Wayne and Caroline are leaving his expensive restaurant, and Aldo has presented her a rose. " 'A very lovely lady,' he said to Wayne and smiled at him and turned to welcome another couple" (224).

Restaurants and jealous husbands figure in each of the last three stories of the collection. When Leo's wife calls home she says she's with the used-car salesman at a restaurant whose

name she at first can't recall and then identifies as New Jimmy's.
Leo tries to call her back a few minutes later but is told that the
restaurant has closed for the evening. No doubt she and the
man she is trying to persuade to buy the car had been at a
restaurant at some point that night, but her phone call may
have been a ruse to conceal her true whereabouts. As we will
soon see, the last and title story of the collection concerns a very
jealous husband who will try to drown his sorrows at still another restaurant. Wayne and Caroline's relationship is on the
rocks, and Arthur Salzman underlines the continuity between
their situation and that of the married couple of the story just
before when he writes that "an expensive dinner at Aldo's was
intended to be the inauguration of that phantom second
chance that Leo and Toni had blown in the previous story"
(67).

They seem to think that spending a great deal of money
on food and entertainment—the visit to Aldo's was just the
"first of the extravagances they had planned for that evening"
(217)—will improve their marriage. Leo and Toni had been
just as extravagant, but their marital discord apparently dated
from the problems to which their extravagance led. Their in-
come had increased because Toni had gone back to work selling,
and "for a while they didn't know how to spend the money"
(208). They bought the convertible, and "bicycles for the
kids" which because of his impending bankruptcy "he had
sent to his mother's for safekeeping" (210)—otherwise "What
Is It?" would have repeated its predecessor story's motif of
a missing bicycle. There were "some big parties back there,
some fine travel. . . . Food, that was one of the big items.
They gorged on food. He figures thousands on luxury items
alone" (210).

We are not told whether Wayne has reason to fear that his
wife will leave him for anyone in particular, but he is clearly in
danger of her leaving. "Is there a chance for us?" he asks.
"Maybe so," she answers, but also says, "Tonight, right now, at
this minute, I just can't say what I'm going to do. I'll just have
to see" (222). She is evidently on the brink of deciding to walk
out of the marriage. We do get a glimpse of what is driving

them apart when Wayne says "I don't mind admitting I'm not much of a . . . connoisseur. I don't mind admitting I'm just a lowbrow. Not like the group you've been keeping with lately" (220).

"Will You Please Be Quiet, Please?"

Ralph Wyman must have felt the same way about his wife Marian. Though they both prepared to become high school teachers, Marian soon advanced more rapidly in their chosen profession than her husband: "Marian was offered a post as a *French* and English *instructor* at the junior college at the edge of town, and Ralph had stayed on at the high school" (228; emphasis added). In Aldo's restaurant, Wayne was outclassed by his wife, who had to bail him out when he showed himself totally incapable of dealing with the waiter.

> "Could I have a soup spoon?" Wayne asked.
> "Sir?"
> "A soup spoon," Wayne repeated.
> The waiter looked amazed and then perplexed. He glanced around at the other tables. Wayne made a shoveling motion over his soup. Aldo appeared beside the table.
> "Is everything all right? Is there anything wrong?" "My husband doesn't seem to have a soup spoon," Caroline said. "I'm sorry for the disturbance," she said.
> "Certainly. *Une cuiller, s'il vous plaît,*" Aldo said to the waiter in an even voice. He looked once at Wayne and then explained to Caroline. "This is Paul's first night. He speaks little English." (221)

It must have been rather galling to Wayne that Caroline should feel obliged to apologize for his uncouth behavior, and that Aldo should now communicate directly with her, bypassing him.

Marian Wyman's superior ability as a *French instructor* is even anticipated in the restaurant story, in an almost uncanny

way, when Caroline finds herself in the position of giving "instruction" to Wayne about ordering in French: " 'What about
one of these *French* dishes, Wayne? . . . ' She placed her finger
in *instruction,* and then she narrowed her eyes at him as he
located the language, pursed his lips, frowned, and shook his
head. 'I don't know,' he said. 'I'd kind of like to know what I'm
getting' " (218; emphasis added).

Ralph Wyman can remember getting the feeling on their
Mexican honeymoon that he didn't quite fit in Marian's world.
It was a late afternoon, and she was leaning over the balustrade
of their *casita;* Ralph gazed upon her from the dusty road
below. "Her hair was long and hung down in front over her
shoulders, and she was looking away from him, staring at something in the distance. . . . [T]he whole incident put Ralph in
mind of something from a film, an intensely dramatic moment
into which Marian could be fitted but he could not" (227). We
are almost given enough clues to identify, if not which film, at
least the mythic scene it dramatizes. For later in the story (in a
passage Carver added) Ralph is deeply moved by another
freeze-frame of a long-haired woman: "Ralph saw the woman
toss her hair as she got into the car: He had never seen anything so frightening" (238). We know from other things the
narrator says that Ralph is sexually repressed. In Mexico he
had been "secretly appalled by the . . . open lust he saw" (227).
He was of the opinion that "there was a great evil pushing at
the world . . . and it only needed a little slipway, a little opening" (239).

Why should he find the sight of the woman tossing her hair
"so frightening"? Because she embodies the mythical long-
haired Medusa, whose horrible face turned to stone the men
who gazed at her, and who, as Freud pointed out, embodies
the female sexual organ: "Medusa's head takes the place of a
representation of the female genitals" ("Medusa's Head," 213).
Perseus slew the monster by cutting off her head, having taken
the precaution of viewing her only through her reflection in
his shield. What is particularly frightening for a Ralph Wyman
in this regard would be, according to Freud, the terror of castration:

> We have not often attempted to interpret individual mytho-logical themes, but an interpretation suggests itself easily in the case of the horrifying decapitated head of Medusa. To decapitate = to castrate. The terror of Medusa is thus a ter-ror of castration that is linked to the sight of something. Numerous analyses have made us familiar with the occasion for this: it occurs when a boy, who has hitherto been unwill-ing to believe the threat of castration, catches sight of the female genitals, probably those of an adult, surrounded by hair, and essentially those of his mother. ("Medusa's Head," 212)

On the same evening that Ralph is frightened by the woman tossing her hair, he soon afterwards comes face to face with an even more graphic "representation of the female genitals" in the toilet of Jim's Oyster House where it is, precisely, in close association *with hair:* "Inside, in line behind three other men, he found himself staring at opened thighs and vulva drawn on the wall over a pocket-comb machine. Beneath was scrawled EAT ME, and lower down someone had added *Betty M. Eats It —RA 52275"* (241).[8]

8. This telephone number seems, intriguingly, to have a connection with the scene earlier that evening in which Ralph, paying for a drink at the bar, "pulled out some change, examined it in his hand. A quarter, nickel, two dimes, two pennies. He counted as if there were a clue to be uncovered. He laid down the quarter and stood up, pushing the change back into his pocket" (237). In the original version of this story, published in *The Best American Short Stories 1967,* the number of pennies was not specified, and the sentence in which he counted as if there were a code to be uncovered did not appear (51). That sentence, of course, recalls the one, likewise added for the book version of these stories, in "How About This?" in which Harry studied the dates of the licence plates nailed to the barn door "as if he thought their sequence might disclose a code" (188). While that added sentence appears to allude to the way that the sequence of the stories in this collection seems to form a hidden code, the allusion hidden here may be to the telephone num-ber scrawled on the restroom wall. The change Ralph counted amounts to fifty-two cents, corresponding to the first two numbers in 52275, while the second two numbers constitute the change he had left after leaving a quarter on the bar. Only the last number remains unaccounted for. The prefix RA repeats the first two letters of Ralph's own name.

Despite his horror at the woman whose tossing hair caught his eye, Ralph may have been originally attracted to his wife by her long hair. "Marian Ross wore her hair long and favored high-necked sweaters and always went around with a leather purse on a long strap swinging from her shoulder. Her eyes were large and seemed to take in everything at a glance" (226). Each element of this description seems to allude to Perseus's encounter with Medusa: the long hair to Medusa's (which was actually writhing serpents), the high-necked sweaters to her decapitation, the leather purse both to Perseus's name and to the leather purse (the *kibisis*) he put the head in (for Medusa's eyes still had the power of turning men to stone), and Marian's large and all-seeing eyes to Medusa's deadly gaze.

If we look in detail at the Mexican honeymoon scene, "the one vision he would always remember and which disturbed him most of all" (227), we will once again find these elements of myth. "Her hair was long and hung down in front over her shoulders, and she was looking away from him, staring at something in the distance. She wore a white blouse with a bright red scarf at her throat" (227).[9] Fortunately for Ralph, she was looking the other way—Perseus too made sure to avoid eye contact with the monster he had been sent to slay. The bright red scarf at her throat not only echoes the "high-necked sweaters" she had favored in their courting days but is a modern-day incarnation of the blood that encircled Medusa's neck when Perseus struck his decapitating blow. The latter-day version of Perseus's reddened sword appears when Ralph, in conversation with his wife, remembers this scene: "He looked down at his hands and noticed they had the same lifeless feeling they had had when he had seen her on the balcony. He picked up the red grading pencil lying on the table and then he put it down again" (233).

9. Later in the story, at Jim's Oyster House Ralph notices that the men in the band are wearing white shirts "with little red string ties around their necks" (240). This would appear to confirm Freud's suspicion that part of the horror of Medusa is the equation of decapitation with castration, for what had been an attribute of Ralph's Medusan wife has now become a threat to his own sex.

The moment of actual physical violence he inflicts on his wife
—when she finally confesses, under his insistent prodding, to
having gone considerably beyond a kiss with Mitchell Anderson
one evening two years before—has its own way of echoing that
mythical violence: " 'No, no,' she said, *throwing her head back*"—
as if awaiting the blade. "She began to pant in her fright. She
tried to *head him off*" (236; emphasis added), as Medusa tried to
"head off" Perseus with the one weapon she possessed, her
head (the sight of it, that is).

The horrifying scene in "Why, Honey?" now takes on a new
meaning—or rather a previously suspected one resurfaces.
Perhaps it was violence after all that Carver, if not actually the
son, had in mind. For if Medusa, as Freud claimed, is the
mother, then when the son asked his mother to kneel, to assume the position of the victim of the executioner's blade, he
was in fact, whether he realized it or not, reenacting that classic
decollation. In retrospect all this now seems to have been anticipated by the other scene where someone chops off a woman's
head, the chapter in Burroughs's *The Princess of Mars* that so
fascinated the boy in "Nobody Said Anything" that he read it
five times and then reenacted by doing the same thing to the
fish. Carver's stories are likewise carved in half (as far as the
sequential stories that seem so much to be cut out of the same
cloth are concerned), cut into pieces so that both their appearance together between the covers of a single volume and the
very order of their appearance there can give the reader
enough clues to begin to reconstruct what seems to be missing.

I say *seems* to be, for there is no guarantee that what is
missing will be found. After all, Carver may be giving us only
the semblance of a hidden meaning or narrative to be discovered. We may only be inebriated with the text as Ralph surely
was with grief and alcohol when he went past the main dining
room (and the bar and the dance floor) of Jim's Oyster House,
past the restroom where he saw the drawing on the wall,
through "another door at the other end of the corridor" (242)
where men were playing cards. Their "silent movements"
seemed to him "heavy with meaning," and so does the silence
that inhabits Carver's writing.

But there is something that draws us to that back room, to the hidden and more distant story within these stories, to the kind of silent yet echoing gestures and moments in the story of which even this back room in Jim's Oyster House is yet another instance. This deeper exploration of the restaurant, while standing for the deeper exploration of the story, parallels as well the invitation Aldo extended to Caroline and Wayne in the story before: " 'Would you like to see the wine cellar and the private dining rooms?' 'Very much,' Caroline said. 'I will have someone show you around when you have finished dining' " (221–22). When that moment arrives, their night out together will have gone so poorly that Wayne will say to his wife, "I don't want any guided tour of this place" (223), though Caroline will promise Aldo to accept his invitation on a future visit. "Next time, I should like to have your permission to check things out a little, but this time we simply must go" (224). Ralph and Marian do some exploring of dark rooms in Mexico—"they both enjoyed visiting the decayed churches and the poorly lighted museums" (227)—but it's Ralph alone who, with his restaurant explorations, really follows up on the invitation declined in the story before. What he saw in Mexico, however (his disturbing vision of Marian), does form an essential part of *our* exploration of the hidden dimensions of this story.

3

What We Talk About When We Talk About Love

In the *Paris Review* interview Raymond Carver said of *What We Talk About When We Talk About Love*, "it's a much more self-conscious book in the sense of how intentional every move was, how calculated. I pushed and pulled and worked with those stories before they went into the book to an extent I'd never done with any other stories" (*Conversations*, 44). Considering how much Carver revised the stories in *Will You Please Be Quiet, Please?* before they went into that volume, and how much those revisions made it a remarkably "self-conscious book," we have reason to expect that this collection will open itself to the same kind of reading as its predecessor. If a hunting license is needed—and if, like Emily's father in "How About This?" we were hunting out of season before—we have one now.

Yet it won't be easy, for *What We Talk About* is the most minimalist of Carver's collections. The stories here have been pared to the bone, especially by comparison to their original versions and by comparison to the lesser cuts made in the early versions of the stories in *Will You Please* and *Cathedral*. In this volume Carver went the farthest he ever had towards a terseness that is almost silence; the expansive stories of *Cathedral* will show a complete reversal of direction.

"Why Don't You Dance?"

We recall that "Fat," the first story in *Will You Please,* featured a narrator who, referring to the person to whom she had told what happened, points out to us that "I've already told her too much" (6). Now although the first story in *What We Talk About* is told by an omniscient narrator who doesn't figure in the story, at the very end the story is retold, much more briefly, by one of the participants. In fact she is obsessed with retelling it: "She kept talking. She told everyone." Yet we also learn that "There was more to it, and she was trying to get it talked out. After a time, she quit trying" (10). Both narrators refuse to continue, the one in "Fat" because she's told too much already, the one in "Why Don't You Dance?" because she's given up trying to express it. That resignation to the impossibility of telling what happened or of telling what it meant is especially characteristic of the taciturn stories of this collection, but the feeling that there is something more than first appears is a constant in Carver, and it is surely significant that both collections should begin by reminding us of that fact.

The story she gave up trying to get talked out is about a man, apparently abandoned by his wife, who decides to have a yard sale of all the contents of his house. As a result, the house is turned inside out.

> In the kitchen, he poured another drink and looked at the bedroom suite in his front yard. The mattress was stripped and the candy-striped sheets lay beside two pillows on the chiffonier. Except for that, things looked much the way they had in the bedroom—nightstand and reading lamp on his side of the bed, nightstand and reading lamp on her side.
>   His side, her side. (3)

Everything happens twice in these opening lines of the story—and of the collection. The bedroom that used to be inside the house has now been replicated on the lawn. Her side of the bed duplicates his. Even on the level of the words, in a kind of interior rhyme, "-striped" comes within a letter of "stripped."

And not only the bedroom, but the kitchen, the living room, the whole house has been brought outside. "He had run an extension cord on out there and everything was connected. Things worked, no different from how it was when they were inside" (4).

It will have been no accident, surely, that the collection should begin this way, if the stories here are going to repeat themselves in sequence as much as those in the preceding volume did, for the house that exists in two versions—before and after, inside and outside—will have provided a useful introduction to the volume, telling the reader what the waitress-narrator of that other first story might have termed "too much already": how the book is put together.

"Viewfinder"

That it is put together that way is apparent from the manner in which the second story repeats the first. For in "Viewfinder" too a man, likewise abandoned by his wife, has decided to replicate his house—not, this time, by putting the furniture on the lawn, but by hiring a Polaroid photographer to take some two dozen pictures of it from every conceivable angle. "We moved around the house. Systematic" (14). When the photographer had showed him the first print he "took the picture from him. There was a little rectangle of lawn, the driveway, the carport, front steps, bay window, and the window I'd been watching from in the kitchen" (12). As the man in the story before put it, "things looked much the way they had" before.

In a half-dozen other ways, Carver's second story seems to replicate his first—or, in imitation of what the first man did, to remove its contents and rearrange them in another context.

The husband in "Viewfinder" offers hospitality to a stranger and receives thanks in return: " 'Come in,' I said. 'I just made coffee.' . . . 'Thanks for the coffee' " (11, 14). So did the husband in "Why Don't You Dance?": " 'You kids, you'll want a drink,' the man said. . . . 'Thank you,' she said" (7, 8).

There is buying and selling going on in both stories. In

"Viewfinder" the photographer is selling the husband the pictures of his house, while in the first story the husband is offering the contents of his house to a young couple who happen upon the scene.

Bargains are struck. "I can give you a rate," the photographer said. "Three for a dollar. If I go any lower, I don't come out" (14). The husband in the other story is less worried about coming out ahead. The girl tells the boy, "Whatever they ask, offer ten dollars less" (6), and every time he does the offer is accepted—down to forty dollars for the bed, fifteen for the TV.

The photographer "adjusted the shutter" (14) of his camera; the boy turned on the television set and made "little adjustments" (4)—improving the picture in both cases. When the photographer returned from using the homeowner's bathroom "tucking in his shirt" (12) he was repeating a gesture the boy in the first story had performed when he arose from the bed on the lawn he had been trying out with the girl: "the boy stood up and tucked in his shirt" (5).

The husband in the second story "had a headache" and the coffee he's drinking and offers to his guest is "no good for it" (13); the boy in the first says of the alcohol his host has offered him, "It goes to your head. I'm getting it in the head" (8).

The husband in "Viewfinder" "waved" (15) at his guest (from the roof where he has climbed to get his picture taken); the other husband, when asked how much money he wanted for the desk, "waved his hand at this preposterous question" (7). What one can and cannot do with one's hands is of more than usual importance in these stories because the photographer in "Viewfinder" has none. His arms are fitted with chrome hooks instead, so that when the husband waves from his roof "the man with no hands waved back with his hooks" (15). The girl in the first story responds with *her* arms too: " 'Dance with me' [to the record the homeowner had put on his stereo on the lawn], the girl said to the boy and then to the man, and when the man stood up, she came to him with arms wide open. . . . She pulled the man closer. 'You must be desperate or something,' she said" (9).

Remembering those last words of "Why Don't You Dance?" —"There was more to it, and she was trying to get it talked out. After a time, she quit trying"—and bearing in mind all those details of that first story about replicating that are themselves replicated in the second, one might well wonder if "Viewfinder" isn't perhaps another attempt at telling what it is the girl could not get talked out. Or perhaps the real telling somehow lies in the combination of the two stories, so that together they make some progress toward getting it talked out that could not be made by either one alone.

If it is the idea itself of replication that needs talking out, it is easy to see how this could be true. Yet it seems that something more is at stake, especially because the second of these stories appears to locate in its viewfinder an autobiographical glimpse, a kind of portrait of the artist in the corner of the frame: "There was a little rectangle of lawn, the driveway, the carport, front steps, bay window, and the window I'd been watching from in the kitchen. . . . I looked a little closer and saw my head, *my head,* in there inside the kitchen window. It made me think, seeing myself like that. I can tell you, it makes a man think" (12). As "Viewfinder" underwent revision after its appearance in the *Iowa Review* that image came into clearer focus. Originally Carver wrote, "I looked closer and saw *the outline of* my head . . . behind the kitchen window *and a few steps back from the sink*" (50; emphasis added), and the two sentences of reflection on the significance of this discovery had not yet appeared. Not only was he farther back from the window than he is now, but he had been *behind* the window, which emphasizes that distance, while now he is simply *inside* it, the window serving as the frame. This increasingly clear image of the narrator in successive versions of the story parallels the shift from third- to first-person narration in successive versions of what now appears to have been much the same story—from "Why Don't You Dance?" to "Viewfinder." We get a clearer fix on the husband whose wife left him and who responds by replicating his house in another format when the person telling us the story becomes the man in question.

In the kind of subplot that can shed a telling light on the

main plot of the story, the husband in "Viewfinder," "trying to
think of something to say" to make conversation with the photographer he invited in for coffee, tells him, " 'Three kids were
by here wanting to paint my address on the curb. They wanted
a dollar to do it. You wouldn't know anything about that, would
you?' It was a long shot. But I watched him just the same. . . .
'I work alone,' he said. . . . 'What are you saying?' he said. 'I was
trying to make a connection,' I said" (13). There is, of course, a
connection to be made, for on the next page the photographer
will offer him a quantity discount on the pictures that will echo
these three who wanted to earn a dollar: "Three for a dollar"
(14). It's a connection crying to be made, by the reader if not
by the narrator, but it seems a totally meaningless one. It's just
there—an echo internal to the story that has no justification for
its being except to be an echo. Yet if it will ultimately lead the
reader to make the connection, it will put that reader in
the shoes of the husband who is trying to make one too. If the
reader is a literary critic and is therefore, like the husband,
"trying to think of something to say" about the story, that
reader ought eventually to make the connection I am about to
make: the other husband, in the other story, did succeed in
making a connection—one that completed the illusion that replicated his house on the lawn. "He had run an extension cord
on out there and everything was *connected*. Things worked, no
different from how it was when they were inside" (4). It is a
connection that names itself, which reminds us how important
words are in these stories. In our trying to break through the
silence that surrounds them, words—the choice of words, and
in particular the choice of words that are repeated—are almost
all we have to go on. Connections themselves speak, but we're
still going to have to work at finding out what they are saying.

"Mr. Coffee and Mr. Fixit"

Of the seventeen stories that Carver said he "pushed and
pulled and worked with" before they went into this collection,
"Mr. Coffee and Mr. Fixit" may have undergone the most re-

vision. As "Where Is Everyone?" in the Spring 1980 issue of *TriQuarterly,* it was about four times longer. When Carver selected the story to appear in *Fires: Essays, Poems, Stories* in 1983, two years *after* the publication of *What We Talk About,* he went back to the original, longer version (and title)—which suggests that the changes he made in it for *What We Talk About* may have had more to do with how it might fit the specific requirements of that volume than with a commitment to brevity.

The most important revision it underwent for *What We Talk About* is indicated by the change of title. "Where Is Everyone?" comes out of a passage, suppressed here, in which the narrator-protagonist telephones his mother, who asks if he is calling from home. " 'I'm not at home,' I said. 'I don't know *where everyone is* at home. I just called there' " (212; emphasis added).[1] "Mr. Coffee and Mr. Fixit" refers, respectively, to the "Mr. Coffees in every office" (20) of the aerospace company where Ross, the lover of the narrator's wife, used to work before he became an alcoholic and to the derogatory nickname the narrator gave him because he "spent his time repairing things, now that he had no regular job" (18). The title thus ironically alludes to the before and after of Ross's life, his former glory and his present failure. Much of what is cut out in the longer version concerns persons in the narrator's life other than Ross: his mother, wife, son, daughter, and late father. The pared-down version that concerns us here, like its title, focuses more closely on Ross and on his relationship to the narrator. In the longer version, he tells us that "I never met the man, though we talked on the phone a few times" (204; 173); that line was subsequently dropped, with the result that the reader of "Mr. Coffee and Mr. Fixit" has no reason to assume that they have not in fact made each other's acquaintance.

---

1. The sentence that repeats the title is absent from the *Fires* version of the story (181), which is strange because Carver habitually works his titles into his stories. The context is still there, however, for in both versions of "Where Is Everyone?" the protagonist calls home and no one answers. References will be given parenthetically in the text to both versions, in the order of publication.

As a result of these revisions the story comes more to resemble its new version's immediate predecessor in the collection, which concerned the encounter of two men of whom the first was the protagonist-narrator and the second a man who has a lot in common with Ross. Both Ross and the photographer for example are permanently disabled in limb or limbs because of an injury inflicted on them by a member of their former immediate family. Ross "walked with a limp from a gunshot wound his first wife gave him" (18), while the photographer told his host, " 'I had kids once. Just like you,' he said. I waited with the cups and watched him struggle up from the sofa. He said, 'They're what gave me this.' I took a good look at those hooks" (13–14).

Both Ross and the photographer pose as masters of a craft; they are both technicians. The photographer boasts of the quality of his work: "Don't I know what I'm doing? Let's face it, it takes a professional" (12). Ross used to be an "aerospace engineer" (17). "He told Melody [the narrator's daughter] he'd worked on the moon shots . . . was close friends with the astronauts" (20). The place where he had worked was "a modern operation. . . . Cafeteria lines, executive dining rooms, and the like. Mr. Coffees in every office" (20).

In both stories the narrator is said to have something in common with the other man: "I had kids once. Just like you," we have just seen the photographer say; he will say it again, through an eloquent if mysterious gesture (how exactly, we wonder, did he lose those hands?), when the narrator tells him how his family left him. "I said, 'The whole kit and kaboodle. They cleared right out.' 'Look at this!' the man said, and again he held up his hooks" (14). The narrator of the other story tells us "we had things in common, Ross and me, which was more than just the same woman. For example, he couldn't fix the TV when it went crazy and we lost the picture. I couldn't fix it either" (19). They were also both alcoholics. "He was in his mid-thirties when he went under. Lost his job and took up the bottle. I used to make fun of him when I had the chance. But I don't make fun of him anymore," the narrator confides in us, alluding to his having become an alcoholic himself ("drinking a fifth a day" [19]). "God bless and keep you, Mr. Fixit" (19–20), he continues, having come to the realization that they are brothers—perhaps even twins—under the skin.

As this story underwent its transformation from "Where Is Everyone?" to "Mr. Coffee and Mr. Fixit" its plot was condensed, as I have said, into the narrator's discovery of how much he resembles his former rival, Ross. Given that, together with the degree to which Ross resembles the photographer in the immediately preceding story, the next step to which Carver's geometry (in the sense in which it is practiced in the Fifth Book of Euclid's *Elements,* the science of ratios and proportions) invites us is to ask to what extent the narrator of "Viewfinder" sees a double of himself in the photographer. Is he that narrator's brother too—his secret sharer, his double? The question assumes a certain urgency in light of whatever horror happened to that man's hands.

The extraordinarily compelling scene with which "Mr. Coffee and Mr. Fixit" begins points the way to an answer.

> I've seen some things. I was going over to my mother's to stay a few nights. But just as I got to the top of the stairs, I looked and she was on the sofa kissing a man. It was summer. The door was open. The TV was going. That's one of the things I've seen.
>
> My mother is sixty-five. She belongs to a singles club. Even so, it was hard. I stood with my hand on the railing and watched as the man kissed her. She was kissing him back, and the TV was going. (17)

What we discovered in the title story of *Will You Please Be Quiet, Please?* provides what is needed to understand the full import of this passage: the presence in Carver of the figure of Medusa — Medusa, in Freud's words, as "a terror of castration that is linked to the sight of something . . . sight of the female genitals . . . essentially those of his mother" ("Medusa's Head," 212). Note the emphasis on sight in Carver's very first sentence: "I've seen some things"—and then its repetition at the end of the paragraph: "That's one of the things I've seen." In analyzing the previous collection, we had to view one story ("Why, Honey?") through the perspective of another ("Will You Please Be Quiet, Please?") in order to find the connection Carver was making between Medusa and the mother. Here, on the other hand, it is openly displayed before our eyes, for clearly what the narrator has seen is the mother's sexuality in action.

This mother's son tries to make proper allowance for that sexuality, even at her advanced age, but finds it hard to do: "My mother is sixty-five. She belongs to a singles club. Even so, *it was hard.*" That an impression of hardness should arise from his staring at his mother at such a moment makes it hard not to see Medusa in action here, turning the men who gazed upon her into stone. The joke did not escape Freud: "The sight of Medusa's head makes the spectator stiff with terror, turns him to stone. . . . For becoming stiff means an erection. Thus in the original situation it offers consolation to the spectator: he is still in possession of a penis, and the stiffening reassures him of the fact" ("Medusa's Head," 212). At least it's a joke when Carver's narrator says *it was hard,* one that turns upon the double sense of both *it* and *hard.*

"But just as I got to the top of the stairs, I looked. . . . it was hard. I stood with my hand on the railing and watched": that the climactic discovery should come just as he had finished mounting the stairs is entirely appropriate if Freud was right to say, in *The Interpretation of Dreams:*

> Steps, ladders or staircases, or, as the case may be, walking up or down them, are representations of the sexual act. . . . It is not hard to discover the basis of the comparison: we come to the top in a series of rhythmical movements and with increasing breathlessness and then, with a few rapid leaps, we can get to the bottom again. Thus the rhythmical pattern of copulation is reproduced in going upstairs. Nor must we omit to bring in the evidence of linguistic usage. It shows us that "mounting" is used as a direct equivalent for the sexual act. (390, 390n)

"I stood with my hand on the railing and watched": given the ambiguity of *it was hard,* might not this railing, which inclines upward at an angle as the stairs ascend, stand for something else—for the part of the body the beholder of Medusa would like to assure himself is still there?

Consider how the following passage in "Viewfinder" might reveal a latent sense beneath its surface meaning.

> He plucked at his crotch.
> "Here's coffee," I said.
> He said, "You're alone, right?"
> He looked at the living room. He shook his head.
> "Hard, hard," he said.
> He sat next to the camera, leaned back with a sigh, and smiled as if he knew something he wasn't going to tell me.
> "Drink your coffee," I said. (12–13)

The photographer's smile that meant he knew a secret was added to the story for its appearance in this collection, which gives us leave to wonder if this untold something has something to do with what this story may have in common with "Mr. Coffee and Mr. Fixit."[2] Might the secret the photographer knows be that the loss of hands can stand for the lopping off of something else? (And might he know something about what "Hard, hard" can really mean?) If the railing in the staircase scene is what I think it is, then the narrator there is coming dangerously close to repeating the photographer's gesture of plucking at his crotch. There's nothing risky (or particularly risqué) about it in "Viewfinder" alone, for the photographer had just returned from a visit to the narrator's bathroom. "I heard the toilet flush. He came down the hall, zipping and smiling, one hook holding his belt, the other tucking in his shirt" (12). His plucking was simply a matter of adjustment.

---

2. One thing they have in common, by the way, is coffee—as we can see from the coffee the narrator of "Viewfinder" keeps offering his guest: " 'Come in,' I said. 'I just made coffee.' . . . I wanted to see how he would hold a cup" (11). "Here's coffee. . . . Drink your coffee" (12–13). A veritable Mr. Coffee—so that the title of the second story could be alluding to the first, and these two stories resemble the offices in the aerospace plant where Mr. Fixit used to work—each one with its own coffeemaker.

But when we view "Viewfinder" in the context of the stories before and after, more is perhaps at stake.

We have already seen how his tucking in his shirt echoed the way the boy in "Why Don't You Dance?" "tucked in his shirt" (5) as he got up from lying on a bed with his girlfriend. That scene had a definite sexual undertone: " 'How does it feel?' she said. 'It feels firm,' he said. . . . 'Kiss me,' she said" (5). They don't actually do anything on the bed on the lawn, but the thought does occur. " 'Wouldn't it be funny if,' the girl said and grinned and didn't finish" (5).

And we can now see how the missing hands in "Viewfinder" may be turning up in "Mr. Coffee and Mr. Fixit," which begins and ends with them: the hand the narrator has on the railing in the opening scene, and the hands—likewise the narrator's— that need attention in the very last line of the story: "Myrna [his wife] said, 'Wash your hands' " (20). Between these two appearances, we hear about some motionless ones: "Nobody lifted a hand around Mr. Fixit's house" (19). Cut off from their immediate context, these three appearances of a hand or hands make a great deal of sense as manifestations of the effect of the Medusan vision on the story. The hand the narrator laid on the railing (and perhaps somewhere else) may be the focus of his guilt and thus need cleansing; hands no one can lift recall what Medusa has turned to stone.

If we imagine that the photographer's severed hands are somehow related to the castration that is part of the Medusan scene with which the next story begins, then we should look for some allusion to that mythical moment in "Viewfinder" itself in order to confirm that such a reading is possible. Fortunately, there is one, and well placed too. It is in fact the final scene of the story, which anticipates the stair-climbing that is immediately to follow, on the first page of "Mr. Coffee and Mr. Fixit," with a somewhat more difficult ascension:

> I went inside and got a chair. I put it up under the carport. But it didn't reach. So I got a crate and put the crate on top of the chair.
>
> It was okay up there on the roof.

I stood up and looked around. I waved, and the man with no hands waved back with his hooks.

It was then I saw them, the rocks. It was like a little rock nest on the screen over the chimney hole. You know kids. You know how they lob them up, thinking to sink one down your chimney.

"Ready?" I called, and I got a rock, and I waited until he had me in his viewfinder.

"Okay!" he called.

I laid back my arm and I hollered, "Now!" I threw that son of a bitch as far as I could throw it.

"I don't know," I heard him shout. "I don't do motion shots."

"Again!" I screamed, and took up another rock. (14–15)

"It was then I saw them"—after climbing all the way up, just as the sudden vision in the next story will come—"just as I got to the top of the stairs I looked." And what does he see, these rocks, this nest, this hole? Medusa herself, in the hole (her sex) and the nest (her maternity), together with her handiwork, her victims, the men she turned to stone—now figured, ironically, as her children, lying like eggs in her nest. The narrator is jubilant for the first time in the story, exulting in his freedom to cast off the past, to free himself from the bonds of the woman who had abandoned him.[3] That at least is the impression one would have received from his gesture, even if one were unaware of the mythic resonance of his act. The original version of "Viewfinder" ties the scene even more closely to the myth by allowing the narrator the sensation of flying away as Perseus did on winged Pegasus after his encounter with Medusa: " 'Once more,' I called. I picked up another rock. I grinned. I felt I could lift off. Fly" (52). The photographer warns that he doesn't do "motion shots," but that is precisely

3. The woman who abandoned him was his wife, although ultimately Medusa is the mother. Yet "Mr. Coffee and Mr. Fixit" unites the two in its Medusa scene: "back in those days, when *my mother was putting out*, I was out of work. My kids were crazy, and my wife was crazy. *She was putting out too.* The guy that was getting it was an unemployed aerospace engineer" (17; emphasis added).

what the narrator wants: to be frozen in the act on film. Should
he accomplish that, he would have turned himself into a victim
of the kind of paralyzing gaze by which Medusa had made
those rocks, yet come out of it alive. The viewfinder of the title
now reveals itself to be the equivalent of Athena's shield: by
passing the Gorgon's gaze through the frame of its reflecting
surface, Perseus was able to withstand the force of those eyes.[4]

Two passages from the original, longer version of "Mr. Coffee and Mr. Fixit" reveal further depths to the Medusa narrative haunting Carver's text. And it is important to go back to
that version, for Carver went back to it too. It reappeared, as I
pointed out earlier, with the original title "Where Is Everyone?"
in *Fires* two years after the publication of *What We Talk About*,
in very nearly the same form as the 1980 *TriQuarterly* version.

In the first of these passages the mother is symbolically
decapitated: "The one time she had had too much to drink,
years before (I heard this from my dad who laughed about it
when he told it), they'd gone to a little place outside Eureka
and she'd had a great many whiskey sours. Just as they got into
the car to leave, she started to get sick and had to open the
door. Somehow her false teeth came out, the car moved forward a little, and a tire passed over her dentures" (210–11;
180).[5]

The second passage offers an entirely different conclusion
to the story. In "Mr. Coffee and Mr. Fixit" the narrator is
reunited with his wife: " 'Honey,' I said to Myrna the night she
came home. 'Let's hug awhile and then you fix us a real nice
supper.' Myrna said, 'Wash your hands' " (20). In "Where Is
Everyone?" he goes to his mother's, and it's she who fixes sup-

---

4. In the original version the frozen-action shot is achieved. " 'I don't
know,' I heard him say. 'You moved,' he said. 'We'll see in a minute,' and in
a minute he said: 'By God, it's okay.' He looked at it. He held it up. 'You
know,' he said, 'it's good' " (52).

5. This could also be interpreted, despite the sex of the victim, as a
symbolic castration—turning back on the castrating Medusa her own secret
weapon. "A tooth being pulled out by someone else in a dream is as a rule to
be interpreted as castration" (*The Interpretation of Dreams*, 422n). It is true that
she took her own teeth out, but someone else—the father—destroyed them.

per for him and tells him "Wash your hands. It's ready" (212; 182). The hug, too, comes from her: "She leaned over and hugged me" (212; 182). Most interesting of all, in the last sentence of this version of the story he has fallen into a state of paralysis, as if the maternal Medusa had caught him in her gaze. And this happens as he is lying on the same couch where he had seen his mother engaged in that shocking behavior in the opening lines of the story: "She drew the blanket over me. Then she went into her bedroom. . . . I lay there staring at the TV. . . . I couldn't hear it, but I didn't want to get up. I kept staring until I felt my eyes close. . . . I lay there. I didn't move" (213; 183).

"Gazebo"

The next story begins, as did its predecessor, on an upstairs sofa: "We are sitting *on the sofa* in one of the *upstairs* suites" (21; emphasis added). "Mr. Coffee and Mr. Fixit" opened, we should recall, with the narrator mounting the steps to his mother's apartment: "But just as I got to the top of the *stairs*, I looked and she was *on the sofa* kissing a man" (17; emphasis added). This time, in "Gazebo," it's the narrator who's on the sofa, and the woman in his embrace is his wife. Some of their sexual play had been pretty picturesque: "That morning she pours Teacher's over my belly and licks it off" (21). They are managing a motel, and Holly is confronting Duane with her knowledge of his affair with Juanita, with whom he had gotten into the habit of having a quickie "in whatever unit she was in when she was making her cleaning rounds" (26). Like the offices in Ross's aerospace company with Mr. Coffees in every one, the motel rooms are interchangeable—either for Duane and Juanita, or, now that they have decided to work out their problems with a long discussion, for Duane and Holly: "We are sitting on the sofa in one of the upstairs suites. There were any number of vacancies to choose from. But we needed a suite, a place to move around in and be able to talk. So we'd locked up the motel office that morning and gone upstairs to a suite" (21).

One sometimes gets the impression that these stories are like those interchangeable rooms. The upstairs suite with the sofa certainly starts off sounding like the upstairs apartment with the sofa with which the previous story began, but let's look at this couple a little more closely. All four partners are alcoholics: Myrna first met her lover at an AA meeting that her husband should have been attending but he was "drinking a fifth a day" (19) instead; Duane tells us that "the truth is we were both hitting it pretty hard. Booze takes a lot of time and effort if you're going to do a good job with it" (26). While "Mr. Coffee and Mr. Fixit" is the story of a husband and an unfaithful wife who get back together in the end, "Gazebo" is a sort of mirror image of that, the story of a wife and an unfaithful husband who work through their problem (*his* problem) and look forward to a new beginning. "We'd reached the end of something, and the thing was to find out where new to start" (27).

Now these two stories did not entirely become the mirror image they are of each other with regard to the basic outline of their plot until their appearance together in *What We Talk About*. For the last clause of the sentence I have just quoted from "Gazebo," which speaks of a new start, did not appear in the original version (36). They had indeed "reached the end of something" in that first version, and they did go on to reminisce, as they do in the book, about the gazebo out back of the old couple's house where they stopped once for a drink of water. But it's not clear whether it's the end of their discontent that they've reached, or the end of their marriage. It is still not clear even in the present version of the story, but at least they are now looking "to find out where new to start."

But it is the other story that has undergone the most far-reaching change in order to form the complement it now does to "Gazebo." As we have seen, "Where Is Everyone?" concluded with the narrator spending the night at his mother's. The title itself of that version alluded to the fact that his wife has not come back from her paramour Ross, for it anticipates what he will tell his mother when she asks if he is calling from home.

"I'm not at home. I don't know where everyone is at home. I just called there" (212). In fact, it is clear from part of his conversation with his mother that his wife is still seeing Mr. Fixit. " 'It hurts me to tell you, but . . . Cynthia [her name in that version] is seeing another man.' 'That's okay,' I said. 'I know that. . . . His name is Ross and he's an alcoholic. He's like me' " (212; 182). But at the end of "Mr. Coffee and Mr. Fixit" his wife does come back home: " 'Honey,' I said to Myrna the night she came home." (20).

At the same time that the title of "Where Is Everyone?" is changed to "Mr. Coffee and Mr. Fixit," some additions to each story bring into play a new strand of connections. The new title appears now in the text, after the description of the aerospace firm where Ross used to work: "Mr. Coffees in every office. Mr. Coffee and Mr. Fixit" (20). The form it takes, two names linked by an *and,* is echoed in the way the sentence "I'd say to my wife, I'd shout it, 'I'm going to kill him!' " (204; 173) is revised to "I'd say to my wife, 'I think I'll get a *Smith and Wesson*' " (18; emphasis added). A similar addition to "Gazebo" sets up an echo with those echoes in "Mr. Coffee and Mr. Fixit": "You weren't my first, you know. My first was Wyatt. Imagine. Wyatt. And your name's Duane. *Wyatt and Duane*" (28; the emphasis indicates what was added to the original version [37]). We can see Carver's hand here as he "pushed and pulled and worked with those stories before they went into the book," for two lines above the "Smith and Wesson" he added to "Mr. Coffee and Mr. Fixit" he also added "Ross. What a name!" (18), which enriches the resonance of the echo the line I have just quoted from "Gazebo" sets up with Holly's fairly derogatory comment about her husband's (and former boyfriend's) name.

"I Could See the Smallest Things"

The gazebo of the title in the preceding story represented a kind of lost paradise of marital bliss. Duane and Holly were driving on a hot dusty road and stopped at a house to ask for a drink of water.

"Those old people must be dead," she goes, "side by side out
there in some cemetery. You remember they asked us in for
cake? And later on they showed us around? And there was
this gazebo there out back? It was out back under some trees?
. . . men used to come around and play music out there on a
Sunday, and the people would sit and listen. I thought we'd
be like that too when we got old enough. Dignified. And in a
place. And people would come to our door." (28)

"I Could See the Smallest Things" takes a closer look at what is
"there out back" behind the house, and it is not a pretty sight.

Nancy's husband Cliff is fast asleep, but she is disturbed by
the sound of the fence gate. She goes to the window and finds
that the moon is so bright that "I could see the smallest things"
—the open gate, the lawn chairs, the clothesline, even the
clothespins on the line. Unable to sleep (like "The Student's
Wife," who likewise looked out to see the world infused with
whiteness, though from the dawn, not the moon) she goes
downstairs, makes tea, smokes a couple of cigarettes, and finally
decides to go see about the gate. "I peered around the backyard
before I stepped off the porch" (32) and found their neighbor
Sam Lawton leaning on one of the two fences that separate
their houses—after a disagreement, Cliff and Sam had each
built his own fence. " 'Want to see something?' he said" (repeating the story's original title). "I looked and saw some wormy
things curled on a patch of dirt. 'Slugs,' he said. 'I just gave
them a dose of this,' he said, raising a can of something that
looked like Ajax. 'They're taking over' " (33–34). The back
yard that in the story before held an irenic image of conjugal
contentment now reveals, when one looks closely enough, disgusting "slimy things" (35), serpents in Eden.

When one looks closely enough at these two stories, the
smallest things, like these slugs, begin to emerge. Nancy tells
us, "It felt funny walking around outside in my nightgown and
my robe. I thought to myself that I should try to remember
this, walking around outside like this" (33). Duane had likewise
said to Holly that they should remember to remember: "Holly,
these things, we'll look back on them too. We'll go, 'Remember
the motel with all the crud in the pool?' " (28)

In Arthur Saltzman's reading of the story the farmhouse
with the gazebo in the back had been for Holly a dream that
she wanted "to transplant . . . to their motel" (108). He is right,
for she had concluded her description of the farmhouse cum
gazebo with the wish that "people would come to our door," as
they do now to the door of the motel office to demand hospitality. Having retreated to that upstairs suite to hash out their
differences, Duane and Holly have become oblivious to the
ringing phone or to the rattling door. Nancy, on the other
hand, was troubled by the noise from the gate: "I couldn't get
to sleep. . . . I thought about the gate standing open" (32). A
strikingly parallel pair of lines places Nancy for a moment in
the position of someone demanding entry to paradise. When
she was still upstairs in the bedroom, looking out the window
to marvel at how the full moon so illumined the backyard that
one could see the smallest things, she tells us, "I put my hands
on the glass to block out the moon" (31). On the other side of
that glass, at least on the other side of the brief space separating
these two stories, Holly "look[s] out the window" of the upstairs
suite, down into the parking lot, and sees two cars parked in
front of the office, the drivers standing at the door. "There's a
woman there too, and she has her face *up to the glass, hand
shielding her eyes,* peering inside" (24; emphasis added).

The paying customers they once welcomed have become
unwanted invaders, like the pests Sam seeks to destroy. Lawton's slugs and his efforts to eradicate them find two other
counterparts in "Gazebo" as well. There is a funny resemblance
between his cleaning out his backyard with something like Ajax
and Juanita scrubbing the motel bathrooms with what could
well have been the very same cleanser. Holly's husband, on the
other hand, has given up the battle, and as a result algae have
done to the motel pool what the slugs are threatening to do to
the yard. "I stopped cleaning the pool. It filled up with green
gick so that the guests wouldn't use it anymore" (26).

"Sacks"

Originally entitled "The Fling," "Sacks" recounts a meeting between a father and a son who have not seen each other for some time, not since the father's divorce in the wake of the fling he had with a woman who sold household products door to door. Les Palmer, a book salesman who was in California on business, has decided on the spur of the moment to have a brief visit with his father between planes at the Sacramento airport. His father seizes the occasion to confess all the sordid details of his affair. In the original version of the story the son, who is also the narrator, berates himself silently for being a poor listener; in the much-shortened present version these reflections have been eliminated, but we can still see him taking a glance at his watch as his father drones on. And the father still complains of his son's incomprehension: "You don't know anything, do you? You don't know anything at all. You don't know anything except how to sell books" (45).

The change of title of "The Fling" to "Sacks" gives emphasis to an internal echo that had already been there. When Les first sees his father "standing where everyone else was—behind the gate, that is" he is holding "a white confectionary sack" (38) with candy inside for the son to take back to his family. When the father first met Sally Wain she was holding a sack too. "I ask her to step in. . . . She didn't know whether she should or not. Just stands there holding this little paper sack and the receipt with it" (39)—a delivery for his wife, who wasn't at home. So the father, standing at the airport gate, repeats the gesture Sally made at his door. Given the hint the title makes that this story may be about that repeated gesture, we might be led to say that the father is to the son as Sally Wain was to the father, that the father is perhaps unconsciously seeking to restage the encounter he had had with Sally Wain. If he approaches his son as Sally approached him—that is, standing at the door (the gate) with a sack—then perhaps his son will respond to his demand for understanding, love, and affection as well as he had responded to whatever Sally Wain's inner need might have been that allowed her to make no resistance to his advances. In fact, she apparently longed for contact just as much as he did: "Well, I kissed her then. I put her head back on the sofa and kissed her, and I can feel her tongue out there rushing to get in my mouth" (42). The original version of the story spelled this out in some detail: "He wanted something. He was trying to involve me in it someway, all right, but it was more than that, he wanted something else. . . . Maybe simply a gesture on my part, a touch on the arm, perhaps" (151). There is some confirmation of this at the conclusion when the son's disinclination to show much sympathy for his father's plight finds its correlative in his having, through negligence, left the sack behind. "We shook hands. That was the last I've seen of him. On the way to Chicago, I remembered how I'd left his sack of gifts on the bar. Just as well. Mary didn't need candy, Almond Roca or anything else" (45).

Evidently the son took his mother's side in the divorce, since it was clearly his father's adultery that brought it about. He doesn't want to be his father's confidant because he'd rather be his antagonist, if it came to that. Another internal echo underlines, however faintly, this potential enmity. It is prepared by the moment we have just been considering, that first glimpse of his father "standing . . . behind the gate" with the sack in his hand; this time we should focus our attention on the gate. Its counterpart can be found at the high point of his father's story: he was in bed with Sally Wain when "this car pulls into the driveway and somebody gets out and slams the door. 'My God,' she screams. 'It's Larry!' I must have gone crazy. I seem to remember thinking that if I run out the back door he's going to pin me up against this big fence in the yard and maybe kill me" (44). That doesn't happen, but the encounter of father and son at a gate itself repeats this imagined encounter with a jealous rival at a fence on the level of the events of the story if not on that of the father's unconscious motivation as in the case of the sacks. The son, of course, could be considered a jealous rival in the lover's triangle he forms with his parents and could well feel that his father by his actions has forfeited any genuine claim to his mother's affections.

The gate in this instance was not the kind attached to a

fence. Yet the gate in the immediately preceding story was, and
that story too featured a disagreement between two men in-
volving a fence. "Sam and Cliff used to be friends. Then one
night they got to drinking. They had words. The next thing,
Sam had built a fence and then Cliff built one too" (33). In the
perspective opened up by the contiguity of these stories—
neighbors in Carver's collection, linked by a fence—we can see
that the father standing at the airport gate with a sack in his
hand bears a strange resemblance to the man standing behind
one of the fences whose gate had awakened Nancy, standing
there holding "a can of something" (the poisonous powder he
sprinkled on the slugs, anticipating the powdery confectioner's
sugar sprinkled on almond roca). The resemblance increases
when we realize that Sam Lawton's "silvery" hair and "tan-and-
white shoes" (33) are echoed in the "*white* hair" and "*brown* Sta-
Prest pants" of Les Palmer's father.

   More telling perhaps are certain changes Carver made in
these stories for their appearance in the book. Both narrators
begin the story by looking out the window and telling us how
much they can see. The second sentence of "Sacks" reads:
"From my hotel window I can see too much of this Midwestern
city" (37). Originally it had been: "From my hotel room window
I can look out and see much of this gray midwestern city" (139).
In its present version it more closely parallels the sentence on
the first page of "I Could See the Smallest Things" in which
that title appears: "Everything lay in moonlight, and I could
see the smallest things" (31). "I can see" recalls "I could see"
better than does "I can look out and see"; the alteration of
"much" to "too much" brings it closer to the superlative of "the
smallest things." For its part, the sentence in "I Could See the
Smallest Things" was revised too in the direction of closer resemblance, for it had originally read "the smallest things came
to my attention" (29) instead of "I could see. . . ."

   When the father in "Sacks" is in bed with Sally Wain, just
before her husband suddenly shows up, "I'm telling myself I
better remember that pretty soon I got to get up and go" (44).
That line was changed from "At the same time, I was awake
and I remember thinking that pretty soon I'd have to get up

and go home" (149). The revision introduces the idea of *telling oneself* to remember, instead of just remembering. It thus comes more closely to resemble the thought Nancy had about the necessity of remembering: "I thought to myself that I should try to remember this, walking around outside like this" (33), which, if we remember, already echoed talk in "Gazebo" about future remembrance.

Both stories end with the narrator having *failed* to remember: "It was then that I remembered I'd forgotten to latch the gate" (36). "On the way to Chicago, I remembered how I'd left his sack of gifts on the bar" (45).

"The Bath"

The next story is to a considerable extent about forgetting to pick up something very much like the confection the son in "Sacks" left behind—a chocolate birthday cake special-ordered from a bakery. The parallel is tightened by Carver's decision to pare down the contents of the sack the father offered the son. Originally they had been "some Almond Roca for Mary, a Cootie game for Ed, and a Barby Doll" (140); now the game and the doll have been replaced by "some jelly-beans for the kids" (38), so that the sack contains only confectioner's products, the more closely to anticipate the baker's creation: "The cake she chose was decorated with a spaceship and a launching pad under a sprinkling of white stars. The name SCOTTY would be iced on in green as if it were the name of the spaceship" (47).

In a passage that was added to the original story, Les tells us that it was "just as well" that he had forgotten the confectionary sack because his wife "didn't need candy, Almond Roca or anything else. That was last year. She needs it now even less" (45). It's a puzzling statement, since we are not told why she doesn't need it. Another addition to the text earlier in the story points in the same mysterious direction. In the original version, when his father asks, "How's Mary and the kids?" Les Palmer tells us "I looked at him closely before answering. Of course, he didn't know we'd been living apart for nearly six months. 'Everyone's fine,' I answered" (140).[6] In the present version, we are told that the answer is false but we are not told why: " 'Everyone's fine,' I said, which was not the truth" (38). That everyone is *not* fine could conceivably be attributed to the trauma of divorce, but it is vague enough to have other, more disturbing causes. And it is harder to see why a divorce would mean that his wife had no need for "Almond Roca *or anything else.*" Is she ill—or dead?

The only thing we know for certain is that we don't know. Information gleaned from "The Fling" doesn't exactly count when it comes to answering a question like this. It is no longer the same story, not only because Carver has changed the title but by virtue as well of its appearing in this collection. The proximity of Les Palmer's forgetting to pick up the sack with candy for his family to Scotty's mother's forgetting to pick up his birthday cake in "The Bath"—together with all the evidence we have so far seen of how Carver's neighboring stories seem capable of half-hidden interaction—exerts an almost sinister tugging on those revised lines when we come to the realization that Scotty will have no need of the birthday cake because he is in the hospital, trapped in a coma from which he shows no signs of awakening. That he was struck by a car as he and another boy were "passing a bag of potato chips back and forth between them" (48) suggests that transferring sacks, which has already happened twice in the story just before, can have disastrous consequences.

If we read these two stories one after the other, the son's having forgotten to pick up the sack his father left him returns to haunt the tormented parents in "The Bath" in the form of the brutish baker who persists in making mysterious and nagging phone calls to the Weiss residence. " 'There's a cake that wasn't picked up.' That is what the voice on the other end said" (49). "He picked up the receiver and shouted, 'Hello!' The

6. Thus echoing Sam Lawton's answer to the same question from Nancy: " 'Sam,' I said, 'how's everybody?' 'They're fine,' he said" (34).

voice said, 'It's ready' " (50). The parents had taken turns watching by their son's hospital bed; first the father, and then the mother, went home for nourishment and to take a bath (hence the title). The father had answered both these calls. At the conclusion of the story, it is the mother's turn.

> The telephone rang.
> "Yes!" she said. "Hello!" she said.
> "Mrs. Weiss," a man's voice said.
> "Yes," she said. "This is Mrs. Weiss. Is it about Scotty?" she said.
> "Scotty," the voice said. "It is about Scotty," the voice said. "It has to do with Scotty, yes." (56)

The indeterminacy with which "Sacks" ended—the chilling ambiguity of Les Palmer's wife having no need of what was in the sack—is repeated here. Who is calling? Mrs. Weiss thinks it is the hospital, but we know what she apparently does not know, that the baker has called twice already to complain that they have not picked up, and more importantly not paid for, the cake. The baker knows the boy's name was Scotty because it was to have been inscribed on the rocketship, so it is natural that he would say that "it has to do with Scotty." Yet all this does not necessarily mean that it *is* the baker. We may have been given that knowledge only in order to be made to think that it is.

An event on the immediately preceding page might suggest to us that Mrs. Weiss is indeed deceived in thinking it is a doctor calling. As she was leaving the hospital she had lost her way and stumbled into a waiting room where an equally anxious family took *her* to be someone from the hospital who had news about *their* son. " 'Nelson,' the woman said. 'Is it about Nelson?' " (55)—anticipating the very words Mrs. Weiss will ask the mystery caller: "Is it about Scotty?" Yet even this anticipation of the final scene does not definitively prove that it is the baker calling. Just as with the two calls from the baker that came to Mr. Weiss, the only thing we can know for certain is that it will tend to make us think we know who is on the other end of the line.[7]

"Tell the Women We're Going"

The next story begins with what almost amounts to a recollection of the innocent scene just before the catastrophe in "The Bath" of the two boys "walking to school" (48) and sharing the contents of that sack. For it begins with an account of two other boys who "went through grade school and junior high together" (57), and then on to high school, sharing everything along the way: "wore each other's shirts and sweaters and pegged pants . . . dated and banged the same girls . . . bought a car together" (57). Jerry married first, had two daughters, then Bill found a wife too. They continued to spend a lot of time in each other's company, especially weekends.

"It was a Sunday at Jerry's place the time it happened. The women were in the kitchen straightening up. Jerry's girls were out in the yard throwing a plastic ball into the wading pool" when Bill noticed that "Jerry was getting to be deep, the way he stared all the time and hardly did any talking at all" (59). They decided to get away and go for a drive. After two hours of shooting pool in a bar, they spot two girls pushing their bicycles on the highway. Sharon and Barbara decline the invitation to ride in their car. Having correctly surmised that the girls are on their way to Picture Rock, Jerry and Bill drive on up to wait for them there.

And thus does the first paragraph's statement that they "banged the same girls" come horribly to have another meaning, though it is Jerry alone who does the banging. Bill "never knew what Jerry wanted. But it started and ended with a rock. Jerry used the same rock on both girls, first on the girl called

---

7. That when the story is retold, at much greater length, in "A Small, Good Thing" in *Cathedral* it *will* turn out to be the baker still leaves us in the dark about who it is here.

Sharon and then on the one that was supposed to be Bill's" (66). End of story.

But not quite: "it started and ended with a rock" is a curiously haunting phrase because it challenges us to remember exactly when it did start. For before Jerry picked up that rock there was already one in the name of the place where the fatal rendezvous occurred, Picture Rock. There is something haunting about that place name too, for we have already seen a story conclude with a *picture* of a *rock*, one in fact heaved with some violence: "I got a rock, and I waited until he had me in his viewfinder. . . . I laid back my arm and I hollered, 'Now!' I threw that son of a bitch as far as I could throw it" (15).

Medusa haunted that scene in "Viewfinder," as we learned from paying attention to such details as the rocks in the nest over the hole. The man on the roof having his picture taken as he hurled the rocks was experiencing the triumph of striking back at the wife who had left him; Jerry, it appears, is striking back in anger at the entrapment of his marriage: "Guy's got to get out" (60), he had said to Bill as they left their wives behind for their escape to the open road. Bill had earlier noticed "how much older Jerry looked, a lot older than twenty-two. By then Jerry was the happy father of two kids and had moved up to assistant manager at Robby's, and Carol had one in the oven again" (59). The wife, that is, in both cases has assumed the proportions of a monster who castrates her husband either by abandoning him to wallow in helpless self-pity (in "Viewfinder") or by enchaining him to family responsibilities in the prime of his youth (in "Tell the Women We're Going").[8]

But there is still more to the way this scene at Picture Rock loops back to the network of connections we first saw in "Viewfinder," especially if we focus our view, as always, on the immediately preceding story. For there is something strangely

8. That the title itself is in the imperative mood while its appearance in the story takes the form of a statement of fact—"I'll tell the women we're going" (60)—gives some impetus to this interpretation. It practically amounts to a declaration of independence.

familiar about that menacing baker in "The Bath": "he wore a
curious apron, a heavy thing with loops that went under his
arms and around his back and then crossed in front again
where they were tied in a very thick knot" (47-48). We have
seen such an apparition before, in the figure of the photographer who made the pictures of the rocks: "I knew how he held
the camera. It was an old Polaroid, big and black. He had it
fastened to leather straps that looped over his shoulders and
went around his back, and it was this that secured the camera
to his chest" (11–12).

What possible connection could there be between baking
and photography? The fact of the matter is that this particular
baker actually uses photography in his work:

> Saturday afternoon the mother drove to the bakery in the
> shopping center. After looking through a loose-leaf binder
> with photographs of cakes taped onto the pages, she ordered
> chocolate, the child's favorite. The cake she chose was deco-
> rated with a spaceship and a launching pad under a sprin-
> kling of white stars. The name SCOTTY would be iced on in
> green as if it were the name of the spaceship. (47)

It is a very thick knot indeed: To what extent is the baker the
reincarnation of the similarly-outfitted photographer who
froze the action in which the narrator was engaged? Has Scotty
become "iced"—frozen into stasis—too?

Of course he has. That is exactly what happened to him
when he fell into his deathlike sleep. The intriguing thing is
that the coma did not immediately follow the accident:

> The birthday boy did not cry. But neither did he wish to talk
> anymore. He would not answer when the other boy asked
> what it felt like to be hit by a car. The birthday boy got up
> and turned back for home, at which time the other boy waved
> good-bye and headed off for school.
>   The birthday boy told his mother what had happened.
> They sat together on the sofa. She held his hands in her lap.
> This is what she was doing when the boy pulled his hands
> away and lay down on his back. (48–49)

What it immediately followed was his sitting on the sofa with his mother. In the context of "The Bath" alone this only adds to the pathos. But in the larger context Carver's short story sequence demands it points to something else. For we have seen what the effect can be of seeing one's mother on the sofa in that opening scene of "Mr. Coffee and Mr. Fixit," where she becomes a vision of Medusa. She was sitting there with another man then, but when the narrator returns to that sofa at the end of the version of the story "Where Is Everyone?" tells, and his mother joins him there—"she made a bed for me on the sofa . . . and sat down at the end of the sofa" (212; 182)—and he later lies back on that same sofa, he finds himself unable to summon the will to rise: "I didn't want to get up . . . I lay there. I didn't move" (213; 183).

Disaster ensued in the immediately preceding story ("Sacks") too when a man sat down with a woman on the living room sofa: "I sit down on the other end of the sofa from her . . . I put her head back on the sofa and I kissed her" (42). And when it was over, "I fixed up the sofa and turned over the cushions" (43). In each instance *sofa* has been substituted here for the original *couch* (144–45), with the result that the scene of mother and son on the sofa in "The Bath" comes even closer to becoming an eerie repetition of this seduction scene.

We had earlier seen the significance of the narrator's *mounting* the stairs to discover his mother on the sofa *in flagrante delicto* in the opening scene of "Mr. Coffee and Mr. Fixit," which had been immediately preceded by the closing moment of "Viewfinder" that found the husband climbing up, with some difficulty, to the roof of the garage to discover the rocks covering his chimney. Now the encounter at Picture Rock that recalls that prior scene of pictures and rocks was prepared for in the same way: Bill and Jerry had to *climb* a steep path to get to the girls. Picture Rock was "a high, sloping, black mound of rock, part of a low range of hills" (64). So steep was the path that Bill had to stop "to catch his breath. . . . He was too winded to speak" (65–66). In the same way that it was "just as I got to the top of the stairs" (17) that the narrator of "Mr. Coffee and Mr. Fixit" tells us he looked and saw his mother on the sofa, it was at the very summit of the climb, where "the path began to drop," that Bill "looked and saw the girls" (66). A small detail from the accident scene in "The Bath" now falls into place, for it turns out that the son who fell into suspended animation after sitting on the sofa with his mother had shown signs of trying to climb up something too: "At an intersection, without looking, the birthday boy stepped off the curb, and was promptly knocked down by a car. He fell on his side, his head in the gutter, his legs in the road moving as if he were climbing a wall" (48).

"After the Denim"

James Packer, a retired accountant, accompanies his wife Edith to their weekly neighborhood bingo game. But because they arrive late, he finds that their usual parking space is occupied by an old van and that their seats inside the bingo hall have been taken by a young hippie couple dressed in denim. His indignation increases when he spies the youth cheating by playing a card he hasn't paid for, even more when the girl wins the evening's jackpot. Later, as they are returning to their car, he makes the further discomforting discovery that the van in their parking space belongs to the young couple.

James's hostility is clearly a generational one, as Edith realizes. " 'Don't you pay it any attention,' she said. 'They're not hurting anybody. They're just young, that's all' " (70). He has been displaced by these representatives of the younger generation, displaced from his lucky bingo seats and his parking place. "It's not lucky if you have to start out walking half a mile just to play" (68).

A repeated gesture underscores the extent to which the couple in denim are a younger version of the Packers. When James complains that there wouldn't be so many cars if they had been on time, Edith replies, " 'There'd still be as many. It's just we wouldn't have seen them.' She pinched his sleeve, teasing" (68). Later, inside the bingo hall, "Just as the Packers came up, the girl turned to the fellow with her and poked her finger at a number on his card. Then she pinched his arm" (70).

The title of the story appears in the text when Packer thinks of how the difficulties he and Edith are now facing—his wife is showing symptoms of serious illness—will one day have to be confronted by the couple in denim: "If only they had to sit with him in the [doctor's] waiting room! He'd tell them what to expect! . . . He'd tell them what was waiting for you after the denim and the earrings, after touching each other and cheating at games" (77). He goes beyond this to wish that they could die in Edith's place. "Why not someone else? Why not those people tonight? . . . Why not them instead of Edith?" (77).

His desire for their death resurrects a telling detail from the previous story. Jerry, who murdered the two girls at Picture Rock, has two little girls of his own. We aren't told that at first, just that he was "the happy father of two kids" and that the weekend barbecue with Bill and his wife was always held at Jerry's house because he had the barbecue "and too many kids to drag around" (59). Only after we are given a hint of the horror to come is the sex of his two children revealed: "It was a Sunday at Jerry's place the time it happened. The women were in the kitchen straightening up. Jerry's girls were out in the yard" (59). Despite his victims' being probably only slightly younger than his own twenty-two years, it would appear that his violence toward them acts out his anger toward not only his wife but his own children—all the more so for the fact that his story appears between the possibly fatal injury of a child in "The Bath" (an injury that came from, as did the girls' in "Tell the Women We're Going," a roadside encounter) and a murderous wish directed toward the younger generation in "After the Denim." We should recall as well that the photographer who so insisted on the similarity between his situation and that of the abandoned husband and father who hurled rocks from his roof laid the blame for his stumps on his children: "I had kids once. Just like you. . . . They're what gave me this" (13).

In yet another way does James Packer appear to follow in the footsteps of the two young men in the story before. He does so by following, quite literally, in the footsteps of the young couple as they all come out of the bingo parlor. "The Packers filed out of the assembly hall along with the rest, somehow managing to fall in behind the fellow in denim and his girl. . . . 'Let those people get ahead of us,' James said into Edith's ear. 'I can't stand to look at them.' Edith said nothing in reply. But she hung back a little to give the couple time to move ahead" (75). When he returned home he thought back to "that sauntering, arrogant gait as the two of them moved just ahead" (77). Now all this recalls the initial encounter of Jerry and Bill with the girls riding their bicycles, even though that involved a more complicated choreography of following and waiting for the other party to move on. "They'd just passed an old pickup loaded with furniture when they saw the two girls" (61). After a mile or so, Jerry decided to turn around. "He slowed when he came nearly even with the girls. . . . He waited for the cars to pass so he could pull a U" (62). They pull on ahead and wait for the girls to catch up. They try to engage them in conversation. "They kept bicycling and Jerry kept driving." A car behind them honks its horn. "He pulled off a little and let the car go around. Then he pulled back up alongside the girls" (63). Bill, in the passenger seat, is not having much success, so Jerry "fed the Chevy gas and pulled up off onto the shoulder so that the girls had to come by on his side" (64). Having determined that the girls are headed for Picture Rock, they drive on to wait for them there. They allow the girls to get ahead of them on the path up the cliff to the rock.

This ascent has its echo in Packer's story too. For as he sits with his bingo card and the beans to cover the numbers, he is reminded of a legendary climber. "He shook the beans in his fist. Something came to him about a boy who'd thrown some beans out a window. The memory reached to him from a long way off, and it made him feel lonely" (71–72). The beans Jack unintentionally sowed led to the kind of jackpot to which the beans Parker held in his fist could have led that night had he not been so unlucky. The young man's girlfriend won it instead —"a ninety-eight-dollar jackpot!" (75)—and since they were occupying the Packers' usual seats their luck should have been his.

"Tell the Women We're Going" has two protagonists—Jerry, who does the deed, and Bill, who "had just wanted to fuck. Or even to see them naked. On the other hand, it was okay with him if it didn't work out" (66). When Jerry "used the same rock on both girls" Bill was, apparently, just a spectator, as he had been earlier, when Jerry was first married to Carol, and Bill was still single. When Bill would come over to visit, and Jerry and Carol would begin to fondle each other in front of him, "he'd have to get up and excuse himself and take a walk. . . . Or sometimes Jerry and Carol would head off to the bathroom, and Bill would have to move to the kitchen and pretend to be interested in the cupboards and the refrigerator and not trying to listen" (58). James Packer, whose resemblance to Jerry Roberts we have already explored, embodies the spectatorly qualities of this other protagonist as well. Like Bill Jamison (whose last name recalls Packer's first) he finds himself standing at the refrigerator and trying not to listen. On their return home from the bingo game, Edith went into the bathroom to confirm whether the bleeding she had first noticed in the restroom at the bingo hall has indeed returned. "After a time, Edith came out of the bathroom . . . and said, 'I guess I'll have to see Dr. Crawford in the morning. I guess there really is something happening down there' " (76). After she went to bed, James Packer "went to the refrigerator. He stood in front of the open door and drank tomato juice while he studied everything inside. Cold air blew out at him. He looked at the little packages and the containers of foodstuffs on the shelves" (76). He evidently had not really wanted that glass of tomato juice, for "he shut the door and spit the last of the juice into the sink. Then he rinsed his mouth. . . . He went to the bedroom door and listened for a time. He felt unworthy to be listening" (77). It might have struck us as a little strange that Jerry and Carol "would head off to the *bathroom*," but the narrator explains that there is no bedroom in their tiny apartment, just a hide-away bed in the living room. Though thus fully justified in the context of that story, however, the detail of their having gone there nevertheless serves another purpose, as we can see now—that of enabling the scene where James Packer pretends to be interested in the refrigerator and feels guilty about listening to make an even richer echo, since what he feels unworthy to hear is Edith's private reaction (alone in her bedroom does she weep?) to what she discovered in the bathroom.

"After the Denim" concludes in a strange way. Packer is for some reason sleeping in the guest room, and not with his wife. Before turning in for the night, he "took up his basket of embroidery, and then settled himself in the chair. He raised the lid of the basket and got out the metal hoop. There was fresh white linen stretched across it. Holding the tiny needle to the light, James Packer stabbed at the eye with a length of blue silk thread. Then he set to work—stitch after stitch—making believe he was waving like the man on the keel" (78).[9] This is a reference to a photograph he had seen in the foyer of the bingo hall of "a boat that had turned over, a man standing on the keel and waving" (69). Has Packer, who had taken up knitting too—he "pushed aside his knitting basket" before reaching for his embroidery—become feminized?

He may well feel castrated, if the hostility he feels towards the young man prompted him to remember the story of Jack and the Beanstalk. For the fairy tale is exceedingly relevant, particularly to the generational conflict at work here. Having once, in his youth, been the Jack who had the beans, Packer has since become the vanquished giant. Having once, that is, been the younger generation, he has become the older one, the father, symbolically emasculated by the son when he chops down the massive phallic beanstalk to escape with the giant's treasure. Jack was a thief; so too was the young man in denim, whom James saw "put down a bean on a card he hadn't paid for. . . . 'That fellow over there who has our place is cheating. I can't believe my eyes' " (72).

9. Though silk and not denim, the thread's color evokes the blue-jeans costume of the couple who had taken James and Edith's seats.

"So Much Water So Close to Home"

That concluding image of Packer pretending to be waving like a man on the keel of an overturned boat certainly connotes some kind of downfall. The giant fell to earth; the man on the capsized vessel may have come close to falling in the water.[10] The water into which he may yet fall and drown should no one respond to his waving announces all the water so near at hand in the next story, which was anticipated as well by all the water just outside the bingo parlor, both before the game ("They could hear the surf breaking on the rocks at the bottom of the cliff behind the building" [69]) and after ("James thought sure he could hear the surf over the sound of engines starting" [75–76]). The title appears in the story and finds its explanation when Claire asks her husband why he had to go miles away to fish when there was "so much water so close to home" (83), a creek and a pond just down the road. On the last page, in a passage that did not appear in the original version of this story, Claire will speak, like James Packer, of water so close one can *hear* it: "I can't hear a thing with so much water going" (88).

And the drowning death that may await the man on the overturned boat announces the horrible discovery Claire's husband Stuart will make on his fishing expedition: "They saw the girl before they set up camp. Mel Dorn found her. No clothes on her at all. She was wedged into some branches that stuck out over the water" (81). The fishermen didn't want to interrupt their vacation to contact the police. "They pleaded fatigue, the late hour, the fact that the girl wasn't going anywhere." Later they return to the river to "keep the body from drifting away. . . . One of the men—it might have been Stuart—waded in and got her. He took her by the fingers and pulled her into shore. He got some nylon cord and tied it to her wrist and then looped the rest around a tree." The bizarre combination of threading and aquatic disaster that came together when Packer

---

10. Waving from the *keel*, the highest point he could attain on the overturned boat, he at the same time evokes the memory of the man who waved to the photographer from the top of his garage (15).

stitched embroidery while "making believe he was waving like the man on the keel" reemerges here in the tying and knotting performed for the floating corpse.[11]

Stuart's refusal to allow anything, even the discovery of a dead girl's body, to stand between him and his fishing recalls James Packer's pouting response to finding that the denim couple had taken over his regular table. "This is regular Friday night bingo for the people of this community," he complained, as if they had no right to be there at all. On the other hand, Stuart's angry denial that he had done anything wrong in not immediately reporting the body to the police brings him and Claire to repeat almost word for word the exchange that had taken place between Packer and the young man he had discovered cheating at bingo.

> "I see what you're doing," James said.
> The man turned around. "Pardon me?" he said and stared. "What am I doing?"
> "You know," James said. (73)

> "Tell me what I did wrong. . . .
> "You know," I say. (80)

And Packer's command to Edith as they found themselves uncomfortably close to the denim couple on their way out of the bingo hall to "let those people get ahead of us"—which already recalled the maneuvers in which Bill and Jerry had been engaged in the story before that when they tried to pick up the girls—is echoed in turn by Claire's effort to shake the man in the pickup truck who was following her too closely on the way to the funeral of the girl who died. "I keep slowing at the wrong times, hoping he will pass" (86). What happened two stories back threatens to happen again here: "On a long clear stretch

---

11. Tying the corpse down so that the water wouldn't carry it away was anticipated as well by what the Packers saw on their way from their car to the bingo hall: "They stopped under the street lamp at the corner. It was a damaged street lamp, and wires had been added to support it. The wires moved in the wind, made shadows on the pavement" (69).

he goes past. But he drives along beside for a bit. . . . We look each other over. Then he waves, toots his horn, and pulls on up ahead. I slow down and find a place. I pull over and shut off the motor. I can hear the river down below the trees. Then I hear the pickup coming back. I lock the doors and roll up the windows" (86).

The girl in the water had in fact been murdered. In the original version of the story she had been strangled, though we are not told how she died here. We are however told an intriguing detail about the death of another girl, whose murder is recalled to Claire's mind by this death. Like the girls two stories back, she was slain by two men—"The Maddox brothers. They killed a girl named Arlene Hubly where I grew up. They cut off her head and threw her into the Cle Elum River" (83). The intriguing thing about her death is the circumstance that recalls what was evoked in the death of the girls at Picture Rock: like Medusa (a name "Maddox" evokes), she had her head cut off. Another detail, this one concerning the girl in the water whom Stuart and his friends found, calls forth once more that ancient but psychoanalytically powerful myth: "the trout they'd caught were hard because of the terrible coldness of the water" (82)— hard too, perhaps, because those fish may have seen the petrifying face of the dead girl. She was apparently floating face down in the water, for when Claire imagines herself to be the victim she sees herself prone. "I look at the creek. I'm right in it, eyes open, face down, staring at the moss on the bottom, dead" (83). Her husband must have told her what the original version of the story did in fact make explicit: "Mel Dorn found the girl floating face down in the river" (43; 187); when Stuart (who it "might have been") pulled her by her fingers closer to shore she was "still face down." [19] Eyes open, as Claire imagined her, and staring face down, she would have been in an excellent position to cast her hardening gaze onto the fish. And, signifi-

---

12. The story appeared in *Furious Seasons*, and, like "Sacks," was reprinted in *Fires* in its original version after its appearance in this collection. Page references are given in order of publication. This reprinting, as it did for "Sacks," justifies my mining it for material here.

cantly, the men may have never seen that face, for not only was she face down the entire time, but they seem to have avoided visual contact: "They didn't look at the girl again before they left" (44; 188). Even in the present version there is evidence that her face must be kept from sight: When Claire attends the girl's funeral she finds that there is no viewing of the deceased —"The casket is closed and covered with floral sprays" (86).

"The Third Thing That Killed My Father Off"

In the original version of "So Much Water So Close to Home" the naked corpse found "*wedged* into some branches" had been "lodged" (43; 187) there. Carver's change prepares the way for a parallel to emerge between that body and the one the boy narrator of the following story discovers in a flood-swollen river: "We came to Dummy's fence and found a cow *wedged* in up against the wire. She was bloated and her skin was shiny-looking and gray. It was the first dead thing of any size I'd ever seen. I remember Orin took a stick and touched the open eyes" (100; emphasis added). Other eyes in this story that catch the young narrator's eye are those of the fish in Dummy's pond ("I could see their big, heavy-lidded eyes watching us as they went by" [97]) and the "glittery little eyes" of Dummy's wife. "The first time I saw her," the boy Jack tells us, anticipating what he will say a few pages later about the "first dead thing" he had ever seen, "I saw those eyes" (91). That sentence was not present in the original version of the story, which appeared in *Furious Seasons*. Here it serves to tighten the connections between woman and fish, a linkage that surfaced in "Nobody Said Anything" in the green and decapitated fish that paralleled the green decapitated woman in R's favorite reading and between woman and death, which has come to the fore in the stories most recently read here. Eyes, as they are here, have been the connecting medium: eyes that kill, eyes whose gaze must be avoided.

With so much water so close to home, Claire had asked her husband, why go so far to fish? Dummy, the mute half-wit acquaintance of the narrator's father in "The Third Thing That Killed My Father Off," looked as if he had that problem solved when he decided to stock the pond a half-mile behind his house with black bass shipped in from Louisiana. This was particularly the case in that bass were not native to his region of the country. "A lot of people I knew had never seen a bass except for pictures. But my father had seen plenty of them when he was growing up in Arkansas and Georgia, and he had high hopes to do with Dummy's bass, Dummy being a friend" (92). One would have had to go quite far from home to fish for bass. The only trouble was that Dummy came to love his fish so much that he never fished there, nor would he allow the narrator's father to do so.

So protective was Dummy of his fish that the boy's father said "You'd reckon the fool was married to them fish, the way he acts." "From what I hear," someone else said, "he'd do better to put that fence round his house" (94). For Dummy's wife had the reputation of flirting with other men. In the end he lost both the woman and the fish. Unlike the fishermen in the story before who wisely tied the girl's body to a tree to keep the river from carrying it away, Dummy was powerless to save his fish when the floods came that February, forming a channel that connected his pond with the nearby river and carrying off his fish. And he had no fence to rein in his wife, who after the flood was seen "sitting in the Sportsman's Club with a big Mexican fellow" (101). Not too long after that the news came that Dummy "did in his wife with a hammer and drowned himself" (102).

We had seen the hammer before, of course, when the baby bass arrived in barrels crated in pine lath and Dummy "took out a hammer and a tire iron. . . . He undid the other two crates himself, leaving dark drops of blood on the lath where he ripped his hand doing it" (93).

Dummy, who never spoke, gave in death an enigmatic yet eloquent gesture that recalls the waving hand of the man who may be drowning, the man on the overturned keel James Packer pretended to be when he stitched his embroidery (78). Dummy had drowned himself in his pond, and men were dragging for his body. "After a time, an arm came out of the water. It looked like the hooks had gotten Dummy in the side. . . . It seemed to me everything took a bad turn for my father after. . . . That arm coming up and going back down in the water, it was like so long to good times and hello to bad" (103). In other words, a wave.

"A Serious Talk"

A wife's betrayals and a husband's violent response are the subject of "A Serious Talk" as well. And like Dummy, this husband too suffers from an inability to talk.

Burt and Vera's marriage has broken up, but Burt insists on visiting his wife and children on Christmas, even though he is not entirely welcome there, and must, as Vera warned him, "be out by six o'clock because her friend and his children were coming for dinner" (105). After an exchange of presents, Burt sits by the fire under the temporary illusion that he is still in "his house, his home" (106). As his wife and daughter set the dining room table for the evening meal to which he is not invited, however, his rage begins to smolder. "A small wax and sawdust log burned on the grate. A carton of five more sat ready on the hearth. He got up from the sofa and put them all in the fireplace. He watched until they flamed." On his way out, "he saw the pies lined up on the sideboard. He stacked them in his arms, all six, one for every ten times she had ever betrayed him. In the driveway in the dark, he'd let one fall as he fumbled with the door" (106–7).

It left "a halo of pumpkin filling on the pavement" that he notices when he returns the day after Christmas to apologize and to have his "serious talk." "Can I come in and talk about it?" he asks (107). But he doesn't talk about it. He doesn't talk about why he, in Vera's words, "tried to burn the house down" by throwing all those flammable logs on the fire, nor does he address himself to the problems between them. Instead he asks her what time her friend left the night before, provoking an angry response, then asks for something to drink. Vera becomes impatient. "Jesus, Burt. What'd you want to talk about, anyway? I told you I have someplace to go. . . . What is it? Tell me what's on your mind, and then I have to get ready." "I wanted to say I was sorry." "You said that" (109).

Vera excuses herself to go to the bathroom. The phone rings twice, the voice asking "Is Charlie there?" The second time Burt leaves it off the hook. Vera returns, replaces the receiver. "There were things he wanted to say, grieving things, consoling things, things like that" (111), but he never gets around to saying them. When the phone rings a third time— "It's someone wanting Charlie"—Vera takes the call in the bedroom. Alone in the kitchen, Burt washes the grease off the carving knife and saws through the cord.

Incensed, Vera demands that he leave. "He picked up the ashtray. He held it by its edge. He posed with it like a man preparing to hurl the discus" (112). He doesn't throw it at her but takes it with him to the car. "He was not certain, but he thought he had proved something. He hoped he had made something clear. The thing was, they had to have a serious talk soon. There were things that needed talking about, important things that had to be discussed" (112–13).

Burt wants to have his serious talk, but when he has the opportunity to do so he is incapable of saying all those things he wanted to say, "grieving things, consoling things, things like that." He speaks instead through his gestures—cutting the telephone cord, making as if to hurl the ashtray—believing that "he had proved something . . . had made something clear." But as far as the woman with whom he wishes to communicate is concerned, his furious sign language signifies nothing but a violence and anger she'd rather do without. As he departs he absurdly carries the ashtray—"a big dish of stoneware they'd bought from a bearded potter" (110)—with him (as he had carried off the six pies the day before, any one of which by its shape would have made a better discus than the ashtray). The last two sentences of the story suggest just how ridiculous a gesture it was: "He started the car and put it into reverse. It was hard managing until he put the ashtray down" (113).

The last we saw of Dummy was a wordless gesture too—the

arm rising mysteriously out of the water. It too bore a meaning-less burden: "The arm went back down and then it came out again, along with a bundle of something" (103). And like Burt, Dummy was incapable of having a serious (or any other kind of) talk. "I don't think he was really deaf. . . . But he sure couldn't talk. That was for certain" (90).

On second thought, Burt's gesture of posing with the stone ashtray "like a man preparing to hurl the *discus*" has a certain surprising eloquence. For there were, as he said to himself, "important things that had to be *discussed*." And Burt's rebus permits him as well to take his place alongside the other stone-throwing and woman-stoning husbands in *What We Talk About When We Talk About Love.*

"The Calm"

Another discussion threatens to erupt into violence in "The Calm." And we may have found the "Charlie" that the insistent phone calls were for in the preceding story. This "Charles" is, as it happens, someone the narrator thinks he's seen before but cannot quite place. Of the three men he can see from his van-tage point in the barber's chair, "Two of the men waiting I'd never seen before. But one of them I recognized, though I couldn't exactly place him" (115). After some reflection, the narrator tells us, it came to him: "And then I saw him in a cap and uniform, little eyes watchful in the lobby of a bank." He had to restore him to his original context, his bank guard's uniform, before he could recognize his face. The reader of these stories in sequence could well undergo the same experi-ence, thinking perhaps that "Charles" is a curiously familiar name but not at first being able to recall why.

"The barber put a hand on top of my head to turn me for a better look. Then he said to the guard, 'Did you get your deer, Charles?' " (116) It turns out he didn't, exactly. He had wounded the deer, but gave up trying to track him down to put him out of his misery, despite the animal's having left "a good trail. . . . Blood on the ground and blood on the leaves" (118).

He became more interested in arguing with his drunken son. "I boxed his goddamn ears for him, that goddamn kid. He's not too old. He needed it. So the point is, it got too dark to trail, what with the kid laying back to vomit and all" (118).

Carver has left a trail of sorts too. For the *"trail* of smoke stains [that] rose up the bricks to the mantel" (108; emphasis added) that Burt had left in the wake of his angrily throwing five wax and sawdust logs on Vera's fireplace in "A Serious Talk" was not originally there. In the first version of the story the same event had taken place, but there was no *trail:* "It was true, the fireplace had black smoke stains reaching up the bricks toward the mantel" (24). The trail that shows up there now allows us to trace the passage of the rewriting authorial hand and reveals how much of a "self-conscious book" this is, as Carver said in the *Paris Review* interview, "how intentional every move was, how calculated."

As Charles tells his tale to the barber, the older of the two other men in the barbershop becomes more and more perturbed at his violation of the rules of good sportsmanship. As the other of the two men points out, the wounded buck will have suffered an unnecessarily slow death from "the coyotes . . . the crows and the buzzards" (118). And besides that, Charles had shot the deer for nothing, since he wasn't able to bring in the carcass for venison. The waste recalls Burt's theft of the half-dozen pies, five more than he could have possibly eaten, and one of which he ruined when he dropped it in the driveway. "The older man put his cigarette out and turned to the guard. . . . 'You ought to be out there right now looking for that deer instead of in here getting a haircut.' 'You can't talk like that,' the guard said. 'You old fart. I've seen you someplace.' 'I've seen you too,' the old fellow said" (119)—both of them echoing what the narrator had said to himself at the beginning of the story. Charles threatens to box his ears; the older man dares him to try it; the barber calls for peace.

In the original version the older man had not in fact remembered seeing him. "Well, I haven't seen you before. I'd recollect if I'd seen your fat face before" (35). It makes more sense that he should remember seeing him now, now that "The

Calm" appears right after "A Serious Talk"—now that we too can remember having heard of someone with that name.

"Popular Mechanics"

For the third straight time, a discussion threatens to turn violent—and this time really does. A husband and wife, splitting up, are fighting for possession of the baby. The husband tries to pry it from his wife's grasp: "He worked on her fisted fingers with one hand and with the other hand he gripped the screaming baby up under an arm near the shoulder. . . . She would have it, this baby. She grabbed for the baby's other arm. She caught the baby around the wrist and leaned back. But he would not let go. He felt the baby slipping out of his hands and he pulled back very hard. In this manner, the issue was decided" (125).

Charles had been reproached in "The Calm" for not caring enough about the deer to do what had to be done to put it out of its misery. All he cared about, apparently, was bringing home something to eat, for he seemed to put the deer completely out of his mind once he discovered that his father had killed another deer in his absence. And when he expresses regret for what had happened, it wasn't for the deer's suffering but for its size: "Pity too. He was a big old son of a bitch. So in answer to your question, Bill, I both got my deer and I didn't. But we had venison on the table anyway. Because it turns out the old man has got himself a little spike in the meantime. Already has him back to camp, hanging up and gutted slick as a whistle" (118–19).

Both the husband and the wife, in this version of King Solomon's decision, both got the baby and didn't too, if, as it appears, the infant was torn apart by their tug of war. That "the issue was decided," as the concluding words of the story say, must mean that possession became moot with the serious injury, or even death, of the child. The mechanics of what happened probably were that the arm was broken or dislocated or even torn off at the shoulder, for the father's gripping "the screaming baby up under an arm near the shoulder" was darkly anticipated by the story's first lines: "Early that day the weather turned and the snow was melting into dirty water. Streaks of it ran down from the little *shoulder*-high window" (123; emphasis added).[13]

"Everything Stuck to Him"

The story that follows that one concerns a husband and a wife and the baby they fight over but ends much more happily. A hint of the Solomonic halving "Popular Mechanics" evoked and which Carver had earlier retold in "Nobody Said Anything" (the fish R and the other boy divided) can be seen in this father's joyful marveling "at the infant who had half his features and half the girl's" (130). A rift does threaten at first when he insists on going hunting with a friend and she doesn't think he should because their child shows signs of illness. "I don't want to be left alone with her like this. . . . The girl said, I'm your wife. This is your baby. She's sick or something. Look at her. . . . You're going to have to choose, the girl said. Carl or us. I mean it" (132–33). But although the husband goes through the motions of putting on his hunting clothes and assembling his equipment, starting the car, and clearing the windshield, he doesn't go. When he comes back inside, his wife and child are asleep. He starts frying bacon for breakfast; she awakes and puts her arms around him, apologizes for her harsh words, and makes a batch of waffles. He sits down to eat but accidentally spills the plate of waffles and syrup all over him. "The boy looked down at himself, at everything stuck to his underwear" (134)—hence the title. They laugh together

13. Removing the baby's arm might be taken, in the context that unites this story with "Viewfinder," as retribution for what the photographer claimed his children did to him. That it is in fact what happened is suggested by William Stull's meditation on the last word of the story: "The Latin root of 'decide' (*de-caedere*, to cut off) indicates just what fate the hapless 'issue' suffered" ("Beyond Hopelessville," 3).

and promise never to fight again. The entire story is told by the father to the grown-up daughter who was that child.

The storyteller remembers once more how "They had leaned on each other and laughed until the tears had come, while everything else—the cold, and where he'd go in it—was *outside,* for a while anyway" (135; emphasis added). "Popular Mechanics" had begun with a description of the cold darkness that lurked outside but, by contrast with the story that would follow, that had made its way, tragically, inside: "Cars slushed by on the street *outside,* where it was getting dark. But it was getting dark on the *inside* too" (123; emphasis added).

The two stories are in other ways remarkably each the complement of the other, so much so that it is as if "Everything Stuck to Him" were the missing half of its predecessor, as if the baby torn in half were emblematic of the complementary relationship the two stories bear. One wife wants her husband to stay; the other wants him to leave: "I'm glad you're leaving! she said" (123). "Just get your things and get out" (124). One husband wants to leave the baby behind with its mother; the other wants to take it with him. One story is about something (waffle syrup and "everything") getting stuck to something else (his underwear); the other is about something (the baby) coming unstuck.

But, in a somewhat larger perspective, "Everything Stuck to Him" combines the main features of the *two* stories that precede it. We have seen how the father in "Popular Mechanics" who was so caught up in his desire to have the baby that he causes it grievous harm responds to the hunter in "The Calm" who was so caught up in his own desires—firing at the deer without taking sufficient care to make a clean kill, beating his son instead of going after the wounded deer—that he was guilty of wanton destruction. "Everything Stuck to Him," by being about a man who wants to go hunting but who foregoes that pleasure for the sake of his baby, combines and reconciles the conflicts of these two preceding stories.

"What We Talk About When We Talk About Love"

In the title story of the collection, two couples are sitting around talking and drinking gin: Mel, a cardiologist; his wife, Terri; the narrator, Nick; and his wife, Laura. Terri recalls her lover Ed, who used to beat her. "He dragged me around the living room by my ankles. He kept saying, 'I love you, I love you, you bitch' " (138). Mel argues that such violent behavior couldn't have been love, while Terri maintains that it was. Mel recounts Ed's threats against his life, and Ed's eventual suicide.

Mel then wants to give what to him is the definitive example of true love. He had performed surgery on an elderly couple who were gravely injured in a car accident. They were given only a 50 percent chance of survival. Becoming increasingly drunk from the gin as he tells this story, Mel gets sidetracked and says that if he could be reincarnated he'd like to come back as a knight. "You were pretty safe wearing all that armor. . . . what I liked about knights, besides their ladies, was that they had that suit of armor, you know, and they couldn't get hurt very easy. No cars in those days, you know? No drunk teenagers to tear into your ass" (148–49). Nick replies that the armor had its disadvantages—danger of suffocation, heart attacks from the heat.

Brought back to the story of the old couple, Mel describes them as bandaged head to foot in casts, side by side in the same hospital room. "Little eye-holes and nose-holes and mouth-holes. . . . Well, the husband was very depressed for the longest while. Even after he found out that his wife was going to pull through. . . . I'd get up to his mouth-hole . . . and he'd say . . . it was because he couldn't see her through his eye-holes. . . . Can you imagine? I'm telling you, the man's heart was breaking because he couldn't turn his goddamn head and *see* his goddamn wife" (151).

Getting sadder and sadder with the gin, Mel announces that he wants to place a call to the children from his former marriage. This brings him to the subject of his ex-wife, who is allergic to bees, and to his fantasy of going to her house dressed like a beekeeper. "You know, that hat that's like a helmet with the plate that comes down over your face, the big gloves, and the padded coat? I'll knock on the door and let loose a hive of bees in the house. But first I'd make sure the kids were out, of course" (153).

The couples had spoken of going out to eat in a new restaurant, but everyone now seems to lack the energy to move. Mel spills what gin remains in his glass. The narrator concludes, "I could hear my heart beating. I could hear everyone's heart. I could hear the human noise we sat there making, not one of us moving, not even when the room went dark" (154).

Earlier, sunlight had "filled the kitchen from the big window behind the sink" (137). "The afternoon sun was like a presence in this room, the spacious light of ease and generosity. We could have been anywhere, somewhere enchanted" (144). But as Mel, the picture of confidence and good humor at the beginning of the story, becomes increasingly morose and increasingly drunk, darkness enters, the enchantment fades, and silence descends. Darkness invades the room in the last line of the story, by contrast with the cold that was kept outside in the last line of "Everything Stuck to Him": "While everything else —the cold, and where he'd go in it—was outside, for a while anyway" (135). And we have seen how that last line contrasted with the opening of "Popular Mechanics": "It was getting dark on the inside too"—which now finds its ultimate echo in the last words of the title story: "when the room went dark." Certainly Mel's comment on Terri's former lover Ed—"The kind of love I'm talking about, you don't try to kill people" (139)— has its applicability to the love, or whatever it was, that impelled the father and mother to tear their child apart.

The sunlight whose splendor and gradual disappearance parallel the course of the friends' conversation and mood had provided the observant narrator with an instructive parable that is immediately applicable to this story, and ultimately to all those in the volume to which it gives its title. "The sunshine inside the room was different now, changing, getting thinner. But the leaves outside the window were still shimmering, and I stared at the pattern they made on the panes and on the Formica counter. They weren't the same patterns, of course" (150).

They would have been the same patterns, evidently, had not the different surface—the counter top as opposed to the window panes—given the shadow of the leaves a different context in which to appear. The narrator's meditation appears between Mel's talking about knights in armor and his description of the old couple in their casts—he had begun the story of the injured couple before bringing up the knights but had not yet spoken of their casts. By the time he begins to describe their head-to-toe carapace with tiny holes for eyes, nose, and mouth, we are ready to apply the parable to the evident similarity between chivalric armor and these body casts: different surface, different contexts, thus different patterns—yet the same original projection. Mel clearly has this image of body armor so much on his mind that it keeps coming out in different images—of which there is of course a third, the beekeeper's protective gear.

Yet the parable of the patterns has greater relevance than what it can tell us about what is going on in Mel's mind. This instance of the same basic image in three different patterns— knight's armor, plaster casts, and beekeeper's outfit—enacts within a single story, and perhaps not by chance in the *title* story, what is enacted by all the stories in the collection. Every two stories (and sometimes three) display too the same basic image in different patterns, in different contexts. Like the elderly husband who knew his wife was right next to him but grieved because he couldn't see her, the stories too seem at times to be half-aware of the nearly identical mate that lies right next to them and almost yearn to break out of their boundaries to make the connection already half-visible beneath the surface. I am thinking of such moments as the mysterious telephone call for Charlie in one story that is answered, in a way, by the Charles in the next whom the narrator thinks he's seen before but can't at first remember where, or of the two sequential stories in *Will You Please Be Quiet, Please?* where a character says something "not really knowing what he meant," or of neighboring stories about neighbors, and other neighboring stories about a fence, or of the man in "Viewfinder" who was just "trying to make a connection" while his counterpart in

"Why Don't You Dance?" had already made sure, thanks to his extension cord, that "everything was connected." The elderly couple in their plaster casts enact the same phenomenon within "What We Talk About" that the stories they stand for do: placed between the description of knights in their armor and a beekeeper in his head-to-toe protective garb, they are flanked on either side by similarly covered bodies—different patterns from the same basic image—just as, on a more intimate level, each member of the couple has a similarly enveloped double for a neighbor.

Between the narrator's reflection on the way the shadow of the leaves projected differently on different surfaces and Mel's description of the old couple in their casts, Mel paused to stare at the narrator's wife and said, "Laura, if I didn't have Terri and if I didn't love her so much, and if Nick wasn't my best friend, I'd fall in love with you" (150–51). The husband in the immediately preceding story had expressed the same sentiment: "Sally was the girl's sister. She was striking. . . . The boy used to say to the girl, If we weren't married, I could go for Sally" (130). Like these marriages—Mel and Terri's and the young couple's in "Everything Stuck to Him"—these stories too could have turned out differently. Their constituent parts—characters, gestures, images, and turns of phrase—are sometimes so similar that we might wonder if they are not perhaps interchangeable.

"One More Thing"

Carver's short story collections tend to conclude with their title story. This is at least what happens with *Furious Seasons, Will You Please Be Quiet, Please?* and *Cathedral.* Thus the actual concluding story to *What We Talk About* gives the appearance by its very title of being an afterthought to the title story, a postscript to the book's real conclusion, "one more thing" to add on the topic that was discussed at such length in the story just before. Indeed, for a moment we might have thought we *were* still in that discussion, or its aftermath, when on the first page of "One More Thing" we see Rae say to her mother "Tell him *what we talked about*" (155; emphasis added).

As it happens, Carver has made such drastic cuts since the original appearance of this story that we never do get a clear idea of what they were talking about. In its first version it was that "If he"—Rae's father, L.D.—"wants to stop drinking, all he has to do is tell himself to stop. It's all in his head. Everything's in the head" (28). The closest the revised version comes to that is Rae's insistence that "it's all in his head" (156)—*what* it is that was in his head is left unsaid. L.D. at one point comes close to repeating the gesture the cardiologist host had performed at the end of the preceding story: "Mel turned his glass over. He spilled it out on the table" (153). Here, L.D. "hit the table with the flat of his hand. . . . His glass fell on its side and rolled off" (156).

L.D., whose wife, Maxine, is telling him to pack up and leave, picked up a jar of pickles and threw it through the kitchen window. " 'I'm going. . . . It suits me to a tee. You're nuts here, anyway. . . . There's another life out there. Believe me, this is no picnic, this nuthouse.' He could feel air from the hole in the window on his face. 'That's where I'm going,' he said. 'Out there,' he said and pointed" (157). He was pointing to the fresh air coming from outside through that hole in the window, the fresh air of liberty, of freedom from the oppressive atmosphere of life at home. Now Carver too has punched a hole where there wasn't one before, adding "one more thing" to the story the better to make it fit in the sequence, just after "What We Talk About" with its talk of "little eye-holes and nose-holes and mouth-holes" (151) and of knights who "suffocated in all that armor" (149) from lack of air (their holes were too small). For that sentence had originally read, "He could feel the draft of air from the window on his face" (29)—the same basic idea, but without the *hole*. Sometimes less is more; sometimes an additional absence, another "hole" in the text, will allow more to take place between the lines. For the hole opened up here is at the same time a breach in the wall that divides this story from its neighbor.

4

Cathedral

"Feathers"

Before and after" (14), Bud said, holding up an "old plaster-of-Paris cast of the most crooked, jaggedy teeth in the world" (12) next to his wife Olla's orthodontically straightened ones. It is one of several sights Jack and Fran have to endure on their visit to Bud and Olla's house. Another is the pet peacock that wanders into the house during dinner, is "smelly" (25), and lets out blood-curdling screams. Still another is their hosts' offspring, "the ugliest baby" Jack has "ever seen," with "no neck to speak of" and "three or four fat chins" (20).

Yet Jack, who narrates the story, is able to say that "that evening at Bud and Olla's was special. . . . That evening I felt good about almost everything in my life. . . . I wished . . . that I'd never forget or otherwise let go of that evening" (25). Fran was of a different opinion. "Fran would look back on that evening at Bud's place as the beginning of the change. . . . 'God-damn those people and their ugly baby,' Fran will say, for no apparent reason." It was a change for the worse: Fran has since cut her lovely long hair and has "gotten fat on me, too" (26), Jack says. They have a child now, but he "has a conniving streak." And Fran and Jack no longer talk to each other very much. Jack's wish that he would never forget that evening was "one wish of mine that came true. And it was bad luck for me that it did. But, of course, I couldn't know that then" (25).

We are thus presented with two differing interpretations of

137

the meaning of the visit. For Fran it was a disagreeable experience, and the beginning of what went wrong in their lives. But
for Jack it had been a glimpse of paradise—though a paradise
that in retrospect he realized he'd never see again—symbolized
by the peacock: " 'They don't call them birds of paradise for
nothing,' Bud said" (23). The baby may have been ugly, but to
Bud and Olla, Jack imagines, "It's our baby" (24). He remembers "Olla giving Fran some peacock feathers to take home . . .
all us shaking hands, hugging each other, saying things" (26).

But is a third interpretation possible? Is "Feathers" about
anything else, too?

From our somewhat different vantage point as nonpartici-
pants in the story, we can make some observations that may
have escaped Jack and Fran. One of them is that this story of
an evening they will both always remember began with an anecdote about the difficulty of remembering. Jack had tele-
phoned Bud once

> to see if he wanted to do anything. This woman picked up
> the phone and said. "Hello." I blanked and couldn't remem-
> ber her name. Bud's wife. Bud had said her name to me any
> number of times. But it went in one ear and out the other.
> "Hello!" the woman said again. . . . I still couldn't remember
> her name. So I hung up. The next time I saw Bud at work I
> sure as hell didn't tell him I'd called. But I made a point of
> getting him to mention his wife's name. "Olla," he said. Olla,
> I said to myself. *Olla.* (4)

The strange thing about this is the resemblance between "Olla"
and "Hello," between what Jack heard her say and what he
couldn't remember. The voice on the other end of the line is
practically telling him the name he is racking his memory to
find. "Olla" and "Hello" are almost the same, yet not quite:
close enough for their similarity to be noticed—by us, if not by
Jack—yet not enough alike for one to be taken for the other.
We might remember that in "Are You a Doctor?" a story whose
plot arises out of a telephone call made to a wrong number,
which was what Jack's abortive call must have appeared to Olla

to have been, Arnold Breit had made a similar transposition of syllables when he thought Cheryl's name was Shirley.

A number of other things in "Feathers" present themselves in pairs, of which one can be taken to stand for the other. When Fran and Jack first arrived, they saw a baby's swing set in the front yard and some toys on the porch. "It was then that we heard this awful squall. There was a baby in the house, right, but this cry was too loud for a baby. . . . Then something as big as a vulture flapped heavily down from one of the trees and landed just in front of the car" (7). It was the peacock, which occupies the stage long before they get to see the baby.

Then there are the teeth, the "before" and "after" Bud is so proud to exhibit (he had paid for the orthodontic work that Olla's parents had not been able to afford). The more closely we examine these teeth, however, the more slippery the notion of before and after becomes. The mold, of course, is just a copy of a prior original: Olla's teeth as they were before the treatment began. So the "before" is a copy, while the "after" is the (revised) original. But there is another copy: "That orthodontist wanted to keep this," Olla announces as she holds the mold in her lap. "I said nothing doing. I pointed out to him they were *my* teeth. So he took pictures of the mold instead. He told me he was going to put the pictures in a magazine." Bud wonders "what kind of magazine that'd be. Not much call for that kind of publication, I don't think" (14).

Yet there still is another copy, another version of this "picture in a magazine." For a few pages later, when Fran asks why Olla decided to get a peacock in the first place, she answers, "I always dreamed of having me a peacock. Since I was a girl and found a *picture* of one *in a magazine*. I thought it was the most beautiful thing I ever saw. . . . I kept that picture for the longest time" (18; emphasis added). So the peacock in their house is the copy of the original magazine picture, which in turn is an echo of the magazine picture mentioned earlier of the mold of Olla's teeth, which in turn . . . : not an *infinite* regression by any means, yet one of significant length.

It is fitting that the first story in Carver's new collection of stories should begin with this evocation of a chain of befores and afters, of originals and copies, of forerunners (the peacock that, in its initial appearance, could be taken for the baby) and avatars (the baby as the later version of the peacock, which had occupied the house, and Olla's affections, first). That, as we have been accustomed to discover by now, is the way his short story sequences appear to be put together: a chain of befores and afters bearing a strange resemblance to each other.

"Chef's House"

In this chain of resemblances the second story in *Cathedral,* like the first, is also about a house that affords a glimpse of paradise lost. This time it is told from the point of view of the wife. Edna had been separated from Wes but accepted his invitation to join him in a place with an ocean view he was renting for next to nothing from a recovered alcoholic named Chef. Wes was on the wagon too. "He said, We'll start over. I said, If I come up there, I want you to do something for me. . . . I want you to try and be the Wes I used to know. The old Wes. The Wes I married" (27).

Things went very well in that idyllic spot. Edna found herself wishing the summer would never end. She put her wedding ring back on. They drank no alcohol. Wes would pick flowers for her, and they'd go fishing. Their children, grown up now, "kept their distance" (29). But one afternoon Chef came by with the sad news that they had to leave. "Chef said his daughter, Linda, the woman Wes used to call Fat Linda from the time of his drinking days, needed a place to live and this place was it." Her husband had disappeared, she had a baby and couldn't afford to live anywhere else.

Wes is devastated. "This has been a happy house up to now, he said. We'll get another house, I said. Not like this one, Wes said. It wouldn't be the same, anyway. This house has been a good house for us. This house has good memories to it" (30). Edna tries in vain to keep Wes from giving up. "I said, Suppose, just suppose, nothing had ever happened. Suppose this was for the first time. . . . Say none of the other had ever happened"

(31). But Wes replies "Then I suppose we'd have to be some-body else if that was the case. Somebody we're not. I don't have that kind of supposing left in me" (32). He can see no future, no more room to continue the fresh start they had been able to make as long as they could live in Chef's house.

And that's about where the story ends. "He seemed to have made up his mind. But having made up his mind, he was in no hurry. He leaned back on the sofa, folded his hands in his lap, and closed his eyes. He didn't say anything else. He didn't have to" (32).

For both Jack and Wes, the house they visit—Jack and Fran for an evening, Wes and Edna for a summer cut short—is an almost magical place where they can see a vision of how life ought to be lived. "This house has been a *good* place for us. This house has *good* memories to it," according to Wes. "That evening I felt *good* about almost everything in my life," Jack had said. Wes speaks of "good *memories*," and Jack made the wish "that I'd *never forget* or otherwise let go of that evening." Though they are at opposite moments in their lives—Jack and Fran at the beginning of their marriage, the child they will have not yet born, and Wes's children already grown—the future for both men is evidently bleak. It's just that Jack didn't know it yet.

Two smaller details from "Feathers" reappear here. The fatness of Bud and Olla's child—"big fat lips . . . three or four fat chins. . . . Fat hung over its wrists. Its arms and fingers were fat" (21)—returns in the name Wes gave its counterpart, Fat Linda, who is the baby's counterpart because both are the off-spring of the owner of the house that afforded that glimpse of paradise. The other recurrence concerns what happens to Jack's attempt to engrave on his memory the name he was so embarrassed at having forgot: "Olla, I said to myself. *Olla*" (4). Now when Wes lies back on the sofa and lapses into silence, Edna tells us that "*I said his name to myself. It was an easy name* to say, and I'd been used to saying it for a long time" (32; emphasis added)—unlike Jack, of course, who was saying that name to himself for precisely the opposite reason: to get so used to saying it that he wouldn't forget. This echo emblema-

tizes the essentially complementary nature of these two opening stories, the first looking toward the future, the second
backward to the past, because their living at Chef's house was
apparently a condition of their living together at all, and this
may be one of the last times Edna will ever pronounce Jack's
name.

"Preservation"

What happens near the conclusion of "Chef's House"—the
way Wes demonstrated his abject surrender to bad luck when
he "leaned back on the sofa, folded his hands in his lap, and
closed his eyes" (32)—is what happens at the beginning of
"Preservation": "Sandy's husband had been on the sofa ever
since he'd been terminated three months ago" (35). "He made
his bed on the sofa that night, and that's where he'd slept every
night since it happened" (35–36). After a discouraging visit to
the unemployment office "he got back on the sofa. He began
spending all of his time there, as if, she thought, it was the
thing he was supposed to do now that he no longer had any
work. . . . It's like he *lives* there, Sandy thought" (36; Carver's
emphasis).

The title of the story, which for once does not actually appear in the text itself, is doubly evoked (1) by the story Sandy's
husband kept rereading as he lay on the sofa of "a man who
had been discovered after spending two thousand years in a
peat bog" (36)—in a state, that is, of almost perfect preservation—and (2) by the sudden demise of the refrigerator, that is
by its inability to *preserve* their food any longer. "I have to cook
everything tonight" (40), Sandy says, and proceeds to clean out
the fridge. She "started taking things off the shelves and putting stuff on the table." Wes "took the meat out of the freezer
and put the packages on the table. . . . He took everything out
and then found the paper towels and the dishcloth and started
wiping up inside" (41). Strangely, Sandy and her husband's
cleaning out the refrigerator and cleaning up the mess inside

repeats what happened on the last page of the preceding story. The refrigerator in Chef's house had not broken down, but since he had informed Edna and Wes that they had to leave they did feel obliged to clean it out—to eat up, that is, what was left inside: "I went in to start supper. We still had some fish in the icebox. There wasn't much else. We'll clean it up tonight, I thought, and that will be the end of it" (33). The idea is not to waste the food they have. Sandy and her husband have a lot more they'll have to eat, way too much, in fact: " 'I've got to fry pork chops tonight,' she said. 'And I have to cook up that hamburger. And those sandwich steaks and the fish sticks. Don't forget the TV dinners, either' " (42).

The refrigerator had given out, Sandy's husband determines, because "we lost our Freon. . . . The Freon leaked out" (41). It's not the only time that gas leaks out in this story. Sandy has decided that they should go to the Auction Barn that evening because they were advertising new and used appliances. Her husband does not share her eagerness: "Whoever said anything about us buying an icebox at an auction?" (44), he asks. Sandy, however, remembers what "fun" (43) it was to go to auctions with her father when she was a child, although her father died in a car he had bought at one of those auctions. It "leaked carbon monoxide up through the floorboards and caused him to pass out behind the wheel. . . . The motor went on running until there was no more gas in the tank. He stayed in the car until somebody found him a few days later" (45).

Her father's death and the icebox's demise respond to each other in interesting ways. A leaking gas caused both events. The faulty car had been an auction bargain—"he said he'd bought a peach of a car at this auction for two hundred dollars. If she'd been there, he said, he'd have bought one for her, too" (45)—while the faulty refrigerator is to be replaced by one bought at auction. Her father's undiscovered body had doubtless begun to deteriorate in those few days as had the food in her fridge: "She opened the door to the freezer compartment. An awful smell puffed out at her that made her want to gag" (39). Sandy doesn't say so, but the association of these two events is surely powerful enough that she could have smelled the memory of her father's corpse when she opened that door and the "warm, boxed-in air came out at her."

"The Compartment"

Sandy's father in the icebox, and especially in the "freezer *compartment*," is answered, too, in an interesting way by the story that follows, in which a *father* has "decided he wasn't going to leave the *compartment*. He was going to sit where he was until the train pulled away" (55; emphasis added). Carver's choice of a title for this story draws attention to this connection to its predecessor. This decision to stay put echoes as well, of course, Sandy's husband's decision to spend the rest of his life on the living room sofa reading about the corpse discovered in a Netherlands bog.

Myers, on vacation, was touring Europe alone. His son, whom he hadn't seen since the divorce eight years before, had written him a letter from Strasbourg, France, where he was studying. Myers had decided to visit him for a few days on his way from Milan to Paris. Myers had always believed that the breakup of his marriage had been "hastened along . . . by the boy's malign interference in their personal affairs" (47). The last time he had seen him they had actually come to blows —the son, thinking he had to defend his mother from his father's anger, "charged him. Myers sidestepped and got him in a headlock while the boy wept and pummeled Myers on the back and kidneys." Myers "slammed him into the wall and threatened to kill him. He meant it. 'I gave you life,' Myers remembered himself shouting, 'and I can take it back!' " (47–48).

In the train compartment, Myers "looked at guidebooks. He read things he wished he'd read before he'd been to the place they were about . . . he was sorry to be finding out certain things about the country now, just as he was leaving Italy behind" (48). But he is tired of trying to make himself understood to foreigners and probably will not spend his whole six weeks of vacation in Europe after all. When he returns from the WC Myers discovers that the expensive Japanese watch he has bought as a gift for his son is missing from the coat he had left behind in the compartment. Through sign language, he tries to ask the other passenger in the compartment if he saw anyone take it, but the man shrugs in incomprehension. Myers stalks out into the corridor but sees no chance of making anyone else understand either.

When he returns to his seat, it comes to him that "he really had no desire to see this boy whose behavior had long ago isolated him from Myers's affections. . . . This boy had devoured Myers's youth, had turned the young girl he had courted and wed into a nervous, alcoholic woman whom the boy alternately pitied and bullied" (54). So when the train pulled into Strasbourg Myers "decided he wasn't going to leave the compartment. He was going to sit where he was until the train pulled away" (55).

As he looks through his compartment window Myers doesn't see his son on the platform. While the train is still in the station, he gets up and opens the compartment door. "He went to the end of the corridor, where the cars were coupled together. He didn't know why they had stopped. Maybe something was wrong. He moved to the window. But all he could see was an intricate system of tracks where trains were being made up, cars taken off or switched from one train to another" (57). What happens at this point is that Myers becomes caught up in that intricate system switching and coupling. He wanders into the second-class car next to his first-class one. The train begins to move. He returns to his car and compartment—but his suitcase is gone. "It was not his compartment after all. He realized with a start they must have uncoupled his car while the train was in the yard and attached another second-class car to the train. . . . He was going somewhere, he knew that. And if it was the wrong direction, sooner or later he'd find it out" (58).

"A Small, Good Thing"

What has happened to Myers is what has also happened to
his story, for Carver's sequences are part of an intricate system
of switching, coupling, and decoupling too, and while Myers's
journey started out in a car coupled at one end to "Preservation," it ended in a car coupled to "A Small, Good Thing,"
which, as it turns out, is a car from another train: a revised
version of "The Bath," from *What We Talk About When We Talk
About Love.*

We know that story. We know how it too, like "The Compartment," concerns a missed appointment: Myers's missed
rendezvous with his son at the Strasbourg station is thus echoed
by the one Mrs. Weiss had made with the baker to pick up her
son's birthday cake. We recall as well how, like the story to
which it is coupled here, this one concerns a gift for the son
that does not get delivered: the expensive Japanese wristwatch
that disappears from Myers's pocket, and all the gifts that
Scotty would not get to open for his birthday. We recall that
just before he was struck by the car, "the birthday boy was
trying to find out what his friend intended to give him for his
birthday that afternoon" (60).

What we didn't know when we read "The Bath"—the identity of the mysterious telephone caller and whether the boy
would survive—is what "A Small, Good Thing" goes to some
lengths to tell us. The caller is the baker whose cake was not
picked up, and after the boy's death, the Weisses go to his
bakery for a confrontation that turns into a reconciliation. The
"small, good thing" the contrite baker offers them is bread.

It is now quite a different story from "The Bath." This
version is in a way more comforting—the scene in the bakery
becomes almost heartwarming—but in another perhaps more
troubling. Coming as it does just after "The Compartment" the
son's death now comes dangerously close to fulfilling the filici-
dal wish Myers had made when "he slammed him into the wall
and threatened to kill him. He meant it. 'I gave you life . . . and
I can take it back!' " Tess Gallagher, in her Introduction to *A
New Path to the Waterfall,* speaks of the persistent image of the

"son as an oppressive figure" (xxiv) in Carver's poetry (she mentions "The Compartment" as well), with particular reference to "On an Old Photograph of My Son," which appears in that collection. The son, a "petty tyrant," bullies his mother in that poem—as had Myers's son ("This boy had . . . turned [his mother] into a nervous, alcoholic woman whom the boy alternately pitied and bullied"): "Hey, old lady, jump, why don't you? Speak / when spoken to. I think I'll put you in / a headlock to see how you like it. I like / it" (86). The poet writes, apparently speaking out of Carver's own ambivalent feelings toward his son, "I want to forget that boy / in the picture—that jerk, that bully! / . . . Oh, son, in those days I wanted you dead / a hundred—no, a thousand—different times." What Carver confesses in "Fires," an essay on what had influenced his writing over the years, gives us some understanding of how he could have felt, as Myers did, that "this boy had devoured [his] youth." In the mid-1960s he was in a busy laundromat keeping a keen eye out for the next available dryer. He also had to worry about his children, who were at a birthday party but whom he would have to pick up as soon as he could get the laundry done.[1] His wife was working that afternoon as a waitress. Every time he thought he had a dryer someone else beat him to it.

> In a daze I moved away with my shopping cart and went back to waiting. But I remember thinking at that moment, amid the feelings of helpless frustration that had me close to tears, that nothing—and, brother, I mean nothing—that ever hap-

---

1. That is, he thinks he remembers it was a birthday party, but he isn't entirely sure: "They were with some other kids that afternoon, a birthday party maybe. Something. . . . As I say, I'm not sure where our kids were that afternoon. Maybe I had to pick them up from someplace, and it was getting late, and that contributed to my state of mind" (32). In light of the fact that in "The Bath" (and later in "A Small, Good Thing") the son dies on his birthday and that the cake was an elaborately iced birthday cake makes the uncertainty of his recollection all the more interesting. Concealed beneath it may be a kind of birthday wish that could be expressed only in a fiction: that his children had never been born.

> pened to me on this earth could come anywhere close, could
> possibly be as important to me, could make as much differ-
> ence, as the fact that I had two children. And that I would
> always have them and always find myself in this position of
> unrelieved responsibility and permanent distraction. . . . At
> that moment I felt—I knew—that the life I was in was vastly
> different from the lives of the writers I most admired. I
> understood writers to be people who didn't spend their Sat-
> urdays at the laundromat and every waking hour subject to
> the needs and caprices of their children. (*Fires*, 32–33)

He did get published—"Neighbors" appeared in *Esquire*—"But
my kids were in full cry then . . . and they were eating me alive"
(39)—as the son in "The Compartment" "had *devoured* Myers's
youth." And then Carver uses a railroad metaphor that puts
him in very nearly the same situation as Myers at the end of
"The Compartment" (the difference being that though Myers
found himself on the wrong track he was still going somewhere): "My life soon took another veering, a sharp turn, and
then it came to a dead stop off on a siding." He is evidently
alluding to his descent into alcoholism, but it is clear that part
of what drove him there was his despair at not having the time
to write, time his children consumed.

How close Myers may be to Carver himself is suggested by
the fact that the protagonist of "Put Yourself in My Shoes,"
whom we saw to bear some remarkable resemblances to the
author, had the same name.

What consolation the baker can offer Ann and Howard
Weiss for the loss of their son as they accept the bread he offers
them at midnight in his bakery and talk on with him into the
early morning hours brings them to about the same point that
Myers's decision to forego meeting his son had brought him.
"He decided he wasn't going to leave the compartment"; "they
did not think of leaving" (89).

Such a dark reading of the story, influenced by Carver's
decision to place it immediately after "The Compartment,"
with its tale of a father's enmity toward his son, contrasts with
William Stull's sunnier interpretation. In "Beyond Hopelessville: Another Side of Raymond Carver," Stull is right, of

course, to say that "A Small, Good Thing" is more hopeful than "The Bath," as Carver himself has indicated in several interviews, but I think he goes too far when he says that here "Carver goes farther still . . . toward a final vision of forgiveness and community rooted in religious faith" (11). Quite correctly calling our attention to the manner in which the Weisses' and the baker's breaking of bread recalls the Last Supper, Stull nevertheless presumes more than I am willing to accept when he argues that "a subtle but pervasive pattern or religious symbols" in the story "suggests the presence of a third kind of love in Carver's work" in addition to erotic and brotherly love: "Christian love." Stull sees the rite of Christian baptism in the baths the parents take: "While their innocent child (a Christlike figure, to be sure) lies suspended between life and death, each of the parents bathes. Carver calls attention to this seemingly incidental action by making it the title of the original story" (12) —as if forgetting his argument that the second story is the Christianized version of the hopeless, secular first.

Stull, who has not only written widely on Carver but has even resurrected some of his early work (in *Those Days*) and certainly done more than anyone else to promote Carver's academic reputation, is the foremost Carver scholar we have, and "Beyond Hopelessville" is probably the most influential article yet to appear on Carver's work. Its principal thesis that the distance between *Will You Please Be Quiet, Please?* and *Cathedral* encompasses a significant movement "beyond Hopelessville" is undeniably correct in general terms, but precisely because of the article's special significance in Carver studies I'd like to take the opportunity to quarrel with its theological conclusion—as well as to indicate that Stull and I do agree on one very crucial point, though we interpret it differently: The slain son *is* a sacrificial victim. In my reading, he is slain by the father, the same father (the father behind the scenes in a number of Carver's stories and poems who is to a startling degree Carver himself, who can become a writer only by sacrificing his son) who in the immediately preceding story, "The Compartment," wishes his son were dead. In Stull's reading, Scotty is a sacrificial son because he is the Son of God: "The child Scotty dies—

painfully, irrationally, unjustly—in a sacrifice that recalls not only the crucifixion but also Christ's teaching. As Jesus makes clear again and again in the Gospels, the child is the emblem of perfect faith: 'Whosoever shall not receive the kingdom of God as a little child, he shall not enter therein' (Mark 10:15). . . . With unwitting cruelty, [the baker] torments the Weisses, taunting them and taking the name of the Christlike child in vain" (12). Stull then cites Matthew 18:6: "But whoso shall offend one of these little ones which believe in me, it were better for him that a millstone were hanged about his neck." The problem here is that Scotty is nowhere depicted in the story as "one of these little ones which believe in me." At most he believes in his birthday, and the likelihood of presents. Nor can the baker be blamed for taking Scotty's name in vain if he was unaware (not having read Stull's article) that the child was "Christlike."

Where Stull, using the King James Version, cites "whoso shall *offend*," the Revised Standard Version gives "whoever *causes* one of these little ones who believe in me *to sin*," a more accurate translation of the original Greek "causes . . . to stumble" *(an skandalisé)*—which resonates intriguingly with what really did happen to Scotty: "the birthday boy stepped off the curb at an intersection and was immediately knocked down by a car . . . the boy got unsteadily to his feet. The boy wobbled a little. . . . He walked home" (60–61). If anyone causes the boy to stumble, it's not the baker but the driver of the car.

Stull is of course right to say that Carver's story recycles elements of the Christian Gospels, but I think it is risky to conclude from that that the story buys into the Christian message itself. "In breaking bread together," Stull writes, "the characters reenact the central rite of Christianity, the Lord's Supper. 'It's a heavy bread, but rich,' the baker says—an apt description of the Eucharist" (12–13). It may be more accurate to say that Carver's characters here achieve, on their own, without divine intervention, a genuine but purely human communion. They don't need God to do it, and Carver doesn't need a Christian conversion to write it. Stull, having brought Carver back into the fold of the "humanist realism" of a James Joyce or a Henry James by arguing that *Cathedral,* in contrast to his earlier stories, is "more expressive, more 'painterly' " (8), seems to want to bring him back into the church as well: "A study of Carver's revisions reveals not only another side of his realism, the humanist side, but also another spirit in his work, a spirit of empathy, forgiveness, and community tacitly founded on Judeo-Christian faith" (6). The way Carver recycles his own stories, particularly in their sequential resonance, allows us to see how he can incorporate elements of a prior narrative into a new one without having to "found" the new one on the old. What I'm criticizing in Stull—that he "reads into" Carver's story the haunting presence of a prior narrative (by another Hand, in this instance)—could be turned against my own reading of Carver were it not for the preponderance of evidence. More importantly, I am *not* suggesting that the second story (of two sequentially linked ones) actually retells the first or is dependent on the first for anything more than the raw material it gives such a strong impression (or illusion) of borrowing. What essential relation it may have with the story it echoes or recycles is likely to be an ironic one, each playing off the other for a greater effect. What's missing from Stull's reading is the very real possibility of irony in Carver's recycling here of the Christian foundation myth.

"Vitamins"

Before Mrs. Weiss told the baker her son was dead, when the atmosphere was still tense with anger—the Weisses' for the baker's sinister phone calls, the baker's for their sticking him with an unbought cake—he had said: "You want to pick up your three-day-old cake? . . . There it sits over there, getting stale. I'll give it to you for half of what I quoted you. No. You want it? You can have it. It's no good to me, no good to anyone now" (85–86). The vitamins in "Vitamins" are a product no one wants either. The narrator's wife tries to sell them door to door but business is terrible. "Nobody's buying vitamins. . . . Middle of winter, people sick all over the state, people dying,

and nobody thinks they need vitamins" (98). The narrator con-
curs: "Vitamins were on the skids, vitamins had taken a nose-
dive. The bottom had fallen out of the vitamin market" (100).

The vitamins are not the only thing in "Vitamins" into
which the cake of the immediately preceding story is transformed, as if it had passed through the distorting process of
dream. Dreams are in fact thematic in the story, as the narrator's wife is plagued by nightmares: "Everybody dreams," she
tells her husband. "If you didn't dream, you'd go crazy. I read
about it. It's an outlet. People dream when they're asleep. Or
else they'd go nuts. But when I dream, I dream of vitamins. Do
you see what I'm saying?" (97) "A dream," Freud wrote in *The
Interpretation of Dreams*, "is a (disguised) fulfilment of a (suppressed or repressed) wish" (194; the parentheses are Freud's).
It is inevitably distorted into a disguise in order to get past the
dream censor of the conscious part of the brain. The raw material for the disguise in which the unconscious clothes its wish
is the "day residue"—the events of the immediately preceding
day. "In every dream it is possible to find a point of contact
with the experiences of the previous day," but dreams "make
their selection" from those immediately previous events "upon
different principles from our waking memory, since they do
not recall what is essential and important but what is subsidiary
and unnoticed" (197). Carver's sequential stories behave in similar fashion: each successive one functioning like a dream, picking up details left over from the immediately preceding story
—details that are generally of quite minor significance there—
and using them as raw material for its own narrative. We earlier
saw Freud's dream analysis emerge as a model for understanding how these stories work when we found that the protagonist
of "Night School" was caught up in the analysis of a dream that
repeated an event that seemed to have come from the immediately preceding story.

The birthday cake, as I was saying, returns in "Vitamins" as
the vitamins themselves. Or rather, the relatively unimportant
detail of the baker's halfhearted attempt to sell Mrs. Weiss the
cake at half price, together with his frustration at being unable
to sell it at all, returns in the form of Patti's inability to unload

her vitamins. Two details about that cake, its having dried out after three days ("There it sits . . . getting stale") and it's having almost become the body of the boy whose name is on it ("Your Scotty, I got him ready for you" [83], the taunting voice on the phone said to the grieving mother *after* her son had died, as if he had his corpse ready for burial), also recur, in the form of something that resembles a piece of stale food: "It looked like a dried mushroom" (106). It is the "dried-up" (107) severed ear of an enemy soldier, brought back from Vietnam by Nelson, a sinister black vet the narrator encounters in the back room of Khaki's Off-Broadway Bar. The narrator was there with Donna, one of his wife's vitamin salespeople, and he had been confident of scoring with her until Nelson sat down at their table and spoiled things by showing them the ear and by proposing to purchase Donna's sexual services.

Other minor details from the immediately preceding story emerge again here. When Ann Weiss realized whom the calls were coming from, she and her husband drove to the shopping center where the bakery was located.

> The sky was *clear and stars were out.* . . . They parked in front of the bakery. All of the shops and stores were closed. . . . The bakery windows were dark, but when they looked through the glass they could see a light in the *back room.* . . . They drove around behind the bakery and parked. . . . She knocked on the door and waited. . . . "I'm closed for business," he said. "What do you want at this hour? It's midnight. Are you drunk or something?" (85; emphasis added)

It was the same hour of night when the narrator of "Vitamins" left work and went with Donna to Khaki's bar: "I'd walked out of the hospital just after *midnight*" (100; emphasis added). The baker complained that he was "closed for business . . . at this hour," while the narrator was in the habit of frequenting the Off-Broadway "because I could get a drink there *after closing hours*" (99; emphasis added). The weather was precisely the same: "It'd *cleared* up *and stars were out.*" The baker's accusation that the Weisses were "drunk or something" was genuinely true in the narrator's case: "I still had this buzz on from the Scotch I'd had." The Weisses had to go to the back room of the bakery, as the narrator goes to the back room of the bar: "The front half of the Off-Broadway was like a regular café and bar. . . . We went through the café and into the big *room in back*" (101; emphasis added).

The recurrence of details is naturally puzzling. Why should the scene in Khaki's bar come this close to repeating the scene in the bakery? What does the confrontation with the black Vietnam vet have to do with the confrontation with the baker? To the extent that Carver's stories recycle residual details from their immediate predecessors as dreams recycle day residue, this question might not really have an answer, because what dreams are devised to express is not the hidden meaning of what happened the day before but the repressed wishes of the unconscious. The day residue is just the clothing of the disguise. With these stories, however, the situation is a little more complicated, for each preceding one is not only a fund of leftover residue to be mined for raw material for the next, but is itself—by virtue of its relation to *its* immediate predecessor, if for no other reason—something like a dream. And of course there are other reasons for saying Carver's stories are like dreams, as "A Small, Good Thing" for instance reveals when it shows itself, as does "The Compartment," to be a dream about the death of his son.

Perhaps it would be more accurate to say a *daydream.* In "The Relation of the Poet to Day-Dreaming" Freud suggests that the imaginative writer is a daydreamer, and that a daydreamer is like a child at play: "Every child at play behaves like an imaginative writer, in that he creates a world of his own or, more truly, he rearranges the things of his world and orders it in a new way that pleases him better. . . . Now the writer does the same as the child at play; he creates a world of phantasy which he takes very seriously" (35). Freud also maintains that daydreams and night dreams are really the same. "Language, in its unrivalled wisdom, long ago decided the question of the essential nature of dreams by giving the name of 'day-dreams' to the airy creations of phantasy. If the meaning of our dreams usually remains obscure in spite of this clue, it is because of the circumstance that at night wishes of which we are ashamed also become active in us. . . . Such repressed wishes . . . can therefore achieve expression only when almost completely disguised" (39). Normally, he writes, we would find other persons' daydreams boring, if not in fact repellent. "But when a man of literary talent . . . relates what we take to be his personal daydreams, we experience great pleasure. . . . The writer softens the egotistical character of the day-dream by changes and disguises, and he bribes us by the offer of a purely formal, that is, aesthetic, pleasure in the presentation of his phantasies" (42–43). So the writer's ability to disguise his daydreams to make them more palatable to the reader performs the same task as the dream work of the unconscious, which disguises its repressed wishes in order to express them without the conscious realizing what they mean. Carver's stories, I believe, are daydreams to the extent that through his art he has made his fantasies palatable to the reader; yet they resemble night dreams to the degree that they treat their immediate predecessor in his short story sequences as day residue to be transformed into the fabric of its disguises. Freud does not say whether the "changes and disguises" the successful writer exerts on his daydreams are consciously or unconsciously done; it is quite probable they are a mixture of both. Certainly what happens in nocturnal dreams is an unconscious phenomenon. We have seen in Carver some evidence of conscious change in the alterations he has made in his stories so that they will "couple" (in the railroad sense) better in sequence. Yet surely much of what we are uncovering here is unconscious as well, and thus all the more intriguing.

But if we are going to try to tackle the question of the reason for the resemblance between the back room of the bakery and the back room of Khaki's bar we must first be sure we are in command of all the details of that resemblance. One parallel that needs to be made more explicit is the one between Nelson and the baker. Both are sinister, in fact downright mean, and both threaten violence. Nelson had *"little* red *eyes"* (102; emphasis added); while Ann Weiss found, when she first

set eyes on the baker, that his *"eyes* were *small,* mean-looking"
(86; emphasis added). Nelson threatens violence by attributing
the thought of it to the narrator: "I bet you thinking, 'Now
here a big drunk nigger and what am I going to do with him?
Maybe I have to whip his ass for him!' That what you thinking?" (104–5). Likewise the baker had made a show of warning
against violence at the very moment he was brandishing a
weapon: "A look crossed Ann's face that made the baker move
back and say, 'No trouble, now.' He reached to the counter and
picked up a rolling pin with his right hand and began to tap it
against the palm of his other hand. . . . The baker continued to
tap the rolling pin against his hand. He glanced at Howard,
'Careful, careful,' he said to Howard" (86).

Yet at this point the resemblance surely ends, for the encounter with Nelson ends on an angry note while the meeting
with the baker is suddenly transformed, when Ann Weiss tells
him what happened to her son, into a reconciliation. Benny,
who was a friend of the narrator's, had brought Nelson over to
be introduced. Unfortunately, they decided to join the narrator
at his table. What begins as a friendly gesture, at least on Benny's part, will soon turn into something much uglier, as Nelson
becomes increasingly aggressive. What began, however, as a
hostile confrontation turned into something much more amia-
ble in the other story when the baker, in sudden contrition,
"cleared a space for them at the table. . . . Howard and Ann sat
down and pulled their chairs up to the table. The baker sat
down, too. 'Let me say how sorry I am,' the baker said" (87).
"Although they were tired and in anguish, they listened to what
the baker had to say. They nodded when the baker began to
speak of loneliness, and of the sense of doubt and limitation
that had come to him in his middle years. He told them what it
was like to be childless all these years" (88–89).

Why is it that these two back-room scenes should bear so
many ties of resemblance and yet turn out so differently? Have
we overlooked something that could resolve this discrepancy?

Well, yes—in one small detail that was added to "The Bath"
when it became "A Small, Good Thing." The family that Ann

Weiss had met in the hospital when she was looking for the elevator in "The Bath"—"she turned and saw a little waiting room, a family in there, all sitting in wicker chairs, a man in a khaki shirt, a baseball cap pushed back on his head, a large woman wearing a housedress, slippers, a girl in jeans, hair in dozens of kinky braids" (55)—has been transformed into a *black* family: "she turned to her right and entered a little waiting room where a Negro family sat in wicker chairs. There was a middle-aged man in a khaki shirt and pants. . . . A large woman wearing a housedress and slippers. . . . A teenaged girl in jeans, hair done in dozens of little braids" (73). One could argue that they were black already because of the "kinky braids" (since changed to "little" ones). But Carver's greater explicitness now makes it possible to see this family as a middle term between the baker and Nelson. Like Nelson, they are black—and the fact that these two consecutive stories should both feature black characters is itself worthy of comment, since there are otherwise so few in Carver's white working-class world. Like the baker, they are in a position to sympathize with Ann Weiss's plight, and to receive her sympathy in return. This was not particularly evident in "The Bath," where the only response Ann elicits when she tells them about her son's accident (he is not yet dead in either story) is that the father shakes his head and repeats his own son's name (56). In the revised version, the father responds to Ann's recital of her plight with an account of what happened to his son. "Our Franklin, he's on the operating table. Somebody cut him. . . . We're just hoping and praying, that's all we can do now" (74).

Not only does Carver strengthen the connection between the two stories by explicitly naming the family as black, but he goes on to give a name to the proprietor of the bar where the narrator encounters the sinister Nelson that comes directly from the description of the black father who commiserated with Ann Weiss. He was "a middle-aged man in a *khaki* shirt and pants," while the Off-Broadway Bar "was run by a spade named *Khaki*" (99; emphasis added). Khaki was a reassuring presence: the narrator might have had reason to fear for his

safety when he frequented this all-black establishment were it
not for Khaki's devotion to preserving the peace, and for his
friendly attitude toward him.

> A story went around once that somebody had followed some-
> body into the Gents and cut the man's throat while he had
> his hands down pissing. But I never saw any trouble. Nothing
> that Khaki couldn't handle. . . . If somebody started to get
> out of line, Khaki would go over to where it was beginning.
> He'd rest his big hand on the party's shoulder and say a few
> words and that was that. I'd been going there off and on for
> months. I was pleased that he'd say things to me, things like,
> "How're you doing tonight, friend?" Or, "Friend, I haven't
> seen you for a spell." (99–100)

Khaki came over at the right moment, when things were getting especially tense with Nelson. "Khaki had a hand on my
shoulder and the other one on Benny's shoulder. He leaned
over the table. . . .'How you folks? You all having fun?' " (106)
Benny assures him that they are, but the narrator takes advan-
tage of Khaki's presence to make his exit. "Khaki was watching
Nelson now. I stood beside the booth with Donna's coat. My
legs were crazy. Nelson raised his voice. He said, 'You go with
this mother here, you let him put his face in your sweets, you
both going to have to deal with me.' We started to move away
from the booth. . . . We didn't look back. We kept going" (107).
      Khaki's name gives us the clue we need. The amiable pro-
prietor of the Off-Broadway Bar is the reincarnation of the
khaki-clad father who commiserates in as friendly a way as their
circumstances permit with Ann Weiss, while Nelson is that of
the baker in his menacing mode. The black father anticipates
the baker's other mode by offering sympathy to Ann Weiss and
receiving hers in return, as does the baker in the final scene.
The bakery and the bar can with appropriateness resemble
each other so much (the clear night sky, the stars, the midnight
hour, the back rooms in both instances) because the baker's two
personae—his sinister side and his commiserating side—are
represented, alternately, by Nelson and Khaki together at the
narrator's table.

In "Fires," Carver tells a curious anecdote that tells us significantly more about just how it was that Nelson came to stand for that menacing baker.

> Not so long ago in Syracuse, where I live, I was in the middle of writing a short story when my telephone rang. I answered it. On the other end of the line was the voice of a man who was obviously a black man, someone asking for a party named Nelson. It was a wrong number and I said so and hung up. I went back to my short story. But pretty soon I found myself writing a black character into my story, a somewhat sinister character whose name was Nelson. At that moment the story took a different turn. But happily it was, I see now, and somehow knew at the time, the right turn for the story. (*Fires*, 29–30)

Nelson's name, as well as his presence in the story at all, was thus due to the purest chance: "This character found his way into my story with a coincidental rightness I had the good sense to trust" (30). But it is a coincidence on top of a coincidence, for his name is the same as that of the son over whom the father in khaki was in anguish in "The Bath": " 'Nelson,' the woman said. 'Is it about Nelson?' . . . The man shifted in his chair. He shook his head. He said, 'Our Nelson' " (55–56). Carver changed the name to Franklin in "A Small, Good Thing": was he covering his tracks? Was the anecdote about the telephone call a ruse? Surely not, yet that phone call itself seems to come right out of this story about the effects of a mysteriously sinister voice on the phone. By comparing in detail the scene in the back room of the bakery with the one in the back room of Khaki's bar we explored the remarkable extent to which the baker who made those calls resembles that "somewhat sinister character whose name was Nelson." Carver's anecdote about the fortuitous event that interrupted, yet influenced the writing of "Vitamins," while appearing to stress how much Nelson's presence in that story is the product of chance, actually reveals how much that story grows out of the one that immediately precedes it in *Cathedral*'s unfolding sequence.

One more incident in "Vitamins" deserves our attention, for its strange resemblance to something that happened in "A Small, Good Thing" can, I think, be interpreted. It takes place early in "Vitamins," quite possibly before Carver's phone rang with the wrong number, because it would appear not to have much to do with Nelson. Yet it has a lot to do with the death of the Weisses' son. Sheila, one of the vitamin sellers working under the narrator's wife, Patti, "passed out on her feet, fell over, and didn't wake up for hours" (93). It happened at a Christmas party Patti gave for her employees. Sheila had had too much to drink. "One minute she was standing in the middle of the living room, then her eyes closed, the legs buckled, and she went down with a glass in her hand. . . . Patti and I and somebody else lugged her out to the back porch and put her down on a cot and did what we could to forget about her" (93). Sheila's sudden collapse into unconsciousness uncannily repeats Scotty's: "he suddenly lay back on the sofa, closed his eyes, and went limp" (61). Why should this be so? What does Sheila have in common with the Weisses' son?

The answer draws us back to our reading of "A Small, Good Thing" as it coupled with "The Compartment"—to the father's daydream of the death of his son. Myers, we recall, had been locked in Oedipal conflict with his son. Although he accused him of turning "the young girl [Myers] had courted and wed into a nervous, alcoholic woman whom the boy alternately pitied and bullied," the son on another occasion had sought to come to his mother's rescue, to show her he loved her more than his father did. It had happened in a family dispute when she began angrily breaking china plates, and Myers uttered what the son interpreted as a threat: " 'That's enough,' Myers had said, and at that instant the boy charged him" (47). Now in the eyes of the narrator of "Vitamins" Sheila, like Myers's son, was a rival for his wife's affections. "One night this Sheila said to Patti that she loved her more than anything on earth. Patti told me these were the words. . . . Then Sheila touched Patti's breast. Patti . . . told her she didn't swing that way" (92–93). Sheila's sudden collapse into unconsciousness, by recalling Scotty's, shows the extent to which a father's jealousy, already invoked in "The Compartment," presides in secret over the events of "A Small, Good Thing." There is absolutely no evidence of this in "A Small, Good Thing" considered by itself— Howard Weiss's expressions of grief are genuine, and heart-rending to read. But when we consider the larger underlying narrative that extends to the stories on either side (not to mention such a text as "On an Old Photograph of My Son") we can see a father's jealousy at work. Sheila, as the rival for his wife's affections, stands—or rather, falls—for the hated son. In our reading of "The Bath" in the context of the stories that accompanied it in *What We Talk About When We Talk About Love,* we found what lay behind the apparently innocent image of a son sitting on the sofa with his mother, which was what Scotty was doing just before he lapsed into the coma from which he never recovered. It is reason enough to justify a father's jealous rage.

When Sheila fell her hand had struck the coffee table, and when she woke the next morning "she was sure her little finger was broken. She showed it to me. It looked purple" (93). Later it grew "as big as a pocket flashlight" (94). "But she'd made a serious pass at Patti, a declaration of love, and I didn't have any sympathy." We have seen before, in "Fat," how phallic fingers can be. This tumescent digit, which though it belongs to a woman in fact belongs to an Oedipal son, has received a symbolically castrating blow.

"Careful"

The next story begins, too, with a woman having apparently fallen into unconsciousness on the living room floor. "Once . . . he stopped on the landing and looked into his landlady's living room. He saw the old woman lying on her back on the carpet. She seemed to be asleep. Then it occurred to him she might be dead. But the TV was going, so he chose to think she was asleep. He didn't know what to make of it" (111–12). It's hard for us to know what to make of it either, for nothing happens later in "Careful" to integrate it into the story, which concerns not the old woman but her lodger, Lloyd, who stumbles across the sight of her deathlike slumber. It's almost as if this woman dead asleep on the living room carpet were something left over from the previous story—a kind of day residue, to use the term from Freud's dream analysis that has, as I have indicated, a certain relevance to how Carver puts his story collections together. Indeed, in the Alton interview Carver said that the germ of a story or poem is for him often, quite literally, residue: "I never start with an idea. I always *see* something. I start with an image, a cigarette being put out in a jar of mustard, for instance, or the remains, the wreckage, of a dinner left on the table. Pop cans in the fireplace, that sort of thing" (*Conversations*, 154).[2] Carver's point of course is that his stories begin with an image. But the choice of images he provides tells us something more, for they are all images of debris, of remnants left over from a previous event.

Two of the remarks the observant Lloyd makes, however, do serve a purpose beyond his awareness, thanks to Carver's practice of planting resemblances in his sequentially occurring stories. That "it occurred to him she might be dead" confirms the suspicion that Sheila's similarly unconscious state was likewise a semblance of death—not hers of course but Scotty's. And that "he chose to think she was asleep" echoes the doctor's words with which the Weisses tried to comfort themselves in the hospital: "Now he simply seemed to be in a very deep sleep —but no coma, Dr. Francis had emphasized" (61). "Howard gazed at his son. . . . Scotty was fine, but instead of sleeping at home in his own bed, he was in a hospital bed" (65). The landlady was evidently not dead, for the lodger later "saw the old woman down in the yard, wearing a straw hat and holding her

2. When Alton later asks Carver about the role of the unconscious in his work, he acknowledges its relevance: "JA: You have a dream motif in many stories [he mentions "The Student's Wife," "Elephant," and "Whoever Was Using This Bed"]. There are several more that involved dreams occurring, and I wonder what importance you place on the unconscious mind and its relation to the kind of surface reality you record. You get at the unconscious only in an indirect way. . . . I wonder if you think about it much. RC: I don't think about it very much. It may be one of those things you don't think about but that's sometimes relevant to your work" (*Conversations*, 164).

hand against her side" (112). That something might be wrong with her hand recalls the injury Sheila's hand received in her descent: "The hand holding the drink smacked the coffee table when she fell" (93). As residue from the immediately preceding story, the scene of the woman asleep on the living room floor persists, even though it seems to have no immediate relevance to the story it finds itself in now. On the other hand, we can see that it has a great deal of relevance to the sequence in which the story appears, confirming the interpretation to which Sheila's collapse gave rise—that she was a figure for the son as rival for the wife's affections.

Sheila's—and Scotty's—reappearance in the form of the woman on the floor is not, however, the residue from which Carver has fashioned his story. That role belongs to another piece of detritus—a classic case perhaps of one man's trash being another's treasure—left over from the story just before: the object of disgust Nelson showed off in the Off-Broadway Bar, the body part retrieved from the corpse of a Viet Cong soldier. "I looked at the ear inside. It sat on a bed of cotton. It looked like a dried mushroom. But it was a real ear, and it was hooked up to a key chain. . . . 'I took it off one of them gooks,' Nelson said. 'He couldn't hear nothing with it no more. I wanted me a keepsake' " (106–7). The whole story recounted in "Careful" turns upon the problem Lloyd is having with his ear: "He'd awakened that morning and found that his ear had stopped up with wax. He couldn't hear anything clearly, and he seemed to have lost his sense of balance, his equilibrium, in the process. For the last hour, he'd been on the sofa, working frustratedly on his ear, now and again slamming his head with his fist" (113). A problem, as it happens, of too much residue.

Lloyd, an alcoholic who has taken up drinking champagne, is living apart from his wife. But Inez does pay a visit to his third-floor apartment that morning, just as he has worried himself into a helpless state over his ear. As he tells her his tale of woe the chain to which Nelson had attached his keepsake (Nelson "took up the chain and dangled the ear. . . . He let it swing back and forth on the chain" [107]) returns here too, in the chain attached to Lloyd's memory of the last time he had this

problem. "My ear's plugged up. You remember that other time
it happened? We were living in that place near the Chinese
take-out joint. Where the kids found that bulldog dragging its
chain? I had to go to the doctor then and have my ears flushed
out" (114–15). Inez is willing to do what she can to help but
unfortunately her nail-file technique (she couldn't find a hairpin) is neither safe nor effective. But she does have the bright
idea of going downstairs to ask his landlady if she "has any
Wesson oil, or anything like that. She might even have some
Q-tips. I don't know why I didn't think of that before. Of asking her" (119).

She returns with baby oil, and some good advice on how to
use it: warm the oil, pour it in the ear, and massage gently.
"She said it used to happen to her husband. . . . She said try
this. And she didn't have any Q-tips. I can't understand that,
her not having any Q-tips. That part really surprises me" (120).
Inez still doesn't understand that putting any solid object into
the ear, whether hairpin or Q-tip, is only going to push the wax
deeper in, though her stubborn insistence on procuring cotton
swabs does serve the purpose of recalling the "bed of *cotton*" on
which Nelson's ear was displayed. However, by following Mrs.
Matthews's instructions to the letter, success is achieved. "He
heard a car pass on the street outside the house and, at the back
of the house, down below his kitchen window, the clear *snick-
snick* of pruning shears. . . . 'I'm all right! I mean, I can *hear*. It
doesn't sound like you're talking underwater anymore' " (121–
22).

So the old woman whose supine state resembled death did
have an important part to play after all. It's just that her unconsciousness, whether from having blacked out or simply from
sleep, still seems a naggingly irrelevant episode, troubling because of its apparent lack of purpose. We went some distance
toward making sense of its presence in the story when we
found how it served to confirm our sense of what was going on
in the sequence at this point. But I think I can now show that
that opening scene has more to do in the story—and not just
in the sequence—than that.

Let us look once more at Lloyd's behavior the day the principal events of the story take place: "He was on the sofa, in his pajamas, hitting his fist against the right side of his head. Just before he could hit himself again, he heard voices downstairs on the landing. . . . He gave his head another jolt with his fist, then got to his feet" (113). At that moment we had no idea *why* he was hitting his head with his fist. We would learn the reason in the next paragraph—that it was because his ear is stopped up—but before we did his self-inflicted blows had the stage to themselves, and they were incomprehensible. And they continue: "Now and again slamming his head with his fist" (113). "He pounded his head a good one" (114). "He whacked his head once more" (116).

All that we have seen up to now of the way the stories in *Cathedral* and in the two earlier collections retain echoes of prior events, words, and gestures should justify my making the following hypothesis. In slamming his fist against his head Lloyd was not only trying to clear the obstruction in his ear, but as a figure for the father in the ongoing narrative hidden in the sequence of these stories he was also trying to inflict on himself the injury his son had suffered—the son whose death he had wished for in "The Compartment," the son who died in "A Small, Good Thing." For the father in "The Compartment" had in fact "*slammed* him into the wall" as Lloyd kept "slamming his head with his fist," while Scotty suffered a "hairline fracture of the skull" (66) that was caused by his head hitting the pavement ("He fell on his side with his head in the gutter" [61]) and died from "a hidden occlusion" (80). An occlusion is the stopping up, the closing, the obstruction of a passage—in Scotty's case something like a blood vessel in the brain, in Lloyd's the auditory canal of his ear.

Something really does *happen* in the buried narrative hidden between Carver's stories: one event succeeds another. The father desires the son's death, then the son dies, and then the father, chastened by the fulfillment of his wish, repents of his desire and tries in his anguish to turn the suffering inflicted on the child upon himself. But then something else takes place, and that is the reason the old woman downstairs who provides the remedy for Lloyd's suffering was first glimpsed passed out on the living room floor as if she were dead, repeating Sheila's collapse that itself repeats the son's. For by her recreation of Scotty's coma she becomes, in the buried narrative the sequence tells, the son (as Sheila had when she took on the son's Oedipal role of rival for the wife's affections). And by providing the cure for Lloyd's head pounding and for his auricular occlusion, she delivers the son's forgiveness. (It is not perhaps by accident that it should appear in the form of *"baby* oil," instead of the cooking oil Inez had originally requested.) That reconciliation, of course, is this father's deepest desire. For the same poem where Carver confesses "Oh, son, in those days I wanted you dead" ends with these words: "But don't / worry, my boy—the pages turn, my son. We all / do better in the future" ("On an Old Photograph of My Son").

These stories tell this story by recycling each other's details (for example, the ear) as dreams do the residue of the immediately preceding day, so it is fitting that Lloyd should doubt the permanence of the cure just effected and fear his malady might return *as he slept:* "He began to feel afraid of the night that was coming. . . . What if, in the middle of the night he accidentally turned on his right side, and the weight of his head pressing into the pillow were to seal the wax again in the dark canals of his ear? . . . 'Good God,' he said. . . . 'I just had something like a terrible nightmare' " (122–23). It is fitting, too, that this fear of falling asleep should invoke not only the fate that befell the son (who fell into a sleep from which he never awoke) but also the dread Patti evidently had of falling asleep and having dreams that offered her no solace, just the same worries that had fatigued her throughout the day. "I even dream of vitamins when I'm asleep. I don't have any relief. There's no relief! At least you can walk away from your job and leave it behind. I'll bet you haven't had one dream about it. I'll bet you don't dream about waxing floors or whatever you do down there" (97). Her husband performs janitorial duties in a hospital. It's a remarkable coincidence that she should complain that her husband doesn't dream of *wax.*

"Where I'm Calling From"

After Inez's departure, even though his ear is, at least for the moment, cleared of its obstruction, Lloyd still must face his other problem—his addiction to champagne. "In the beginning, he'd really thought he could continue drinking if he limited himself to champagne. But in no time he found he was drinking three or four bottles a day" (119). On the next to last page of the story we find him taking a fresh bottle out of the fridge. "He *worked* the plastic cork out of the bottle as *carefully* as he could, but there was still the festive *pop* of champagne being opened" (124; first two emphases added). These words form some resonant echoes. When his ear was stopped up, Lloyd thought that "it felt like it had when he used to swim near the bottom of the municipal pool" (115) and "his ears would *pop*" (116; emphasis added) when he cleared the water out of them by blowing with his mouth and nose closed tight. Before Inez arrived he had been *"working* frustratedly on his ear" (113; emphasis added). And of course the title, already repeated in Lloyd's plea to "Be *careful*" (118; emphasis added), reappears in the adverb that describes how he worked the cork out of the bottle. Not surprisingly, that cork bears a close resemblance to what the landlady once saw emerge from her husband's ear. "this one time she saw a piece of wax fall out of his ear, and it was like a big plug of something" (120).

This conclusion to "Careful" not only recalls the events that had preceded it but anticipates the subject of the story to follow, which takes place at a "drying-out facility" for confirmed alcoholics. Lloyd's favorite drink is what the narrator consumed en route to the sanitarium: "We drank champagne all the way" (138). Early in the story the narrator witnesses the same kind of event that Lloyd had glimpsed as he mounted the stairs to his apartment. Tiny, one of the inmates at Frank Martin's farm, "was *on his back on the floor* with his eyes closed" (128; emphasis added), as Mrs. Matthews had been "lying *on her back on the carpet*" (111; emphasis added) with her eyes closed as if she were asleep. We never find out why she was doing that; Tiny was having a quasi-epileptic seizure, apparently brought on by alcoholism. The narrator spends most of the story listening, primarily to fellow drunk J.P., who first tells him how he fell into a well when he was twelve, and then how he met his wife. Both episodes repeat significant elements of what Lloyd went through in the story before.

> It was a dry well, lucky for him. . . . But he told me that being at the bottom of that well had made a lasting impression. He'd sat there and looked up at the well mouth. Way up at the top, he could see a circle of blue sky. . . . A flock of birds flew across, and it seemed to J.P. their wingbeats set up this odd commotion. He heard other things. He heard tiny rustlings above him in the well, which made him wonder if things might fall down into his hair. . . . He heard wind blow over the well mouth, and that sound made an impression on him, too. In short, everything about his life was different for him at the bottom of the well. But nothing fell on him and nothing closed off that little circle of blue. Then his dad came along with the rope, and it wasn't long before J.P. was back in the world he'd always lived in. (130)

Lloyd described what it felt like to have his ear stopped up in ways that anticipate J.P.'s experience both of being trapped in a cylinder and of hearing how cylinders distort sounds. "When I talk, I feel like I'm talking inside a barrel. My head rumbles. . . . When *you* talk, it sounds like you're talking through a lead pipe" (115). J.P.'s being "at the bottom of that well" recalls Lloyd's memory of being "near the bottom of the municipal pool" (115) when he had had the same sensation in his ears. When the wax was removed, he could hear things like the "rustlings" and the wind blowing over the mouth of the well: "Lloyd heard the sound her breath made as it came and went . . . the clear *snick-snack* of pruning shears" (121–22). J.P.'s terror of something falling on him from above parallels the claustrophobia induced by the sharply slanting ceiling of Lloyd's top-floor apartment. "He had to stoop to look from his windows and be careful getting in and out of bed" (111). That too-low ceiling contributed to the terror he felt at the thought of his ear problem returning: "What if he woke up then, unable to hear, the ceiling inches from his head?" (122–23). J.P. was rescued by clinging to his father's rope; Lloyd had been at the end of his: "he'd tried everything he could think of, and he was nearing the end of his rope" (114).

Lloyd's rescue is evoked in the most remarkable way by the other story J.P. tells. It was Lloyd's wife (with help from the landlady downstairs) who managed to clean out his occluded canal, while what made J.P. fall in love with the woman who became his wife was the fact that she cleaned out obstructed passages for a living.[3] Roxy was a professional chimney sweep with all the traditional regalia of the trade and had shown up to clean the chimney at the house of a friend J.P. was visiting. "She's wearing a top hat, the sight of which knocked J.P. for a loop. . . . She spreads a blanket on the hearth and lays out her gear" (131)—as, with much less aplomb, Inez had "emptied the purse out onto the sofa. 'No hairpins,' she said. 'Damn' " (117). The sexy chimney sweep is "wearing these black pants, black shirt, black shoes and socks. . . . J.P. says it nearly drove him nuts to look at her. She does the work, she cleans the chimney. . . . J.P. and his friend . . . raise their eyebrows when the upper half of the young woman disappears into the chimney" (131).

What are we to make of these two particular bits of recycling: Lloyd's ear blockage transformed into J.P.'s falling into a well and one wife's ear cleaning become another wife's chimney

---

3. In her short story "Turpentine," Tess Gallagher has her narrator tell practically the same tale and make the same connection between the shape of a well and the shape of a chimney: "A chimney sweep had come to our house not long ago. He'd learned his trade in Germany, where the sweeps go to weddings and kiss all the women on the cheeks for luck. He'd told an incredible story about falling into a well at the age of twelve. He'd had to be rescued by his father. . . . His affection for chimneys, he thought, was entirely due to the excitement and danger of his falling into a well when he was twelve" (*The Lover of Horses*, 12). Ginny Skoyles, who tells this story, found that people were always telling her their life stories and confesses that "sometimes I told them back one of the stories someone else had told me. And once in a while I told it back as though it had happened to me. It was harmless enough and it gave me something to say" (60). Gallagher's narrator, in other words, is a thief of stories. In an oddly self-referential way, so too is the author of the story—or Carver, depending on who told it first.

sweeping? Their effect, I believe, is to justify my hypothesis about the sleeping Mrs. Matthews. I had suggested that the person really responsible for curing Lloyd's malady was the landlady, that his wife was only the medium through which her cure was effected, and furthermore that the old lady passed out on the carpet really represented the son, who was symbolically saving his father from his self-inflicted pain. What happens in the first of these two episodes in "Where I'm Calling From" is that the father-son relationship that I had said was behind Lloyd's aural occlusion has now been brought out into the open: here a father rescues a son; in "Careful" it was the other way around. Each story is a complement to the other, as so many story pairs have shown themselves to be. And the wife still has a part to play, but her contribution has been separated out and re-presented in a totally *different* story.

Near the end of "Where I'm Calling From" a scene takes place that both repeats the scene near the beginning of "Careful" in which Lloyd spied on his landlady stretched out on her living room rug and does so in terms of a father-son connection. Lloyd had glanced into his landlady's apartment on his way up the stairs; here, the narrator, in bed with his wife on a Sunday morning, thinks he can hear something outside the window. His wife suddenly remembers who it must be: the landlord, who was going to paint the exterior of the house.

> I push the curtain away from the window. . . . It's the landlord, all right—this old guy in coveralls. But his coveralls are too big for him. . . . And a wave of happiness comes over me that I'm not him—that I'm me and that I'm inside this bedroom with my wife. . . . The old fart breaks into a grin. It's then I realize I'm naked. . . . I can see the old fellow nod to himself like he's saying, "Go on, sonny, go back to bed. I understand." He tugs on the bill of his cap. Then he sets about his business. He picks up his bucket. He starts climbing the ladder. (145)

Everything is reversed. The landlady has become a landlord. The protagonist has changed from voyeur into someone whose nakedness is the object of someone else's gaze—while in both cases the person doing the viewing is climbing up (the stairs, a ladder) at the time. That the landlady represented the son (not Lloyd's son, of course, but the son of the father whose presence haunts these stories from "The Compartment" on) is evidenced by the fact that in this reversal the landlord addresses the narrator—"Go on, sonny, go back to bed"—as if he were a father speaking to his son. It is the reversal, that is, of the landlady as son and the lodger as father. And the forgiveness that I contended the son was extending to his father by offering the remedy that would make him stop slamming his fist against his skull—that filial forgiveness has now become a paternal blessing: "Go on, sonny. . . . I understand."

"The Train"

"The Train," which is inscribed "for John Cheever," begins where Cheever's "The Five-Forty-Eight" leaves off, with Miss Dent holding a gun on the man who had seduced her and then fired her from her job.[4] She had followed him into his train home to Shady Hill, sat next to him, and explained that she had a pistol in her purse. In the darkness past the station parking lot, as Carver picks up the story, "She'd made him get down in the dirt and plead for his life. While the man's eyes welled with tears and his fingers picked at leaves, she pointed the revolver at him and told him things about himself. . . . 'Be still!' she'd said, although the man was only digging his fingers into the dirt and moving his legs a little out of fear" (147). Blake's terror, and especially the way his eyes "*welled* with tears," evokes J.P.'s terrifying experience at the bottom of the well, though it was J.P. who said that "being at the bottom of that well *had made a lasting impression*" (130) on him, and Miss Dent who "*knew she would remember for a long time* the sound he made through his

4. More precisely, it begins just before Cheever's story ends. Miss Dent walks away, leaving Blake in the dirt. When it was safe to do so, he gets up and makes his way home.

nose as he got down on his knees" (148; emphasis added). This persistent memory of the sound of his nose is an even more precise recycling of J.P.'s recollection of a similarly breathy noise: "He heard wind blow over the well mouth, and that sound made an impression on him, too" (130).

How is it that the scene of a son trapped and then rescued from deep in the ground by his *father* gets transformed into one of a *woman* trapping a man and forcing him to "get down in the dirt"? It is that what had been separated into two stories in "Where I'm Calling From"—the plot of "Careful" divided into the episode at the well and J.P.'s courtship of his chimney-sweep wife—has been put together again into one. For Miss Dent, while putting her victim through an experience that re-calls J.P.'s in the well, at the same time bears a significant resem-blance to J.P.'s wife: both are women extraordinarily capable of violence. Miss Dent had "held a gun on a man . . . she put her foot on the back of his head and pushed his face into the dirt" (147), and Roxy "is a woman who can make fists if she has to" (143). "Her hands are broad and the fingers have these big knuckles. This woman broke a man's nose once" (142).[5]

In "The Train" Miss Dent leaves the man groveling in the dirt and goes into the station to wait for the next train back to the city. An odd couple enter, an elderly man wearing stockings but no shoes and a middle-aged woman who speaks to him in a mixture of Italian and English. They seem to be discussing a cocktail party they have just left, and what they say to each other is as opaque to the reader as it must have been to Miss Dent, something about a girl "alone in a house filled with simps and vipers," an "imbecile they call Captain Nick" (150), "*café au lait* and cigarettes, their precious Swiss chocolate and those goddamned macaws" (151), and having to sit through "home movies about Point Barrow, Alaska" (152).[6] There is nothing I can think of in any other Carver story to compare to this bar-

5. The man was J.P., with whom she would trade blows in the troubled years of their marriage (134).

6. Mark Facknitz was also struck by the incoherence of the scene: "We eavesdrop, but learn little. In fact, the more they say, the less we know. Why

rage of pointless information, pointless, that is, until we realize that it does serve at least one function: it puts Miss Dent in the same situation in which "The Train" puts the reader who does not know Cheever's story. Carver after all does not tell us exactly how his story is an homage to Cheever; he doesn't tell us which Cheever story this is the sequel of, or even that this is one. Carver's story in fact can stand alone, just like all the others in *Cathedral* (which is to say that it can also be part of a larger whole, as they are); we don't need to have read Cheever's story to understand Carver's. Yet while all that is true, Carver evidently still felt the need to put in his story some telltale sign that would make the reader feel that he or she has arrived on the scene too late, that a lot must have already happened before the story began.

What happens at the end of the story points in the same direction. As Miss Dent and the man and woman get on the train, "The passengers naturally assumed that the three people boarding were together; and they felt sure that whatever these people's business had been that night, it had not come to a happy conclusion" (155). As the old man had held the waiting room door for the middle-aged woman and then for Miss Dent, so that they emerged onto the platform with Miss Dent between them, this was not an unreasonable assumption. But in fact they were not together; neither had they transacted any business. The extent of their interaction in the waiting room had been: the man and Miss Dent exchanged a "Good evening" (148–49); Miss Dent silently shook her head when the woman said to her companion, "If you really must smoke, *she* may have a match" (149); the woman once referred to Miss Dent in the third person in the midst of an argument with the man (151); the woman eventually did address her directly: " 'You don't say much. But I'll wager you could say a lot if someone got you started. . . . What *do* they call you?' 'Miss Dent. But I don't know

---

is this man in his socks? What is all this about a trip to the North Pole? . . . The growing, inchoate set of questions suggests many meaningful and intriguing stories, none of which can cohere unless Miss Dent asks for elaborations, for sense" (346).

you' " (153); later, Miss Dent almost began to open a conversation, but just then the train pulled into the station. The three people boarding the train were just as much a closed book to the passengers already on the train as the couple's bizarre conversation had been to Miss Dent; more than that, by assuming they were together the passengers raise the same issue that the story itself raises by being an unannounced sequel to Cheever's "The Five-Forty-Eight": are the *stories* together or not?

It is of course the same question that Carver's stories always raise: are they to be read intertextually—in conjunction with the story just finished—or not? Are they all, in this sense, sequels?

"Fever"

Arthur Saltzman accurately observes that the narrator of "Where I'm Calling From" "is at first unwilling or unable to relate his own story. . . . Instead of confessing, the narrator persuades a fellow drunk, J.P., to tell his" (147). The woman in "The Train" makes the same observation about Miss Dent: "You don't say much. But I'll wager you could say a lot if someone got you started. Couldn't you? But you're a sly boots. You'd rather just sit with your prim little mouth while other people talk their heads off" (153). The wife in "Fever" likewise urges the husband she has left to talk it out: "Tell me about yourself," she said on the phone. "He told her the kids were fine. But before he could say anything else, she interrupted him to say, 'I know *they're* fine. What about *you?*' " (165).

"Fever" is the account of Carlyle's eventually successful effort to accept his wife's not coming back. He teaches art at a high school; Eileen ran away with the drama teacher, leaving Carlyle to cope with his two young children alone. After some bad experiences with babysitters, his luck changes dramatically when his wife puts him in touch with the grandmotherly Mrs. Webster. For six weeks things go beautifully, until Carlyle comes down with a severe bout of the flu. His fever and headaches keep him in bed for several days, while Mrs. Webster takes care of both him and the children.

During this time Eileen occasionally telephones to ask how he is and to say that her life has significantly improved since she left him, all in a trendy psychobabble about her "karma" and his that convinces Carlyle she is going crazy. "Eileen must be losing her mind to talk like that" (164). Her perceived insanity is mentioned at least a half-dozen times in the story. On one occasion even Eileen shows that she realizes how strange she must sound: " 'You may think I'm crazy or something,' she said. 'But just remember.' *Remember what?* Carlyle wondered in alarm, thinking he must have missed something she'd said" (168). On another Carlyle tells his girlfriend Carol why he's not going to answer the phone. "It's my wife. I know it's her. She's losing her mind. She's going crazy. I'm not going to answer it" (175). When he falls ill, Eileen advises him to keep a journal of his illness, just like Colette.[7] "She wrote a little book about what it was like, about what she was thinking and feeling the whole time she had this fever. . . . Right now you've just got this discomfort. You've got to translate that into something usable" (181). Carlyle can make no sense of what seemed like pointless advice. "It was clear to him that she was insane" (182).

Miss Dent was crazy too, in fact certifiably insane—had even been institutionalized for it—not in "The Train" but in Cheever's "The Five-Forty-Eight." "Oh, I know what you're thinking," she said as she sat next to Blake on the train, aiming the pistol in his direction from inside her purse.

> You're thinking that I'm crazy, and I have been very sick again but I'm going to be better. It's going to make me better

7. Which makes "Fever" the third story in a row to allude to other writers—John Cheever in the dedication to "The Train," and in "Where I'm Calling From" the author of *The Call of the Wild:* "Jack London used to have a big place on the other side of this valley," Frank Martin told his guests. "Right over there behind that green hill you're looking at. But alcohol killed him. Let that be a lesson to you. He was a better man than any of us. But he couldn't handle the stuff, either" (137).

> to talk with you. I was in the hospital all the time before I
> came to work for you but they never tried to cure me, they
> only wanted to take away my self-respect. . . . Even if I did
> have to kill you, they wouldn't be able to do anything to me
> except put me back in the hospital. (289)

She was evidently insane even before she came to work for him
and did not become so because he seduced her. In Cheever's
story, her vengeance is thus not so much the act of a woman
taking a stand against male injustice as it is the irrational act of
a poor demented soul. We can read Carver's "The Train" and
not realize this about her, as long as we do not follow the hint
his dedicatory lines to Cheever make and track down "The
Five-Forty-Eight." But if we do read Cheever's story and appreciate the extent to which Carver's "Train" is a sequel to it, then
we are also in a position to appreciate the extent to which
"Fever" is a sequel to both, and Eileen's craziness a distant echo
of Miss Dent's. This is particularly evident when we compare
Miss Dent's words: "You're thinking that I'm crazy" (289) to
Eileen's: "You may think I'm crazy" (168). More than this
unites Eileen to Cheever's heroine, for they both also share a
firm belief in the efficacy of the talking cure. "It's going to
make me better to talk with you," Miss Dent had said. And
later: "I won't harm you if you'll let me talk" (290). Eileen's
insistence that Carlyle articulate his thoughts during his illness
finally bears fruit when, in the midst of a splitting headache, he
begins to talk to Mrs. Webster, not about his fever but about
what Eileen's leaving means. "Mrs. Webster, there's something
I want you to know. For a long time, my wife and I loved each
other more than anything or anybody in the world" (184). And
he goes on at considerable length, spilling out all the thoughts
that had been pent up for so long and that had surely contributed, psychosomatically, to his having fallen sick. " 'There, it's
all right,' Mrs. Webster said. She patted his hand. He sat forward and began to talk again." The children came into the
room. "Carlyle looked at them and went on talking." They kept
quiet but started to giggle. "Carlyle went on talking. At first, his
head still ached. . . . But then his headache went away." He had

started "in the middle," after the birth of the children, but now he went back to the very beginning, when he and Eileen had first met. "You just keep talking, Mr. Carlyle," Mrs. Webster said. "Sometimes it's good to talk about it" (185). He talked so much more that the children had time to fall asleep and wake up again.

When he was finally all talked out, not only had his headache disappeared, but at last "he understood [the marriage] was over, and he felt able to let her go . . . it was something that had passed. And that passing . . . would become a part of him now, too, as surely as anything else he'd left behind" (186). Eileen, crazy as she may have seemed to him to be, was right about one thing. "Remember," she had said, "sickness is a message about your health and your well-being. It's telling you things" (181). His fever was trying to tell him something: it was telling him he had something to tell.

In the end it's Carlyle who begins to resemble Miss Dent. It did both of them good to talk it out. And it turns out they had almost the same dreams: earlier in the story, "when the alarm went off, he wanted to keep his eyes closed and keep on with the dream he was having. Something about a farmhouse. . . . Someone . . . was walking along the road carrying something. Maybe it was a picnic hamper. . . . In the dream, there seemed to exist a sense of well-being" (169). "I dream about picnics and heaven and the brotherhood of man," Miss Dent had told Blake (293).

Carlyle has at least one thing in common with Miss Dent's victim, too. Blake's eyes, we recall, had "*welled* with tears and his fingers picked at leaves" (147) (in a passage that recalled J.P.'s terror in the well). Carlyle "felt a *welling* in his chest as he kissed each of his children goodbye" (171).[8]

---

8. Cheever's story may provide the origin, too, for those almost unbearably troubling words the woman's son utters in Carver's story "Why, Honey?" (in *Will You Please Be Quiet, Please?*): "Kneel is what I say, kneel down is what I say, he said, that's the first reason why" (173). For they are what Miss Dent said to Blake: "When the train had passed beyond the bridge, the noise grew distant, and he heard her screaming at him, '*Kneel down!* Kneel down! Do

"The Bridle"

Like Carlyle, and like the Miss Dent of Cheever's story, Betty Holits too finds it helps to talk it out. "And that's fine with me," Marge tells us in "The Bridle." Marge is a hairstylist, and Betty is her customer. "They like to talk when they're in the chair" (198). Marge at the same time manages, with her husband, Harley, an apartment complex where the Holitses have rented a suite. But the more Betty talks the more it appears that the character in this story to which the protagonist of "Fever" bears the most resemblance is her husband, who like Carlyle is referred to by his last name as if it were his first. Holits, like Carlyle, had a wife (before Betty) who "lit out on them" (198), leaving him with two children to raise.

Holits, an unemployed farmer from Minnesota who has moved west with his family to look for work, had earlier developed a passionate interest in horses and bought a racehorse on which he pinned all his hopes. He named it Fast Betty, after his wife, but it didn't exactly live up to its name. When they moved into the apartment complex and were unloading their possessions from the car, Marge had seen him carry in "something [with] straps hanging from it" that she recognized as a horse's bridle (191–92). At the end of the story, after Holits sustains a head injury from a drunken leap one night from the roof of a cabana onto the deck of the pool and the family moves out a week later, Marge goes to clean the vacated apartment. Betty had left the rooms in unexpectedly tidy condition, but there was one thing left behind. "One of the bureau drawers is open and I go to close it. Back in a corner of the drawer I see the bridle he was carrying in when he first came. It must have been passed over in their hurry. But maybe it wasn't. Maybe the man *left it* on purpose" (208; emphasis added). At the end of "Fever" too we had seen Carlyle leaving something behind, the marriage his wife had walked out on: "their life together . . . was

---

what I say. *Kneel down!*' " (293). Note that not only is the command the same, but the accompanying phrase "what I say" appears in both passages. Could the son be speaking the torment of a seduced and abandoned lover?

something that had passed. And that passing . . . would become a part of him now, too, as surely as anything else he'd *left
behind*" (186; emphasis added).

The parallel is even greater if we can place any faith in the
possible pun between the *bridle* Holits left and the *bride* (or
bridal hopes) Carlyle left behind—or in Holits having named
the horse after his wife, so that its bridle, by evoking the horse,
evokes his bride. Betty recognizes the incongruity of the horse
bearing her name: "The Betty part is a joke. But he says it can't
help but be a winner if he names it after me. A big winner, all
right. The fact is, wherever it ran, it lost" (199).

The duplication of Betty's name is itself duplicated by the
odd way Marge duplicates *her* name on the fifty-dollar bills with
which the Holitses paid their first installment of rent: "I write
my name in ink across Grant's broad old forehead: MARGE. I
print it. I do it on every one. Right over his thick brows. People
will stop in the midst of their spending and wonder. Who's this
Marge?" (192) Marge is like Carver in this regard—not that he
keeps writing his name everywhere, but he does keep writing
the same words in different places, both between and within
his stories.[9] The activity in which Marge is here engaged offers
an intriguing case in point, for her disfiguration of U. S.
Grant's forehead is echoed in the climactic later scene of Holits's fall from the cabana roof:

> He dragged up one of the tables and climbed onto that. Then
> . . . he lifted up onto the roof of the cabana. . . . They're eg-
> ging him on. They're saying, "Go on, you can do it." "Don't
> belly-flop, now." "I double-dare you." Things like that.

9. Of which this is, among those published in the three collections studied here, the fiftieth. This would exclude *Furious Seasons,* which stands apart
from the rest of Carver's fiction because of the wholly untypical title story
("unusual among Carver's stories for its disruption of linear progression, its
conflation of dream and reality, and a surprising lushness of style" [Saltzman,
96]) and its not having been published by a major press. It would exclude the
stories in *Fires,* too, which unlike the other collections consists of poetry and
essays as well as stories. I do not think the stories in *Fires* or *Furious Seasons*
exhibit the sequential echoing structure of those considered here.

> Then I hear Betty's voice. "Holits, think what you're
> doing." But Holits just stands there at the edge. He looks
> down at the water. He seems to be figuring how much of a
> run he's going to have to make to get out there. He backs up
> to the far side. He spits in his palm and rubs his hands to-
> gether. . . . I see him hit the deck. . . . Holits has this gash on
> his forehead. (203)

Forehead, that is, is written into both scenes. Now is this done
haphazardly, promiscuously, as are Marge's MARGEs? Or is
there an underlying reason for this echo?

There are actually two.

Holits was trying to make a leap into the swimming pool
from the cabana roof, but he failed because he couldn't run
fast enough: "He seems to be figuring how much of a *run* he's
going to have to make to get out there." He thus came to
resemble his beloved Fast Betty, the horse that could never run
fast enough, that, "wherever it *ran,* it lost." His drunken and
foolish behavior would brand him for life with a scar on his
forehead in which one can read his identification with the horse
whose name is also the name of his wife. Thus does Marge's
gesture of inscribing her name on a man's forehead find its
echo in the trace of another wife's name.

His head injury at the same time recalls the headache and
fever Carlyle suffered in the immediately preceding story, for
as Holits's wound was self-inflicted so too, in the final analysis,
was Carlyle's psychosomatic illness. He fell sick because he
couldn't cope with his wife's having left him (and once he had
talked out all his feelings on that subject, he was suddenly cured
of his headache). Now while Holits's first wife did leave him in
apparently similar circumstances (left him, that is, with two
children to take care of by himself), his second wife Betty didn't.
Yet apparently it was despair that brought him to make his
near-suicidal leap, a despair that we may be able to understand
by paying attention to Marge's meditation on the meaning of
the bridle he left behind, in the concluding words of the story:

> "Bridle," I say. I hold it up to the window and look at it in
> the light. . . . I don't know much about them. But I know that

one part of it fits in the mouth. . . . Reins go over the head and up to where they're held on the neck between the fingers. The rider pulls the reins this way and that, and the horse turns. It's simple. The bit's heavy and cold. If you had to wear this thing between your teeth, I guess you'd catch on in a hurry. When you felt it pull, you'd know it was time. You'd know you were going somewhere.

Clearly, *bridle* here takes on a *bridal* connotation. Holits may have had the bridal bit between his teeth, but he had apparently lost the ability, and more importantly the will, to go where it was telling him to go: "I can't *go* it" (104; emphasis added), he had mysteriously said after he fell. " 'What'd he say?' . . . 'He said he can't go it. . . .' 'Go what? What's he talking about?' " It's understandable, after the failure of his farm and his long period of unemployment. He may have started working again, Marge thinks, just before the accident. But if so his injury and subsequent hospitalization have put an end to that; he no longer seems in full control of his faculties—when their friends wave at his departure he doesn't at first respond but then raises his hand and then "keeps waving at them, even after they've stopped" (207).[10]

Yet he has to keep on *going* all the same, as the conversation between Marge and Harley reveals, with its repeated emphasis on that word: "He asks me where they're going. But I don't have any idea where they're going. Maybe they're going back to Minnesota. How do I know where they're going? But I don't think they're going back to Minnesota. I think they're going someplace else to try their luck" (206).

"Cathedral"

Marge's fascination with the idea of her name cropping up in strange places, in the mouths of strangers—"People will stop

10. Holits has become a strange parody of the man in "Viewfinder" who climbed up on the roof of his garage, as Holits did on the roof of the cabana, and waved.

in the midst of their spending and wonder. Who's this Marge?"
—finds a precise counterpart in the wonderment the narrator
of "Cathedral" feels when his wife plays for him a tape from
her blind correspondent. Before her marriage to the narrator,
she had worked as a reader to Robert, and they had continued
to exchange tapes in the years since. "I was on the tape, she
said. . . . After a few minutes of harmless chitchat, I heard my
own name in the mouth of this stranger, this blind man I didn't
even know! And then this: 'From all you've said about him, I
can only conclude—' But we were interrupted, a knock at the
door, something, and we didn't ever get back to the tape" (212).
Marge's heart-to-heart talk with Betty Holits had suffered a
similar interruption: "I'm starting to tell how it was before we
moved here, and how it's still like that. But Harley picks right
then to come out of the bedroom" (201). And Betty "for some
reason . . . doesn't come back to get her hair done" any more
so the conversation is never resumed. The architecture of Raymond Carver's *Cathedral,* its ongoing sequence of contiguous
repetitions, is about to be broken off too, since "Cathedral" is
the last story in the collection. It is therefore fitting that one of
the last of these repetitions should be about the sudden interruption of discourse.

The narrator is at first annoyed by the news that Robert is
coming to visit. He has never had much to do with blind people
and knows he is going to feel uncomfortable. But Robert is a
jolly sort, who clearly enjoys good food, good whiskey, and
good dope, though it was his first time for the latter. "We
thought we'd have us some cannabis" (220), the narrator tells
his wife when she came back downstairs and encountered the
smell. High on pot, the blind man and the narrator sit up until
late into the evening, listening to a TV program about "the
church and the Middle Ages" (222) for which the narrator
gives Robert a running commentary. He does his best to depict
the spires, the gargoyles, and the flying buttresses. But realizing
the difficulty of describing a cathedral to someone who has
never seen one, he asks, "If somebody says cathedral to you, do
you have any notion what they're talking about?" (223–24)
Robert responds that he knows, since the man on the television

had just said as much, that "they took hundreds of workers fifty or a hundred years to build," that "the men who began their life's work on them, they never lived to see the completion of their work. In that wise, bub, they're no different from the rest of us, right?" (224) If Carver's *Cathedral* is self-naming, then the kind of cathedral it is is one of these unfinished ones, for the nature of its architecture is forever open-ended, each last word always open to the possibility of being succeeded by another.

The last word in this case is the final scene of the story, which finds the narrator trying to draw a cathedral on the "heavy paper" (226) the blind man had asked him to look for (an empty shopping bag served the purpose), pressing down very firmly with the pen so that Robert would be able to follow the tracings with his fingers. "So I began. First I drew a box that looked like a house. . . . Then I put a roof on it. At either end of the roof, I drew spires. Crazy" (227)—then windows, arches, gargoyles, people, and all. The blind man now tells him to close his eyes. " 'Keep them that way. . . . Don't stop now. Draw.' So we kept on with it. His fingers rode my fingers as my hand went over the paper. It was like nothing else in my life up to now" (228). But it *was* like something else, two stories before, in "Fever": " 'Like this, like this,' he said, guiding their hands. . . . 'Suggestion* is what it's all about,' he said, holding lightly to Sue Colvin's fingers as he guided her brush. 'You've got to work with your mistakes until they look intended. Understand?' " (172) Carlyle, we recall, was a high school art teacher. Should we take his advice? Should we work with the products of chance—what in his context are pupils' mistakes but in ours such possibly chance occurrences as the way this passage so strikingly anticipates the one that concludes the book until they look intended?

Or *are* they intended? I think they are intended to make us think, to feel a sense of wonder as we linger in Carver's *Cathedral* to explore some of its more obscure passages, to realize how—as at Chartres, for example—one image in stained glass or statuary responds to another somewhere else in the fabric (Joseph's coat of many colors to Jesus' seamless robe, his fall into the pit to Christ's descent into hell, or the silver cup hidden in the sack of grain to the chalice of the Eucharist). *"Suggestion,"* to adopt another piece of Carlyle's pedagogical advice, "is what it's all about."

Though distributed at different places in "Fever," two other moments anticipate what happens at the end of the title story. "At school, they were just leaving the medieval period and about to enter the Gothic" (176)—as were the narrator and Robert as they kept pace with the television broadcast. The "heavy paper" that Robert asked the narrator to procure, and that was indispensable for the effect he wanted him to create, had already appeared in a drawing "on heavy paper" Eileen had sent him "of a woman on a riverbank in a filmy gown, her hands covering her eyes, her shoulders slumped. It was, Carlyle assumed, Eileen showing her heartbreak over the situation" (164).

Yet the concluding scene where the blind man's fingers "rode" the narrator's as he drew the cathedral while both were high on cannabis recalls as well the conclusion of "The Bridle" when Holits was high on the cabana roof. For in his loser's run he was, as we have seen, acting the part of the horse wearing the bridle with reins that "go over the head and up to where they're held on the neck between the *fingers*. The *rider* pulls the reins this way and that, and the horse turns." And in a significant reversal, while at first it was the narrator who was in charge, drawing the cathedral on the heavy paper so that Robert could then move "the tips of his fingers over the paper" (227) to get some idea of what it looked like, by the time the story ends it's the blind man who is guiding the narrator, riding him with his fingers. He is showing him what it is like to be blind. He tells him to shut his eyes and then to keep on drawing. "His fingers rode my fingers as my hand went over the paper. It was like nothing else in my life up to now. Then he said, 'I think that's it. I think you got it' " (228), as if he were an art instructor congratulating his student. " 'Take a look. What do you think?' But I had my eyes closed. I thought I'd keep them that way for a little longer. . . . 'It's really something,' I said."

In a question-and-answer session at the University of Akron in 1982 Carver said that in his view to build a cathedral was to engage in a collaborative endeavor. "This is a farfetched analogy, but it's in a way like building a fantastic cathedral. The main thing is to get the work of art together. You don't know who built those cathedrals, but they're there" (*Conversations*, 23). He was referring to the collaboration between writer and editor, though surely the kind of joint effort in which the blind man and the narrator are engaged in "Cathedral," which he was then writing or had recently completed, was on his mind. But this uncertainty as to authorship extends to the uncertainty into which *Cathedral*'s stories lead us: to which of these two stories can the origin of the image of the riding fingers be traced—"Cathedral," which was written first, or "The Bridle," which the stories' order places before the other in the total fabric of the work?[11] *Cathedral*, in other words, is a cathedral in the Carverian sense: like the protagonists of its title story, its stories ride each other, depend on each other, collaborate with each other to create together what they could not have done by themselves.

11. After *What We Talk About* "the first story I wrote was 'Cathedral' " (*Conversations*, 44).

5

The Seven Last Stories

I was in my room one night when I heard something in the corridor. I looked up from my work and saw an envelope slide under the door. . . . My name was written on the envelope, and what was inside purported to be a letter from my wife. I say 'purported' because . . . the charges were outrageous and completely out of keeping with my wife's character. Most important, however, the handwriting was not my wife's" (491). Thus begins "Blackbird Pie," one of the seven new, uncollected Carver stories that appear at the end of *Where I'm Coming From: Now and Collected Stories* (1988). The protagonist here is confronted with a textual problem that is not without relevance to the difficulties that face the reader of this story, as well as of the other six. The reader, that is, who has been able up to now to fill in some of the silence that haunts the text of the stories by having recourse to Carver's *other* text—that formed by the collection itself, the sequence in which the stories appear. For there is no other text to call on here, since the separate collection into which these seven stories would presumably have gone will remain forever unfinished, interrupted by Carver's early death. We do not know what other stories might have joined them there, or in what order Carver would ultimately have arranged them, or even if their order would have been significant. The seven appear here, according to an Editor's Note that refers both to them and to the stories that precede them selected from his three last collections, "arranged, generally, in chronological order" (xii). This obedience to the order of com-

position results in a quite different arrangement in the case of
the stories chosen from *Will You Please . . .* , *What We Talk
About . . .* , and *Cathedral,* which serves to underscore the fact
that whatever governed the order in which they originally appeared in those collections was, as we have seen, something
other than chronology.

Like the letter that the husband claims is not in his wife's
handwriting, most of the seven uncollected stories are not written in quite the style to which we have become accustomed.[1]
Unlike Carver's earlier stories, these—at least the first three—
no longer work through what has been left out but through
what has been added, at times even through the cumulative
effect of one thing piled upon another. In "Boxes" the narrator's mother keeps changing her address and keeps complain-
ing about her living conditions. "She continues to talk. She talks
on and on" (420). So too the couple in "Whoever Was Using
This Bed," who stay up conversing from three o'clock in the
morning until sunup, having been roused from their sleep by
a wrong number. Likewise the ex-wife in "Intimacy" who sub-
jects the narrator to a tirade of complaint. Forty-five paragraphs in "Intimacy" begin with "She says." More happens than
that in the story, of course—the narrator drops to his knees,
holds the hem of her skirt, and begs forgiveness, which she
grants—but the insistent, mechanical repetition of these *she
sayses* is something new in Carver's fiction.

"Menudo," on the other hand, in which a man is having an
affair with his neighbor's wife and remembers the time a friend
of his began to concoct a Latin American stew called *menudo* to
rouse him from his depression (which he didn't get to taste
because he fell asleep before it was ready and some other guests
ate it while he slept), is the sort of story that could have appeared in *Cathedral.*

1. Carver told William Stull that these "new stories are different from
the earlier ones in kind and degree" (*Conversations,* 186). In an interview with
Kasia Boddy he said that they "are different in a lot of ways—in ways I can't
really articulate—from the stories that have come before" (*Conversations,*
199).

The same may be said of "Elephant," whose title comes from the animal the narrator had pretended as a boy to be riding when his father let him perch on his shoulders. He regains the sense of letting go he used to feel then when he decides to stop worrying about how he is going to continue to bear his relatives' financial burdens for them; he has not only become the son he used to be but his father too, the elephant who cheerfully gives others a free ride. His son, on the other hand, is pictured—literally, in a snapshot—in a way that invites comparison to the protagonist's memory of how he rode his father's shoulders as a child. He recalled that he "turned loose and held my arms out on either side of me. I kept them out there like that for balance. . . . I pretended he was an elephant" (486). Now a father himself, he receives a letter from his son enclosing a photograph of the son "standing under a big tree with thick limbs hanging down a few feet over his head. In the picture, he wasn't smiling" (481). In the letter the son asks for money and threatens to kill himself by hanging if he doesn't get it. "That would save him the trouble of borrowing a gun. And save us the price of bullets" (481). One can well imagine that the tree looming so menacingly over his head in the picture (with its "thick limbs *hanging* down") is the one he's going to hang himself from. The father's arms, which he once held out for balance (and does once more at the end of the story: "I raised my arms—raised them up level with my shoulders. I was standing there like that, like a goof, when somebody tooted a car horn and pulled off" [489]) are evoked (in the reader's mind, presumably the narrator's too, though not of course the son's) by these "thick limbs hanging down a few feet over his head." For the father's arms hung (out, if not down) above *his* father's head—an inversion of the relationship in the picture, but with the same terms. And in both the picture and the childhood recollection the father is seen as something much larger than the son: an elephant, a "*big* tree." The culmination of this comparison is reached when we realize that the protagonist's recollection of the joy of letting go in the knowledge that his father held him safe ("*I've got you. You won't fall.* When he said that, I became aware of the strong grip of his hands around my ankles. Then I did let go. I turned loose and held my arms out" [486]) finds its negative image (in the photographic sense) in the son's threat to hang himself from the father-tree. For that too would be a kind of letting go—while this son, too, knows that his father won't let him drop, that he'll send the money he's demanding as ransom for his life.

"Errand," however, the last of these seven stories and a re-creation of the last days of Anton Chekhov, is radically different from anything Carver had ever written before. None of his other stories is set in the past or based on an actual person. The errand in question is the one on which Chekhov's widow sends a young waiter from the hotel where her husband has just died: to bring back a mortician for her husband's body without attracting any attention. As the story—and this last volume of fiction Carver published—ends, the young man is just about to leave the room on his errand. Mrs. Chekhov wants him to proceed immediately to his task and not linger to gather up the wineglasses that had held the champagne the doctor had poured and her husband had consumed when it was clear that death was minutes away. A few hours before, the same waiter had brought the glasses and the champagne. "Leave the glasses. Don't worry about them. Forget about crystal wineglasses and such. Leave the room as it is. Everything is ready now. We're ready. Will you go?" (526) Despite her insistence the waiter cannot resist picking up at least one thing, which he feels he must do, almost surreptitiously, in the last lines of the story: "But at that moment the young man was thinking of the cork still resting near the toe of his shoe. To retrieve it he would have to bend over. . . . He would do this. He leaned over. Without looking down, he reached out and closed it into his hand" (526).

The note on which the last story Carver wrote ends is not without a certain resonance in the context these last stories, uncollected as they may be, actually do form. The very title of "Boxes" alludes to what was lying on the floor and bothered the narrator of that story as the cork had troubled the young waiter: "Within a day or two of deciding to move, she'd packed her things into boxes. That was last January. . . . Now it's the end of June. Boxes have been sitting around inside her house for months. You have to walk around them or step over them to get from one room to another. This is no way for anyone's mother to live." Outside on the lawn clumps of grass pose a similar obstacle: "I hear the mower howl and then thud as it picks up a clump of grass in the blade and comes to stop. In a minute, after several tries, Larry gets it going again" (419). The encumbering boxes and grass clumps in "Boxes" are both answered by the leaves strewn about in "Intimacy"—the boxes by the leaves' evoking the same reponse in the narrator as did the boxes (that they ought to be picked up) and the grass clumps by the allusion to another lawn: "There are these leaves everywhere. . . . I can't take a step without putting my shoe into leaves. Somebody ought to make an effort here. Somebody ought to get a rake and take care of this" (453).

These last lines of "Intimacy" so strongly anticipate what will happen at the beginning and the end of "Menudo" that one can well imagine these two stories appearing side by side, as they happen to do here, in the eventual collection Carver might have made of them. The narrator of "Menudo" is even more unable to put up with the accumulation of leaves. On the first page of the story he looks out his window at four A.M. to the house across the street—"Oliver and Amanda's place with the lights on, leaves heaped up under the front windows." Amanda is the woman with whom he's having an adulterous affair. "A couple of days ago, when I couldn't sit still, I raked our yard—Vicky's and mine. I gathered all the leaves into bags, tied off the tops, and put the bags alongside the curb. I had an urge then to cross the street and rake over there, but I didn't follow through. It's my fault things are the way they are across the street" (454). At the end of the story he rakes his yard again (almost as if he, or Carver, had forgotten that this task had already been accomplished fifteen pages before). "I feel I don't have a choice in the matter any longer. It's light out—light enough at any rate for what I have to do. . . . I rake our yard, every inch of it. It's important it be done right, too. I set the rake right down into the turf and pull hard" (469). Next he moves on to his neighbors' lawn, not Oliver and Amanda's

across the street but the Baxters' next door. "In a few minutes
Mrs. Baxter comes out on her porch, wearing her bathrobe. I
don't acknowledge her. I'm not embarrassed, and I don't want
to appear unfriendly. I just want to keep on with what I'm
doing" (470). The last line of the story finds him on his way
across the street to where Amanda lives, evidently to complete
the unfinished business (the raking) to which he had alluded
on the first page: "I look both ways and then cross the street"
(471). It's one way of coping with, or rather avoiding, the difficult situation into which his adultery has led him.

The champagne cork on the floor that the young waiter just
could not bear to leave there, despite the widow's express command that he not touch a thing in the room and that he depart
immediately on his errand—that cork in "Errand" echoes too,
and in a more elaborate way, the central connection underlying
the married couple's marathon conversation in "Whoever Was
Using This Bed." The parallel in this instance is based not only
on the notion of an act of negligence needing correction—the
boxes, leaves, and cork that someone ought to have picked up
—but at the same time on the function a champagne cork is
meant to serve: to plug up something. In Carver's version of
Chekhov's death a lot of attention is paid to this. Dr. Schwöh-
rer, who had had the inspired idea—"one of those rare moments of inspiration that can easily enough be overlooked later
on, because the action is so entirely appropriate it seems inevitable" (519)—of calling for champagne when it was clear that
nothing more could be done for the patient, tried to work "the
cork out of the bottle . . . in such a way as to minimize, as much
as possible, the festive explosion. He poured three glasses and,
out of habit, pushed the cork back into the neck of the bottle"
(520). Later, after Chekhov died and just after the doctor left
the room, "it was at this moment that the cork popped out of
the champagne bottle; foam spilled down on the table" (521).
It was almost as if we were meant to think of the writer's soul
departing his body on its heavenward flight. For at that moment "Olga went back to Chekhov's bedside. She sat on a foot-
stool, holding his hand, from time to time stroking his face.
'There were no human voices, no everyday sounds,' she wrote.

'There was only beauty, peace, and the grandeur of death' "
(521).

What I am thinking of in "Whoever Was Using This Bed"
in speaking of the cork in "Errand" is the key role, and the
double sense, that plugging and unplugging has in that earlier
story. The reason the husband and wife are up in the middle
of the night endlessly talking is that they forgot, literally, to
remove a plug. " 'We should have unplugged the phone. I
guess we forgot. Try forgetting one night to unplug the phone
and see what happens. I don't believe it" (426). What has happened is that someone called with a wrong number at three in
the morning and the protagonists cannot get back to sleep.
They begin to talk about one thing and another and soon get
to the topic of more or less imaginary medical complaints, and
from this to thoughts of death. The husband then brings up a
news item about "this nurse who unplugged six or eight people
from their [life-support] machines" (436). She had started with
her mother and claimed "she thought she was doing everybody
a favor. She said she hoped somebody'd do it for *her*, if they
cared about her." After some discussion of this and similar
cases, the wife asks her husband to promise her "you'll pull the
plug on me, if and when it's ever necessary" (439). He is not
sure he can say that he will promise that, he needs to think it
over. She then asks him if he wants to exact the same promise
from her. He hasn't answered her first question yet and takes
his time before he answers this one. "No. Don't unplug me. I
don't want to be unplugged. Leave me hooked up just as long
as possible. Who's going to object?" (440). One has the feeling
that he finds it a threatening question, and that a wedge is
being driven between husband and wife.

Dawn arrives, and they must get ready to leave for work.
That evening he's finally able to answer her other question.
"All right, if it's what you want to hear, I'll pull the plug for
you. . . . If it will make you happy, here and now, to hear me
say so, I'll say it. I'll do it for you. . . . But what I said about my
plug still stands" (442). Later that night the same caller dials
their number again, and in the last lines of the story the wife
pulls the plug on her husband (the thing he had told her, in

another context, that he did not want her to do) as he's still talking to the woman on the telephone and trying to make her understand that she's made a mistake: "While I'm trying to tell all this to the woman, while I'm trying to make myself understood, my wife moves quickly and bends over, and that's it. The line goes dead, and I can't hear anything" (443). The more or less hidden pun in "Whoever Was Using This Bed" between unplugging a phone and unplugging a life-support system is underscored here when the phone, too, goes "dead." A similar, if more long-distance play (on images if not words) links this story to "Errand," where the autonomous unplugging of the champagne cork marked the doctor's departure and the moment when Olga was left alone with the fact of her husband's death.

That last gesture at the end of "Errand"—the young waiter's disobedience of the widow's injunction to leave everything in the room as it was—acquires even greater resonance when we realize that we have been doing the same thing. We haven't left things quite as they were either but have lingered in the collection of these uncollected new stories to pick up what we might have left untouched, had we been more intent on putting the book behind us once we had finished the last story. Yet it wasn't entirely our fault. Something here made us linger—maybe it was the power of the waiter's example, and perhaps too the way that "Blackbird Pie" poses a textual riddle for which there is no answer, either for the reader of that letter found on the floor (the one his wife slipped in under his door) or for us. We want to linger, that is, at least enough to try to answer it.

I had said that the first three stories and the seventh are departures for Carver. All the more is this true of the sixth, for "Blackbird Pie" is a story based on an obvious impossibility. Among his previous stories only "Why, Honey?," in which it is perhaps impossible to decide whether the son is indeed a monster or the mother an unreliable narrator, comes close. The problem here is the narrator's persistent claim that the letter is not in his wife's handwriting. "But the handwriting *was not her handwriting*. And I ought to know. I consider myself an expert in this matter of her handwriting" (494; Carver's emphasis), having read at least 1850 of her letters in the years since they first courted. "And yet if it wasn't her handwriting, who on earth *had* written these lines?" (494; Carver's emphasis). "I would go so far as to say that every word of this entire letter, so-called (though I haven't read it through in its entirety, and won't, since I can't find it now), is utterly false" (496). Not, he goes on to say, because the charges the letter makes don't have some validity. The sentiments expressed, he says, may even be hers. Yet "the force of the accusations leveled against me is diminished, if not entirely undermined, even discredited, because she *did not* in fact write the letter. Or, if she *did* write it, then discredited by the fact that she didn't write it in her own handwriting!" (496–97; Carver's emphasis).

At one moment we might have thought he had written it himself, without realizing it—a classically unreliable narrator—that he is, in other words, psychotic. For he gives as a second reason for his conclusion that she hadn't written the letter the claim that "my wife *never* underlined her words for emphasis" (496), doing some underlining of his own at that very moment. If *his* style, as his underlining here and elsewhere suggests, is characterized by underlining, then are we to conclude that the letter is actually in *his* handwriting?

In the poem "Egress," in *Ultramarine*, Carver's narrator does in fact write something, comes across it later, and cannot remember having written it—and, like the husband here, *cannot recognize the handwriting:* "I opened the old spiral notebook to see what I'd been / thinking in those days. There was one entry, / in a hand I didn't recognize as mine, but was mine" (44). In "Spell," another poem in the same collection, he speaks in remarkably similar terms of the poem he is writing (and we are reading): "Why, this time next week I won't remember / what I was feeling when I wrote this" (46). What is particularly remarkable is that "Spell" appears in the collection *immediately after* "Egress," so that these two instances of forgetting what one has written (the only two in *Ultramarine*) occur so close to each other that it could seem a kind of joke. Carver has, in other words, "forgotten" that he had just written about that sort of thing—that is, about forgetting what he had earlier

written—in the immediately preceding poem. Like so many of
the sequentially appearing stories, these two sequentially appearing poems appear to allude in a self-referential, metafictional way to their having repeated each other at such close
range.[2]

One of the passages he quotes from the letter suggests another possible connection between what we know of him and
what the letter might show us about its author. The narrator
had begun the story by claiming that even though he no longer
has the letter, having lost or misplaced it, his memory is so
phenomenal that "I can recall every word of what I read. My
memory is such that I used to win prizes in school because of
my ability to remember names and dates, inventions, battles,
treaties, alliances, and the like" (491–92). He then gives a whole
page of examples, in the midst of which the story's title surfaces: "Ask me anything about the Tartars, the Renaissance
popes, or the rise and fall of the Ottoman Empire, Thermopy-
lae, Shiloh, or the Maxim gun. Easy. Tannenberg? Simple as
blackbird pie. The famous four and twenty that were set before
the king" (492).[3] He quotes from that prodigious memory this
passage from the letter: "The time has come and gone for us.
. . . Thee and me. Lancelot and Guinevere. Abélard and Hé-
loïse. Troilus and Cressida. Pyramus and Thisbe. JAJ and Nora

2. There is more than a hint of this phenomenon of repeating what one
has just said because one has forgotten having said it in the title of Carver's
first major collection, *Will You Please Be Quiet, Please?* The title of the collection that followed—*What We Talk About When We Talk About Love*—showed
that Carver was still interested in saying things twice (though not necessarily
to simulate forgetfulness). I am indebted to an anonymous reader of my
manuscript for pointing out these two echoes. Hidden in plain sight, and in
such prominent places, they had escaped my attention, unlike the doubled
envelope that did not escape Dupin's. Displayed nevertheless in the titles of
two of the three major collections whose structural doubling has been the
object of my efforts here, they do announce that things tend to happen twice
in Carver country.

3. Part of the strangeness of the next story, "Errand," as I have said, is
its immersion in history. Its narrator seems as fascinated by the dates of past
events as the narrator of "Blackbird Pie" confesses to be. This is evident from
the very first words: "Chekhov. On the evening of March 22, 1897" (512).

Barnacle, etc." (499). Here the wife sounds strangely like what the husband purports to be, a history buff.

At another juncture in the narrative we might have thought he was right to imagine that someone else must have written the letter, because he hears "a low murmuring from the living room. It was as if somebody were trying to say something over the phone and this somebody were taking pains not to be over-heard" (499). So his wife had a lover! And the lover must have written the letter for her, she not having the courage to write it herself. But it turns out that she had been telephoning the sheriff to report that someone's horses had gotten loose in the fog that night and had strayed into the front yard of their rural house. And she certainly had no lover to take her away, for she hitches a ride eventually with the owner of the horses who had driven up to retrieve them, having originally asked her husband (in a passage of the letter he had not read) to drive her to the bus depot. It becomes quite clear, whatever we might have suspected, that the narrator, unreliable as he may or may not be, had not written the letter when the wife asks him how much of it he had read.[4]

In the end we are left hanging, unable to understand why the husband so insistently claims the handwriting is not his wife's. We cannot conclude that his stubborn resistance to the facts is simply a symptom of his inability to acknowledge the

4. That is, it becomes clear in the context of "Blackbird Pie." Yet in a larger context—one that would include the poem "Late Night With Fog and Horses" (*Where Water Comes Together With Other Water*, 100–101) that tells the same story in a different way—it is not so clear at all that the husband did not write the letter. In an interview with William Stull, Carver says that the story and the poem, like the story "Why Don't You Dance?" and the poem "Distress Sale" (*Fires*, 56–57), were based on the same incident, one that "made such a strong impression on me that I dealt with it first in a poem and then in a story" (*Conversations*, 179). In the version the poem tells, the wife speaks soothing words to the horses that have wandered into the front yard just as she does in the story, but in all other respects the roles are reversed: It is the husband who is leaving the marriage, not the wife; and it is the husband, not the wife, who calls the sheriff about the horses. So, though there is no letter in the poem, had there been one it would have been the husband who wrote it.

justice of her accusations against him, for he does acknowledge
it. "There is some truth, perhaps, to the charges. I don't want
to quibble" (496). "The handwriting business isn't the important thing, of course. How could it be after the consequences
of the letter? Not the letter itself but the things I can't forget
that were *in* the letter" (510). From a feminist perspective, of
course, one could conclude that he's too much of a monstrous
male to recognize that his wife was capable of writing such a
document (or that, once she found the courage to write it, she
was a changed person and that, since handwriting is a reflection
of one's personality . . .). At least one extratextual consideration suggests that there may be something to this angle: The
horses whose eerie arrival on the scene coincides with the appearance under the narrator's study door of this troubling
wifely text seem an inescapable allusion, in the way Carver's
poems have made biographical allusions but his stories until
now had not, to the particular woman in his life who did write,
and this allusion refers to the title and title story of her short
story collection, in which her Irish great-grandfather had been
"a 'whisperer,' a breed of men among the gypsies who were
said to possess the power of talking sense into horses" (*The
Lover of Horses*, 2). In "Blackbird Pie" the wife too speaks to
horses, to the ones that had wandered into their yard: "She
moved forward and put her face against the horse's mane.
'Where did you come from, you big baby?' she said. . . . Then,
as I watched, she began to cry into the horse's mane. . . . My
wife began to croon to the horse. Croon!" (503).[5] "Blackbird
Pie," in other words, may in some way be a testament to the
pressure that builds when two writers inhabit the same household. One of them finds himself writing a story about a man

5. This corresponds to the crooning through which the narrator of Gallagher's "The Lover of Horses" discovered her own powers of language:
"There was a soft crooning of syllables that was satisfying to my ears, but
ultimately useless and absurd. Then it came to me that I was the author of
those unwieldy sounds, and that my lips had begun to work of themselves"
(16).

who refuses to believe the obvious, that his wife is capable of producing such a text.

That the husband in Carver's story should doubt the authenticity of his wife's handwriting sends us in another intertextual direction as well, back once more to that insistent foreign text in the body of Carver's work, John Cheever's "The Five-Forty-Eight." This is the story to which "The Train" was a conscious sequel, and whose echoes we have detected as well in "Fever" and "Why, Honey?" Blake, the former employer Miss Dent confronted with a pistol in the train for having fired her the day after she slept with him, had noticed one thing about her when she was in his employ that did not fit in with what he thought he knew of her: "She had been competent, punctual, and a good typist, and he had found only one thing in her that he could object to—her handwriting. He could not associate the crudeness of her handwriting with her appearance" (283). The uncharacteristic handwriting plays an important role in the story, coming up again when, in her apartment after their sexual encounter, "he noticed on the dresser a note she had written to a cleaning woman . . . the hideously scrawled letters again seemed entirely wrong for her, and as if they must be the handwriting of some other . . . woman" (283). The very strangeness and inappropriateness of the handwriting carried a meaning that Blake did not realize until too late, when he was trapped in the train with her pistol aimed at his ribs, "regretting his failure to have been warned by . . . the handwriting that looked like the marks of a claw" (289) (as in "tooth and claw"— hence, evidently, her name, which Blake, having repressed, found so hard to remember when he first realized she was trailing him). "He tried to remember her name—Miss Dent, Miss Bent, Miss Lent—and he was surprised to find that he could not" (282). She had *bent* for him, had *lent* him her body, and he had *dented* her self-esteem, but she could bite back. In the train—amazingly, now that we have read "Blackbird Pie" and can begin to see that Carver's homage to Cheever didn't stop with "The Train"—she gives him a letter to read and makes him pick it up (as Carver's husband had to pick up the

letter slipped under his study door). And in reading the letter
he becomes *her husband:* " 'I want you to read my letter before
we get to Shady Hill,' she said. 'It's on the seat. Pick it up.' . . .
He picked up the letter from the seat where she had put it. . . .
'Dear Husband,' she had written, in that crazy, wandering
hand" (290).

If we have our doubts about the reliability of the narrator
of "Blackbird Pie," we can perhaps move to safer ground, up
the metafictional ladder, to try to read the text in the story for
which we can have some confidence that Carver, and not the
troubled fictive husband, is responsible. That is the text of the
title, which in Carver's case, as we have earlier had occasion to
observe, is often so seemingly tangential to the story as to constitute a riddle for which a clue is given when the title resurfaces in the text of the story: "Simple as blackbird pie. The
famous four and twenty that were set before the king." The
nursery rhyme has been conflated with the unrelated saying
"simple as pie." We would do well at this point (since the narrator is at this moment bragging about *his* memory) to remember the rest of the rhyme: "Sing a song of six pence, pocket full
of rye / Four and twenty blackbirds, baked in a pie. / And when
the pie was opened, the birds began to sing. / Wasn't that a
dainty dish to set before the king?" If the blackbirds in the title
are these birds, then presumably they can be made to sing. But
how?

The answer, I think, can be found in the textual strategy
the narrator adopts when he returned to the letter after having
heard his wife speaking to someone on the phone. He was now
convinced that "something was afoot" in the house, but he
didn't know what to do about it.

> I sat in my chair and, trembling, picked up the pages of the
> letter once more. But now here's the curious thing. Instead
> of beginning to read the letter through, from start to finish,
> or even starting at the point where I'd stopped earlier, I took
> pages at random and held them under the table lamp, pick-
> ing out a line here and a line there. This allowed me to
> juxtapose the charges made against me until the entire in-

> dictment . . . took on quite another character—one more ac-
> ceptable, since it had lost its chronology and, with it, a little
> of its punch. . . . In this manner, going from page to page,
> here a line, there a line, I read in snatches. (500–501)

What the husband does to the letter is what was done to the
blackbird pie: it was *opened* so that the birds inside could be
released from their imprisonment in pie crust and stuffing, so
that the lines here and there in the letter could be freed from
their immediate context, and in particular from their chronology. It may be with an uncanny sense of déjà vu that we realize
that we have been doing to the seven uncollected stories the
same thing that this apparently unreliable narrator delights in
(or finds relief in) doing to the troubling text before him. It
was what the young waiter's impulsive gesture at the end of
"Errand" seemed to invite us to do, to pick up the instances in
what we've just read where something begs to be picked up.
We too have been juxtaposing lines, with temporary disregard
for immediate context and chronology. A line in the husband's
description of his reader's stratagem itself calls out for just such
treatment: "The entire indictment . . . lost its *chronology*,"
which, especially in light of the evident analogy between the
letter in "Blackbird Pie" and the stories in this collection, should
be set alongside "the stories in this collection are arranged,
generally, in *chronological* order" from the Editor's Note that
prefaces the volume. If we combine and recombine the seven
uncollected stories through their juxtaposable lines we won't be
reading them any longer in their chronological sequence.
  The letter reader's juxtapositions justify our own, for like
the young waiter who picks up the cork at the conclusion of
"Errand" he too is a figure for the reader in the text. We are
invited (despite the voice—the widow's, in this instance—telling us not to) to repeat his gesture: to linger in the text long
enough for some small detail to catch our eye, and not to be
afraid to reach down and pick it up and take it away to puzzle
over later. In "Errand" that insistent detail just happens to be
the cork. That both the waiter and the husband are metafictional representatives of the reader who is invited to imitate

their example is all the more evident for the juxtaposition that the text so clearly demands we make between them. The letter, like the cork, was meant to be picked up off the floor, since his wife had slipped it under his door. This circumstance receives increased emphasis when the husband later compares the letter to a piece of paper he could imagine picking up off the ground among the debris at his feet in a crowded bazaar: "I could recognize her handwriting anywhere in the world. Give me a few words. I'm confident that if I were in Jaffa, or Marrakech, and *picked up* a note in the marketplace, I would recognize it if it was my wife's handwriting" (496; emphasis added).

As I have already pointed out, the marked difference between the chronological order in which the stories taken from the earlier collections appear in *Where I'm Calling From* and the order in which they first appeared in those collections shows that their order in the latter is not chronological. And we have seen considerable evidence in our reading of those collections that their sequence there seems to have been one in which contiguous stories might echo each other. I had said too that we will probably never know what order the seven new stories might have appeared in had Carver lived to complete their sequence, or even if there would be a significant order. I should say at this point that there is sufficient evidence to make us suspect that, while the sequence to which these seven would have belonged would indeed have been characterized by many echoing cross-references, there would have been so many of them that they probably could not have been based on the kind of exploitation of contiguity that characterized his previous volumes. In that sense too, the eventual collection would indeed have been, like the letter that so evidently stands for it in "Blackbird Pie," composed in a style—a "handwriting"—different from the one to which we had become accustomed.

For example, the husband's certainty that his wife could not have written the letter because it wasn't in her handwriting, and that he was an expert on her handwriting because he had seen it so many times, finds a counterpart in "Menudo" when the husband-narrator of that story fantasizes about his mistress in the house across the street "writing me a letter, and somehow she'll get it into my hands later on when the real day starts. Come to think of it, I've never had a letter from her since we've known each other. All the time we've been involved . . . I've never once seen a scrap of her handwriting. I don't even know if she is *literate* that way" (464; Carver's emphasis). In both stories it's a question of knowing, or not knowing, the woman's handwriting. In fact, there is a letter-writing *wife* too in "Menudo," the narrator's first wife, who was remarkable in that way: "Molly, she was the letter writer. She used to write me even after we weren't living together . . . the letters gave me a chill" (464). The chill came from the increasingly insane quality of her letters—like Eileen in "Fever," she began to speak of "karma." But that chill compares interestingly, too, with the shock that the husband in "Blackbird Pie" would feel when he read *his* wife's letter.

The discovery that there was another wife capable of writing upsetting letters besides the one in "Blackbird Pie" and that there was another letter reader who meditated on identifying a correspondent through her handwriting is akin to the discovery that awaited the king when the pie was opened and the blackbirds began to sing. Both the pie and the text of the assembled stories had to be opened (as the husband opened up his wife's letter to a reading based on carving up the text and juxtaposing lines that did not originally appear together) before these birds—these hidden yet corresponding elements in the text—could sing.

It turns out that some of these birds are really birds, for in "Menudo," "birds call out to each other. At least I think they're calling to each other" (471), and in "Errand," "thrushes began to call from the garden below" (521)—as if they were in fact calling to each other, from one story to another. It is not perhaps by accident that the birds that sang on the morning Chekhov died were thrushes, for the European blackbird *(Turdus merula)* of the Mother Goose rhyme (as opposed to the American blackbird) is in fact a member of the thrush family.

Some of the other blackbirds in Carver's pie that sing when the text is opened to juxtaposition are:

1. The champagne that Chekhov got to drink just before he died (to which he alluded in his last, dying words: "It's been so long since I've had champagne" [520]) that responds to the *menudo* the protagonist not only didn't get to consume but also thinks that death will rob him of knowing: "I'll probably die without ever tasting *menudo*" (469).

2. The complaint the husband in "Menudo" makes that he feels "wild *from lack of sleep*" (458; emphasis added) that echoes the complaint of the man who stayed up half the night talking with his wife in "Whoever Was Using This Bed": "I'm bone-tired *from lack of sleep*" (441; emphasis added).

3. The porch light left burning that is extinguished at the end of "Boxes" ("The porch light goes on. . . . They leave the light burning. Then they remember, and it goes out" [424]), and that is still burning in "Menudo" ("Only the porch light is still burning. Amanda must have forgotten it, I guess" [466]).

4. The narrator's realization in "Boxes" that when his mother moves back to California "I'm probably never going to see her again" (421) and the identical realization about his wife that comes to the narrator of "Blackbird Pie": "Something came to me then. *I might never see her again*" (506; Carver's emphasis).

The carving to which Carver's choice of title—"Blackbird Pie"—and his narrator's strategy of reading his wife's letter invite us is what Carver realizes he does when he writes, according to the story he tells in "The Schooldesk," a poem in *Ultramarine*. Outside the window of a cottage in Ireland "an old iron / and wood schooldesk keeps me company. / Something is *carved* into the desk under / the inkwell. It doesn't matter / what; I'm not curious. It's enough / to imagine the instrument / that gouged those letters" (93; emphasis added). The next lines of the poem turn to thoughts of his parents, his grown-up children, his first wife. A few lines later the connection between the carving on the desk's surface and recollection of these "loved ones" becomes clearer: "I bend over the desk / and run my fingers across its rough surface. / Someone laughs, someone grinds her teeth. / And someone, someone is pleading with me. / Saying, 'For Christ's sake, don't / turn your back on me.' . . . I sit on the bench. Lean / over the desk. I can remember / myself with a pen. In the beginning, / looking at pictures of words. / Learning to write them, slowly, / one letter at a time. Pressing down. / A word. Then the next. / . . . Pressing hard. At first / the damage confined to the surface. / But then deeper" (94–95). To write is to carve; Carver, who began with "pictures of words," turns into the literal picture his name evokes. There is no avoiding the damage that writing does, whether it be that inflicted on "my sweet children," as he evokes them here (damage bound to occur from what he realized that day in the laundromat [*Fires*, 32–33]), or whether it be what the critic, if he wants to open the blackbird pie, must perform on the text.

Whatever shape the unfinished volume of stories might have assumed, it is evident that Carver was—with the letter slipped under the door, that instructive text within the text—moving in the direction of an even greater metafictionality, and toward new ways of exploring the possibilities of the intratextual short story collection.

6

Epilogue

His wife gone, the narrator in "Blackbird Pie," still troubled by "the question of the handwriting" (510), suggests one more interpretive strategy—actually two—to supplement that of "picking out a line here and a line there" (501) and setting them side by side. If "my wife writes more letters, or tells a friend who keeps a diary . . . then, years later, someone can look back on this time, interpret it according to the record, its scraps and tirades, its silences and innuendos" (510–11). To read the "silences and innuendos" of Carver's fiction has been our task in these pages and, though to pursue them fully would really be a project beyond the scope of this book, we ought to give some consideration to whether what Carver seems through this narrator to invite us to do could be done. For as the wife could write more letters Raymond Carver has written more than the stories we have read here: the poems of *Fires, Where Water Comes Together With Other Water, Ultramarine, A New Path to the Waterfall*, not to mention earlier collected and uncollected poems (as well as a few stories that did not appear in the collections discussed here). And as the wife could have a friend in whom she confides and who also writes, so too has Carver had for the last decade of his life in Tess Gallagher a confidante who does, of course, write—though so magnificently that she should not be read for what we can glimpse of Raymond Carver except to the extent that such curiosity on our part, sanctioned to the degree by which "Blackbird Pie" invites it, is a pardonable offense.

207

"The poems in *Fires*," as William Stull writes in the *DLB Yearbook 1988*, "written during his turbulent middle years" (209), come from an earlier period than the maturity that has been our focus here. The later three collections were written after *Cathedral*, after Carver moved into Tess Gallagher's house in Port Angeles, Washington, in 1984 (Stull, 209). *Ultramarine* (1986), I believe, is the best of the three: The poems in *Where Water Comes Together With Other Water* (1985) have not yet fully emerged from prose, while *A New Path to the Waterfall* (1989) would doubtless have assumed a somewhat different state— certainly a more unified one—had Carver lived.[1] Though there are some fine poems in it, he had to fill out its pages with quotations from other writers (Chekhov, Milosz, and a half-dozen others).

Ultramarine has the kind of unity one would expect from a collection of poems written in a short space of time and meant to appear together in a sequence. But it has a greater unity than that: it displays an integration that rivals that of the three major story collections analyzed here, in which each poem re-peats turns of phrase from its immediate predecessor and sur-rounds them with a new context. In "This Morning," for example, the first poem in *Ultramarine*, the poet awakens to a beautiful winter morning by the sea, gazes at the water, but finds that, "as usual, my thoughts / began to wander. I had to will / myself to see what I was seeing / and nothing else. I had to tell my self *this* is what / mattered, not the other" (3). The "other," he goes on to explain, is largely made up of the con-cerns of his past life, whether he has done the right things, "tender memories, thoughts of death, how I should treat / with my former wife. All the things / I hoped would go away this morning." The second poem in the collection may be entirely taken, as a note below the title indicates, "from a letter by Re-noir." Entitled "What You Need for Painting," it begins with a

---

1. Carver himself judged *Ultramarine* superior to *Where Water Comes To-gether With Other Water*: "*Ultramarine* seems more considered, somehow, more careful in certain ways" (*Conversations*, 189). "It may be the stronger of the two books" (*Conversations*, 188).

list of some eighteen different colors for the palette, among which is hidden—as the titles of Carver's stories were so often hidden—the title of the collection itself: "*Ultramarine* blue" (5). In the context of the titles of the two volumes of poetry published immediately before and after this one, *Ultramarine* does not seem to do much more than perpetuate the aquatic theme. But the epigraph Carver supplies (the other two have no such explanatory inscription and need none, for both are titles of poems that appear therein) says a lot about the kind of ultramarine blue with which he painted these poems: " 'Sick with exile, they yearn homeward now, their eyes / Turned to the ultramarine, first-star-pierced dark / Reflected on the dark, incoming waves.' —Derek Mahon, 'Mt. Gabriel,' from *Antarctica*, 1985" (ix). If the title of the collection is a quotation from the epigraph, or at least if its echo in the epigraph explains—as its appearance in the epigraph gives us every right to expect that it does explain—what kind of ultramarine the title is talking about, then it is important to realize that it is an ultramarine that originally comes, despite the etymology so evident in the word, not from the ocean but from the *sky*, though it is seen through its reflection on the surface of the waves.[2] Things, in other words, are turned around. And sea and sky are almost inextricably mixed, the sea reflecting the color from the sky that originally had a marine origin. There are *two* ultramarines, each so connected to the other that it is perhaps impossible to determine which came first. So too these first two poems: for in "What You Need for Painting," after the requisite colors and knives, turpentine and brushes, comes—and this, too, evidently from Renoir's letter—"indifference to everything except your canvas." In other words, the need "to will"—and for Renoir too

---

2. The etymology actually has the blue coming not from the sea but from beyond it, which is in fact what Mahon has it doing when he places its origin in the sky beyond the ocean, the night sky whose stars beckon the travelers beyond the ocean where they are to the home to which the stars will guide them: "f. L. *ultra* beyond + *mare* sea. . . . *Ultramarine blue:* A pigment of colouring matter of various shades of blue, originally obtained from the mineral lapis lazuli and named with reference to the foreign origin of this" (*Oxford English Dictionary*).

it was a question of will, since among the prerequisites the poem goes on to list is "an iron will"—"to will / myself to see what I was seeing / and nothing else."

Both poems are about the need to will oneself to focus full attention on *"this"*—the sight of the sea in the first poem, the canvas in the other—instead of on "the other." Like the two ultramarines (the one in the sky and the one seen on the marine surface), these two poems are in one very important regard the same: each speaks of demanding one's attention and of the necessity of not allowing that attention to wander elsewhere. Yet by that very duplication of demand each poem demands that we turn our attention from one poem and give it to the other, or that we turn from the demand to the demand's having been made twice. The sequence of these two poems, if not the poems themselves, is highly self-referential: Carver's is a metafictional poetry.

"An Afternoon," the third poem in the series, is the third act in this minidrama, continuing the theme of the need to keep one's attention on the matter at hand. The poem builds in particular on the motif first introduced in the second poem of the need for a creative artist to obey this stricture, yet returns us to a concern specific to the first poem by recalling what it was that distracted him there.

> As he writes, without looking at the sea,
> he feels the tip of his pen begin to tremble.
> The tide is going out across the shingle.
> But it isn't that. No,
> it's because at that moment she chooses
> to walk into the room without any clothes on. (6)

The creative pen assumes phallic proportions here, transforming itself into a penis whose tip trembles at the sight of the beloved in all her splendor.[3] We may be distracted for a mo-

___

3. Compare the moment in "Nobody Said Anything" when the boy protagonist "had a big boner and she waved me over with her hand [in his fantasy]. Just as I was going to unzip, I heard a plop in the creek. I looked and saw the tip of my fly rod jiggling" (49).

ment from the story so intriguingly told in "An Afternoon" by the realization that this is not the first time the poet's wife has been a source of distraction. Tess Gallagher has declared (at least to me) that there is no irony in Carver.[4] Yet there's something at least a little ironical in the circumstance that Carver's second wife distracts him in "An Afternoon" from what he is trying to keep his mind on, but it was his *first* wife who distracted him from what he was trying to focus his attention on in "This Morning":

> I had to tell myself *this* is what
> mattered, not the other. (And I did see it,
> for a minute or two!) For a minute or two
> it crowded out the usual musings on
> what was right, and what was wrong—duty,
> tender memories, thoughts of death, how I should treat
> with my former wife. All the things
> I hoped would go away this morning. (3)

The irony resides in both wives doing the same thing (distracting him) but with what a difference.

Every poem of *Ultramarine* enacts such an echo as this, and quite often the echo itself addresses its *being* an echo. Near the middle of the collection, "The Phenomenon" tells of seeing "The sun and moon hang side-by-side over the water. / Two sides of the same coin" (79). This sun and this moon are to each other as "The Phenomenon" is to the immediately preceding poem, "Bahia, Brazil," in the brief moment that the reader glimpses the parallel between this astonishing celestial "phe-

---

4. In a conversation 22 February 1990 in which she anticipated what she would say in her introduction to Adelman's *Carver Country: The World of Raymond Carver*. "One of his French translators, François Lascan, had originally misapprehended Ray's stance in the stories as ironic" but told Gallagher that when he saw a photograph of Carver he realized that such a man " 'could never condescend to his characters. I had to retranslate the entire book' " (10). Irony toward his characters is not, of course, the kind I'm talking about here, which could be more accurately described as irony of the text toward itself.

nomenon" and the unnatural contiguity the poet finds equally astonishing there: In Bahia he saw the ghosts of slaves with "arms shackled together. / Jesus, the very idea of such a thing!" (78)[5] Like the slaves, the contiguous poems are linked; like the side-by-side sun and moon, they are "two sides of the same coin." In "Bahia, Brazil," Carver resurrects the old question of whether, if a house were on fire, you would "save the cat or the Rembrandt," with the obvious application in this instance to the slaves: "Lines of men in the street, / as opposed to lines of poetry. / Choose!" (77–78) But in this very moment of quandary, he may have opted for giving poetry the last word, since the lines of poetry are—as those lines turn into the sequence of poems in *Ultramarine*—as linked as the slaves. Indeed, the "side-by-side" phenomenon "over the water" in "The Phenomenon" is linked, on its other side, to the "boat rocking from *side to side*" (81; emphasis added) of the poem that follows it, "Wind." There, another astonishing phenomenon will take place over the water (though closer to its surface), a mysterious "wind / moving across the water" of the Strait of Juan de Fuca.

Future biographers will want to compare Carver's Brazilian poems in *Ultramarine,* "Bahia, Brazil" and "In the Lobby of the Hotel del Mayo," to the ones Tess Gallagher wrote in *Amplitude: New and Selected Poems* (1987) about what they experienced there. In "That Kind of Thing," she recounts a conversation she and Carver had with an American consular official in Bahia in which arises the same question Carver raised in "Bahia, Bra-

5. The brief moment in which the reader will glimpse the parallel—before being distracted from it by the other demands the poem will make on the attention—is itself already inscribed here: the poet first sees the side-by-side sun and moon from his bed, then climbs out of bed slowly, momentarily distracted by fatigue ("I climb from bed / slowly, much as an old man might maneuver / from his musty bed in midwinter" [79]), and then when he looks out of the window again, distracted once more, this time by the splendor of the landscape itself without reference to what is happening in the sky ("when I look out / the window again . . . I'm arrested with the beauty of this place"), he will discover that the celestial phenomenon has vanished: "I move closer to the glass and see it's happened / between this thought and that. The

zil" concerning the cat and the Rembrandt—lines of suffering slaves versus lines of poetry. The consular official, "speaking to Ray: 'I read your stuff. Well / written. But, to be perfectly / honest, too depressing. I have to live / with that kind of thing / down here all the time'" (152). What's the point, in other words, of writing about suffering, or reading about it, when human misery in the streets of Bahia is so overwhelming? In *Amplitude* Gallagher places this poem just after "Refusing Silence," which is not about Brazil but is about, as "That Kind of Thing" is also about, the writer's need to justify her choice of vocation: To "Insist for us all . . . is the job / of the voice, and especially / of the poet. Else / what am I for . . . ? / There are messages to send" (148).

In "If Blood Were Not as Powerful as It Is," another poem from *Amplitude* with a Brazilian setting (along with "In Maceio" and "Sugar"), Gallagher is struck by the sight of a bloody religious icon: "The rays spiking / from his golden head / set off the irregular rays of blood / streaming down" (158). And of another Christ in the same Recife chapel: "A rivulet trickles from his rib cage / and stops without dropping / one precious drop—this heavenly body / that bleeds without bleeding." As if to demonstrate that certain universals underlie historically separate cultures—while allowing us to see that she is just as interested as Carver in planting the same image in two widely divergent yet, by the poetic sequence she creates, side-by-side contexts—the immediately following poem, "Redwing," recounts a myth from the American Northwest about another bloody religious phenomenon.

---

moon / is gone. Set, at last" (79). Yet even this reenactment of the reader's first seeing and then losing (or forgetting) the parallel is itself one of the parallels between this poem and its immediate predecessor. For in "Bahia, Brazil" there are "no sunsets in this place. Light one minute, / and then the stars come out" (77). That is to say, as the moon will suddenly drop below the horizon without warning in the poem to come, here the sun will suddenly do the same (will *set:* compare "sun*sets*" with "*Set*, at last"). In other words, what happens in "The Phenomenon" is also enacted in the intratext these two contiguous poems form: They are "two sides of the same coin."

> The readers of poetry, the writers of
> poetry. Nation inside
> the nation. That rainbow holding briefly over
> the Strait of Juan de Fuca . . . .
>
>   .   .   .   .
> . . . I don't have to think
> of raindrops hanging as light, or to command
> the schoolbook corpses of refraction and
> internal reflection to be dazzled. The myth
> of the Vilela Indians, its rainbow
> a gigantic serpent charmed
> by a small girl until it sheds her
> sway and piecemeal ravages the world, vanquished
> at last by an army of birds—that's good enough
> for me. And victory too, each bird
> dipping itself in the blood
> of the monster. (160)

And so are Christians dipped in the blood of the Lamb (an old-time religion, they say, "that's good enough / for me"). The "nation inside of the nation" of the readers (and writers) of poetry will see what is so strangely the same in Recife, Brazil, and Washington State and appreciate the way this poem acquires increasing power from the way it speaks not only on its own but in answer too to its immediate precursor.[6]

Carver's and Gallagher's poems, in ways that space permits only a glimpse of here, do open themselves to those other interpretive strategies suggested by the reader of "Blackbird Pie": like the author of that troubling letter, Carver has written "more letters"; and like her, he had a companion in whose

---

6. The rainbow in "Redwing" comes after rain, while "If Blood Were Not as Powerful as It Is" concerns, in addition to a certain insistent religious blood imagery, an account of the suffering caused by a prolonged absence of rain, a "drought / five years running" (159). A woman at the door of the church asks for a glass of water, and tries "to drink / deeply enough to get past the fear of the next / thirsting." In this regard, too, "Redwing" responds to "If Blood," as it also does by presenting a religious blood myth in which the poet can wholeheartedly delight in place of the one for which she can barely conceal her disgust, though that disgust is most heavily directed at the

writing we can find something that could help us "interpret
[the] silences and innuendos" of his stories, something in particular to explain why Carver in his next-to-last published story
gave us a model reader who took to reading by juxtaposition.

In "The Gift," the last poem in *Ultramarine*, Carver remembers that on their flight home from South America

> Your breathing said
> you were fast asleep. I covered you with an arm
> and went on from Argentina to recall a place
> I lived in once in Palo Alto . . . .
> .   .   .   .
> The refrigerator stood next to the bed.
> When I became dehydrated in the middle of the night,
> all I had to do to slake that thirst was *reach out*
> *and* open the door. (139; emphasis added)

The memory of how easy it was to reach out to get what he
needed was evidently prompted by the way his arm had
reached out to cover Tess as she curled up next to him to sleep
on the plane. Yet in the reader's mind it could evoke another
memory, that of how in the immediately preceding poem,
"Asia," "ships pass so close to land / a man could *reach out* / *and*
break a branch from one of the willow trees" (137; emphasis
added). These poems reach out to each other and in doing so
reenact the companionship of Tess and Ray whose conjugal
happiness is celebrated in so many of them, but most especially
in "The Gift." "Asia" and "The Gift" have different agendas,
different contexts, different stories to tell, different things on
their minds. So too do these lovers, as "The Gift" goes on to say:

> You tell me you didn't sleep well. I say
> I didn't either. You had a terrible night. "Me too."

---

gold with which the priests have coated their Christ: The "blood . . . would
be golden too, if blood / were not as powerful as it—powerful / enough to
avoid even gold" (158). It is a testimony to the power not so much of Christ's
blood as of blood itself, which is powerful enough to return, freed from its
Christic associations (though not from their echoes), in "Redwing."

We're extraordinarily calm and tender with each other
as if sensing the other's rickety state of mind.
As if we knew what the other was feeling. (140)

There is an almost uncanny sense in which they do seem to know what the other is thinking.[7] And so do the poems. Indeed, what these last two poems are thinking of is the very idea of knowing what the other is thinking, for as the poet in "Asia" gazes from his balcony at the men on the ship headed for Asia, he declares "I can read the faces / . . . I know what they're thinking." Just as in "The Gift" it is "as if we knew what the other was feeling." Yet, he goes on to say, "We don't, / of course. We never do. No matter." Just as the poems, despite their speaking the same words, don't really know it. Yet, in their silence, the innuendo remains that they do.

7. As in "Slippers," the poem just before "Asia," a woman "woke up / *barking* this one night. And found her little dog, / Teddy, beside the bed, watching" (135)—as if she had, in her sleep (for she had been dreaming), assumed something of a dog's consciousness, and as if the dog, intently watching, had divined something of her dream. "Asia," too, it turns out, is about a kind of mystic communication between man and beast: The ship is bound for Asia, and the men on board wave at horses on the shore, who "stand like statues of horses. / Watching the ship as it passes. / Waves breaking against the ship. / Against the beach. And in the mind / of the horses, where / it is always Asia" (138). As if the horses could read the sailors' minds, as if they knew where they were going, and wanted to go there too.

Works Cited

Index

Works Cited

Works by Carver

Collected Fiction

Cathedral. New York: Vintage Books, 1984.
Furious Seasons and Other Stories. Santa Barbara, Calif.: Capra Press, 1977.
What We Talk About When We Talk About Love. New York: Vintage Books, 1982.
Where I'm Calling From: New and Selected Stories. New York: Atlantic Monthly Press, 1988. Reprint. New York: Vintage Books, 1989.
Will You Please Be Quiet, Please? New York: McGraw-Hill, 1978.

Uncollected Fiction

"The Calm." *Iowa Review* 10, no. 3 (1979): 33 37.
"Cartwheels." *The Western Humanities Review* 24 (1970): 375–82.
"A Dog Story." *Perspective* 17, no. 1 (1972): 33–47.
"Dummy." In *Furious Seasons,* 9–26.
"The Fling." *Perspective* 17 (Winter 1974): 139–52; reprinted in *Furious Seasons,* 62–78.
"Gazebo." *Missouri Review* 4, no. 1 (1980): 33–38.
"Night School." *North American Review* 253, no. 3 (1971): 48–50.
"One More Thing." *North American Review* 266, no. 1 (1981): 28–29.
"Put Yourself in My Shoes." *Iowa Review* 3, no. 4 (1972): 42–52.
"A Serious Talk." *Missouri Review* 4, no. 1 (1980): 23–28.

"So Much Water So Close to Home." In *Furious Seasons,* 41–61; in
    Fires, 185–204.
"View Finder." *Iowa Review* 9, no. 1 (1978): 50–52.
"Want To See Something?" *Missouri Review* 4, no. 1 (1980): 29–32.
"Where Is Everyone?" *TriQuarterly* 48 (Spring 1980): 203–13; re-
    printed in *Fires,* 173–83.
"Will You Please Be Quiet, Please?" In *The Best American Short Stories
    1967,* edited by Martha Foley and David Barnett, 37–65. Boston:
    Houghton Mifflin, 1967.

Collected Poetry

A New Path to the Waterfall: Poems. New York: Atlantic Monthly Press,
    1989.
Ultramarine. New York: Random House, 1986.
Where Water Comes Together With Other Water: Poems. New York: Ran-
    dom House, 1985.

Other Collections

Fires: Essays, Poems, Stories. New York: Random House, 1984.
*Those Days: Early Writings by Raymond Carver: Eleven Poems and
    a Story.* Edited by William Stull. Elwood, Conn.: Raven Editions,
    1987.

Interviews

Conversations with Raymond Carver. Edited by Marshall Bruce Gentry
    and William L. Stull. Jackson: Univ. Press of Mississippi, 1990.

Works About Carver

Bellamy, Joe David. "A Downpour of Literary Republicanism." *Mis-
    sissippi Review* 40/41 (Winter 1985): 31–39.
Boxer, David, and Cassandra Phillips. "Will You Please Be Quiet,
    Please?: Voyeurism, Dissociation, and the Art of Raymond
    Carver." *Iowa Review* 10, no. 3 (1979): 75–90.
Chénétier, Marc. "Living On/Off the 'Reserve': Performance, Inter-
    rogation, and Negativity in the Works of Raymond Carver." In
    Critical Angles: European Views of Contemporary American Literature,

edited by Marc Chénétier, 164–90. Carbondale: Southern Illinois Univ. Press, 1986.

Facknitz, Mark A. R. "Missing the Train: Raymond Carver's Sequel to John Cheever's 'The Five Forty-Eight.' " *Studies in Short Fiction* 22, no. 3 (1985): 345–47.

Gallagher, Tess. "Carver Country." Introduction to *Carver Country: The World of Raymond Carver*. Photographs by Bob Adelman. New York: Charles Scribner's Sons, 1990.

———. "Introduction." In *A New Path to the Waterfall*, by Raymond Carver.

Herzinger, Kim A. "Introduction: On the New Fiction." *Mississippi Review* 40/41 (Winter 1985): 7–22.

Saltzman, Arthur M. *Understanding Raymond Carver*. Columbia: Univ. of South Carolina Press, 1988.

Stull, William. "Beyond Hopelessville: Another Side of Raymond Carver." *Philological Quarterly* 64 (1985): 1–15.

———. "Raymond Carver." In *Dictionary of Literary Biography Yearbook 1988*, 199–213. Detroit: Gale, 1989.

Other Works

Barth, John. "A Few Words About Minimalism." *New York Times Book Review*, 28 Dec. 1986: 1–2, 25.

———. "The American New Novel." In *The Friday Book. Essays and Other Nonfiction*, 255–57. New York: G. P. Putnam's Sons, 1984.

———. "Don't Count on It." In *The Friday Book*, 258–81.

———. "The Literature of Replenishment." In *The Friday Book*, 193–206.

———. *Lost in the Funhouse*. New York: Bantam, 1969.

Barthelme, Frederick. "On Being Wrong: Convicted Minimalist Spills Bean." *New York Times Book Review*, 3 April 1988: 1, 25–26.

Cheever, John. *The Stories of John Cheever*. New York: Ballantine Books, 1980.

Fraistat, Neil. *The Poem and the Book: Interpreting Collections of Romantic Poetry*. Chapel Hill: Univ. of North Carolina Press, 1985.

———, ed. *Poems in Their Place: The Intertextuality and Order of Poetic Collections*. Chapel Hill: Univ. of North Carolina Press, 1986.

Freud, Sigmund. *A General Introduction to Psychoanalysis*. Translated by Joan Riviere. New York: Pocket Books, 1952.

————. *The Interpretation of Dreams.* Translated and edited by James Strachey. New York: Avon Books, 1965.

————. "Medusa's Head." In *Sexuality and the Psychology of Love,* edited by Philip Rieff, 212–213. New York: Collier Books, 1963.

————. "The Relation of the Poet to Day-Dreaming." In *Character and Culture,* edited by Philip Rieff, 34–43. New York: Collier Books, 1963.

Gallagher, Tess. *Amplitude: New and Selected Poems.* Saint Paul, Minn.: Graywolf Press, 1987.

————. *The Lover of Horses and Other Stories.* New York: Harper & Row, 1986.

Lohafer, Susan. *Coming to Terms with the Short Story.* Baton Rouge: Louisiana State Univ. Press, 1983.

Luscher, Robert M. "The Short Story Sequence: An Open Book." In *Short Story Theory at a Crossroads,* edited by Susan Lohafer and Jo Ellyn Clarey, 148–67. Baton Rouge: Lousiana State Univ. Press, 1989.

Poe, Edgar Allan. "The Purloined Letter." In *Poetry and Tales,* 680–98. New York: The Library of America, 1984.

Runyon, Randolph Paul. *The Braided Dream: Robert Penn Warren's Late Poetry.* Lexington: Univ. Press of Kentucky, 1990.

————. *Fowles/Irving/Barthes: Canonical Variations on an Apocryphal Theme.* Columbus: Ohio State Univ. Press/Miami Univ. Cooperative Imprint, 1981.

————. "Montaigne's Larceny: Book III's Symmetrical Intertexts." In *The Order of Montaigne's Essays,* edited by Daniel Martin, 58–76. Amherst, Mass.: Hestia Press, 1989.

————. "The Oblique Gaze: Some Evidence of Symmetry in Montaigne's *Essais.*" In *Essays in European Literature for Walter A. Strauss,* edited by Alice N. Benston and Marshall C. Olds, 13–26. Manhattan, Kan.: Studies in Twentieth-Century Literature, 1990.

————. *The Taciturn Text: The Fiction of Robert Penn Warren.* Columbus: Ohio State Univ. Press, 1990.

Schulz, Max F. *The Muses of John Barth: Tradition and Metafiction from "Lost in the Funhouse" to "The Tidewater Tales."* Baltimore: Johns Hopkins Univ. Press, 1990.

Styron, William. *Set This House on Fire.* New York: New American Library, 1960.

Index